2-52

E...
AN

NORTH YORKSHIRE

YORKSHIRE &
HUMBERSIDE

HUMBERSIDE

WEST
YORKSHIRE

SOUTH
YORKSHIRE

LINCOLN

DERBY NOTTINGHAM

EAST MIDLANDS

LEICESTER

NORTH-
AMPTON

CAMBRIDGE

BEDFORD

BUCKINGHAM-
SHIRE

HERTFORD

ESSEX

GREATER
LONDON

SURREY

KENT

SOUTH EAST

WEST
SUSSEX

EAST
SUSSEX

LANCASHIRE

GREATER
MANCHESTER

MERSEYSIDE

NORTH
WEST

CHESHIRE

STAFFORD

WEST
MIDLANDS

WARWICK

OXFORDSHIRE

BERKSHIRE

HAMPSHIRE

WEST
MIDLANDS

SHROPSHIRE

HEREFORD
&
WORCESTER

GLOUCESTER

WILTSHIRE

CLWYD

POWYS

GWENT

AVON

SOMERSET

DORSET

WALES

GWYNEDD

DYFED

WEST
GLAMORGAN

MID
GLAMORGAN

SOUTH
GLAMORGAN

SOUTH WEST

DEVON

CORNWALL

The Economist

POCKET BRITAIN IN FIGURES

The
Economist

POCKET

BRITAIN
IN FIGURES

THE ECONOMIST IN ASSOCIATION WITH
PROFILE BOOKS LTD

Published by Profile Books Ltd,
62 Queen Anne Street, London W1M 9LA

First published 1995

This edition published by Profile Books
in association with The Economist

Copyright © The Economist Newspaper Ltd, 1995, 1996

Material researched and compiled by
Pamela Canetti, Carol Howard, Joanna Malvisi, Liz Mann

Design and makeup Jonathan Harley

The greatest care has been taken in compiling this book. However,
no responsibility can be accepted by the publishers or compilers
for the accuracy of the information presented.

Printed in Great Britain by
The Bath Press

A CIP catalogue record for this book is available
from the British Library

ISBN 1 86197 003 X

Contents

CONTENTS

CONTENTS

CONTENTS

Notes and glossary

Notes

In this new edition of *The Economist Pocket Britain in Figures* we present a detailed overview of where Britain stands today and how it has changed over the years, how its regions vary and how they have changed, and how Britain compares with other countries. The contents list on the previous pages gives a full list of the hundreds of subjects covered in the 13 main sections.

The research for this book was carried out during 1996, using the most up-to-date and most authoritative sources available. The sources used are listed at the end of the book. However, some notes of explanation are necessary.

What is Britain?   Technically, Great Britain includes only England, Wales and Scotland, whereas the United Kingdom includes Northern Ireland as well. In this book we have often used Britain in a broad sense to mean either the United Kingdom or Great Britain, but we have endeavoured to make it clear how much and which parts of the United Kingdom specific data refer to. Statistical data are often collected by region. The map at the beginning and end of this book shows which counties are included in the regions that are most commonly referred to.

Does it all add up?   The simple answer is "No, not always". Because of rounding, individual amounts do not always add up to the totals given. Similarly, percentages may not add up to 100. However, the differences are usually small and of little significance.

Historical quirks   Over time the methods of collecting or reporting data have changed. Collection of data has generally improved, so more recent statistics should be more reliable than those reported decades ago. In some instances the method of reporting data has changed, which makes it inappropriate if not impossible to compare what has happened since the change with what happened before. Where major changes in the method of reporting data have taken place we have, to the best of our knowledge, indicated so in a footnote. In general, the historical data included in this book give as clear a picture of how trends have developed as is possible, but should not be used for strictly accurate comparisons.

Glossary

Balance of payments   The record of a country's transactions with the rest of the world. The current account of the balance of payments consists of visible trade (goods) and invisible trade (income and expenditure for services such as banking, insurance, tourism and shipping, together with profits earned overseas and interest payments). Imports include the cost of "carriage, insurance and freight" (cif) from the exporting country to the importing. The value of exports does not include these elements and is recorded "free on board" (fob). Balance of payments statistics are generally adjusted so that both exports and imports are shown fob; the cif element is included in invisibles.

Confidence indices   CBI: The difference between the percentage of firms (as surveyed by the CBI) reporting an increase in general business optimism in their industry compared with four months ago, and those reporting a decrease. Gallup: A survey of consumers' optimism.

CSO: A longer leading indicator that helps to identify in advance peaks and troughs in the UK economy. It is derived from five indicator series.

Crude birth rate   The number of live births per 1,000 population. The crude rate will automatically be high if a large proportion of the population is of child-bearing age.

Crude death rate   The number of deaths in one year per 1,000 population. Also affected by the population's age structure.

Current prices   These are in nominal terms and do not take into account the effect of inflation.

Enrolment   Gross enrolment ratios may exceed 100% because some pupils are younger or older than the standard primary or secondary school age.

EU   European Union. Members are: Austria, Belgium, Denmark, Finland, France, Germany, Greece, Ireland, Italy, Luxembourg, Netherlands, Portugal, Spain, Sweden and the United Kingdom.

Fertility rate   The average number of children born to a woman who completes her childbearing years.

G7   The Group of Seven. Members are Canada, France, Germany, Italy, Japan, UK and USA.

GDP   Gross domestic product. It is the sum of all output produced by economic activity within that country. GNP (gross national product) includes net income from abroad eg. rent, profits. In measuring GDP, market prices are normally used to value outputs and so include indirect taxes. When GDP is "at factor cost", indirect taxes have been subtracted.

Infant mortality rate   The annual number of deaths of infants under one year of age per 1,000 live births.

Inflation   The annual rate at which prices are increasing or decreasing. The most common measure is the change in the consumer price index. The underlying rate is usually arrived at by excluding mortgage interest payments. The producer price index tracks the prices of domestically produced goods when they leave the factory.

Life expectancy   The average length of time a newborn baby can expect to live.

Marginal tax rate   The rate of tax paid on extra units of income.

Money supply   A measure of the "money" available to buy goods and services. Various definitions of money supply exist. Those used here are narrow (M0): notes and coins in circulation, and broad (M4): notes and coins and sterling deposits at all UK banks and building societies.

OECD   Organisation for Economic Co-operation and Development. The "rich countries club" established in 1961. Now has 28 members.

Population density   The total number of inhabitants divided by the surface area.

Real terms   Figures are adjusted to allow for inflation.

Reserves   The stock of gold and foreign currency held by a country to finance any calls that may be made for the settlement of foreign debt.

Trade-weighted exchange rates   This measures a currency's depreciation (figures below 100) or appreciation (figures over 100) from a base date against a trade-weighted basket of the country's main trading partners.

Part I

THE LAND AND THE ENVIRONMENT

Regions and counties

The United Kingdom

England

Sq km

North			
Cleveland	597	Merseyside	655
Cumbria	6,824	**West Midlands**	
Durham	2,429	Hereford & Worc.	3,923
Northumberland	5,026	Shropshire	3,488
Tyne & Wear	540	Staffordshire	2,715
Yorkshire & Humberside		Warwickshire	1,979
Humberside	3,508	West Midlands	899
North Yorkshire	8,309	**East Midlands**	
South Yorkshire	1,559	Derbyshire	2,629
West Yorkshire	2,034	Leicestershire	2,551
North West		Lincolnshire	5,921
Cheshire	2,331	Northamptonshire	2,367
Greater Manchester	1,286	Nottinghamshire	2,160
Lancashire	3,070	**East Anglia**	
		Cambridgeshire	3,400

Norfolk	5,372	Kent	3,735
Suffolk	3,798	Oxfordshire	2,606
South East		Surrey	1,677
Bedfordshire	1,236	West Sussex	1,988
Berkshire	1,259	South West	
Buckinghamshire	1,877	Avon	1,332
East Sussex	1,795	Cornwall	3,559
Essex	3,675	Devon	6,703
Greater London	1,578	Dorset	2,653
Hampshire	3,779	Gloucestershire	2,653
Hertfordshire	1,639	Somerset	3,452
Isle of Wight	380	Wiltshire	3,476

Wales
Sq km

Clwyd	2,430	Mid Glamorgan	1,017
Dyfed	5,766	Powys	5,077
Gwent	1,377	South Glamorgan	416
Gwynedd	3,863	West Glamorgan	820

Scotland
Sq km

Borders	4,670	Lothian	1,756
Central	2,627	Strathclyde	13,529
Dumfries &		Tayside	7,502
Galloway	6,370	Orkney	976
Fife	1,308	Shetland	1,433
Grampian	8,707	Western Isles	2,898
Highland	25,304		

Northern Ireland
Sq km

Antrim	3,046	Fermanagh	1,849
Armagh	1,326	Londonderry	2,108
Down	2,466	Tyrone	3,260

Counties: from biggest to smallest

Sq km

1	Highland	25,304	38	Down	2,466
2	Strathclyde	13,529	39	Clwyd	2,430
3	Grampian	8,707	40	Durham	2,429
4	North Yorkshire	8,309	41	Northamptonshire	2,367
5	Tayside	7,502	42	Cheshire	2,331
6	Cumbria	6,824	43	Nottinghamshire	2,160
7	Devon	6,703	44	Londonderry	2,108
8	Dumfries & Galloway	6,370	45	West Yorkshire	2,034
9	Lincolnshire	5,921	46	West Sussex	1,988
10	Dyfed	5,766	47	Warwickshire	1,979
11	Norfolk	5,372	48	Buckinghamshire	1,877
12	Powys	5,077	49	Fermanagh	1,849
13	Northumberland	5,026	50	East Sussex	1,795
14	Borders	4,670	51	Lothian	1,756
15	Hereford & Worcester	3,923	52	Surrey	1,677
16	Gwynedd	3,863	53	Hertfordshire	1,639
17	Suffolk	3,798	54	Greater London	1,578
18	Hampshire	3,779	55	South Yorkshire	1,559
19	Kent	3,735	56	Shetland	1,433
20	Essex	3,675	57	Gwent	1,377
21	Cornwall	3,559	58	Avon	1,332
22	Humberside	3,508	59	Armagh	1,326
23	Shropshire	3,488	60	Fife	1,308
24	Wiltshire	3,476	61	Greater Manchester	1,286
25	Somerset	3,452	62	Berkshire	1,259
26	Cambridgeshire	3,400	63	Bedfordshire	1,236
27	Tyrone	3,260	64	Mid Glamorgan	1,017
28	Lancashire	3,070	65	Orkney	976
29	Antrim	3,046	66	West Midlands	
30	Western Isles	2,898		(Met. County)	899
31	Staffordshire	2,715	67	West Glamorgan	820
32	Gloucestershire	2,653	68	Merseyside	655
33	Dorset	2,653	69	Cleveland	597
34	Derbyshire	2,629	70	Tyne & Wear	540
35	Central	2,627	71	South Glamorgan	416
36	Oxfordshire	2,606	72	Isle of Wight	380
37	Leicestershire	2,551			

Mountains, rivers and parks

Highest mountains
Metres

1	Ben Nevis	Highland	1,342
2	Ben Macdhui	Grampian	1,310
3	Braeriach	Grampian	1,294
4	Cairn Toul	Grampian	1,292
5	Cairn Gorm	Grampian	1,244
6	Aonach Beag	Grampian	1,237
7	Càrn Mor Dearg	Highland	1,222
8	Aonach Mor	Grampian	1,218
9	Ben Lawers	Tayside	1,214
10	Beinn a'Bhùrid	Tayside	1,196

Longest rivers
Kilometres

1	Severn	354
2	Thames	346
3	Trent	297
4	Aire	259
5	Ouse	230
6	Wye	215
7	Tye	188
8	Neùe	161
9	Clyde	158
10	Spey	158
11	Tweed	155

National parks

		Area sq km	Established
1	Lake District	2,292	1951
2	Snowdonia	2,142	1951
3	Yorkshire Dales	1,769	1954
4	Peak District	1,438	1951
5	North York Moors	1,436	1952
6	Brecon Beacons	1,351	1957
7	Northumberland	1,049	1956
8	Dartmoor	954	1951
9	Exmoor	693	1954
10	Pembrokeshire Coast	584	1952
11	Norfolk and Suffolk Broads[a]	303	1989

a The Broads are given the same protection as the national parks.

Pollution and waste

Emissions
Tonnes, m

	Carbon dioxide	Per unit of GDP[a], £m	Methane	Per unit of GDP[a], £m	Sulphur dioxide	Per unit of GDP[a], £m
1970	181	518	5.17	14.8	6.43	18.4
1971	175	490	5.14	14.4	6.06	17.0
1972	171	464	4.96	13.4	5.79	15.7
1973	181	457	5.20	13.1	6.01	15.2
1974	169	433	5.09	13.1	5.51	14.1
1975	165	427	5.22	13.5	5.37	13.5
1976	166	417	5.13	12.9	5.18	13.0
1977	170	417	5.11	12.5	5.16	12.7
1978	171	407	5.12	12.2	5.23	12.4
1979	180	416	5.16	11.9	5.54	12.8
1980	163	385	5.15	12.2	4.90	11.6
1981	157	377	5.15	12.3	4.44	10.6
1982	154	362	5.12	12.0	4.21	9.9
1983	152	345	5.10	11.6	3.86	8.8
1984	147	325	4.28	9.5	3.72	8.3
1985	153	328	4.72	10.1	3.73	8.0
1986	157	321	4.85	9.9	3.90	8.0
1987	158	309	4.79	9.4	3.90	7.6
1988	158	294	4.66	8.7	3.83	7.1
1989	156	283	4.59	8.4	3.72	6.8
1990	158	286	4.52	8.2	3.75	6.8
1991	159	295	4.48	8.3	3.56	6.6
1992	155	288	4.34	8.1	3.49	6.5
1993	151	275	4.17	7.6	3.20	5.8

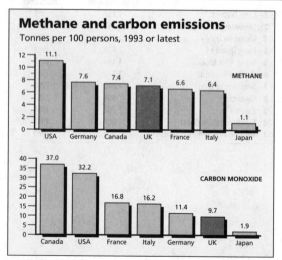

Methane and carbon emissions
Tonnes per 100 persons, 1993 or latest

METHANE: USA 11.1, Germany 7.6, Canada 7.4, UK 7.1, France 6.6, Italy 6.4, Japan 1.1

CARBON MONOXIDE: Canada 37.0, USA 32.2, France 16.8, Italy 16.2, Germany 11.4, UK 9.7, Japan 1.9

a GDP measured at 1990 prices.

Black smoke	Per unit of GDP[a], £m	Nitrogen oxides	Per unit of GDP[a], £m	Carbon monoxide	Per unit of GDP[a], £m
1.03	2.9	2.32	6.6	4.54	13.0
0.92	2.6	2.29	6.4	4.85	13.6
0.80	2.2	2.28	6.2	4.87	13.2
0.81	2.0	2.41	6.1	5.05	12.7
0.77	2.0	2.29	5.9	4.90	12.6
0.67	1.7	2.27	5.9	4.80	12.4
0.65	1.6	2.32	5.8	4.93	12.4
0.67	1.6	2.34	5.7	5.03	12.3
0.63	1.5	2.38	5.7	5.13	12.2
0.64	1.5	2.48	5.7	5.14	11.9
0.56	1.3	2.39	5.7	4.9	11.6
0.53	1.3	2.33	5.6	5.36	12.8
0.53	1.2	2.31	5.4	5.49	12.9
0.51	1.2	2.33	5.3	5.46	12.4
0.47	1.1	2.32	5.1	5.17	11.5
0.55	1.2	2.42	5.2	5.40	11.5
0.57	1.2	2.51	5.1	5.64	11.6
0.53	1.0	2.63	5.1	5.92	11.6
0.49	0.9	2.71	5.0	6.24	11.6
0.48	0.9	2.75	5.0	6.60	12.0
0.46	0.8	2.73	5.0	6.54	11.9
0.47	0.9	2.63	4.9	6.59	12.2
0.58	0.9	2.50	4.7	6.32	11.8
0.44	0.8	2.35	4.3	5.64	10.3

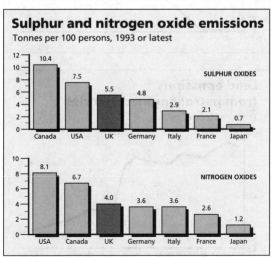

Sulphur and nitrogen oxide emissions

Tonnes per 100 persons, 1993 or latest

SULPHUR OXIDES

Canada	USA	UK	Germany	Italy	France	Japan
10.4	7.5	5.5	4.8	2.9	2.1	0.7

NITROGEN OXIDES

USA	Canada	UK	Germany	Italy	France	Japan
8.1	6.7	4.0	3.6	3.6	2.6	1.2

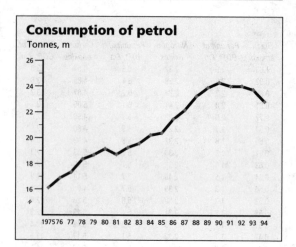

Consumption of petrol
Tonnes, m

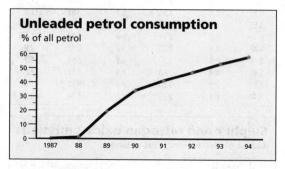

Unleaded petrol consumption
% of all petrol

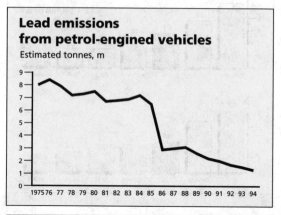

**Lead emissions
from petrol-engined vehicles**
Estimated tonnes, m

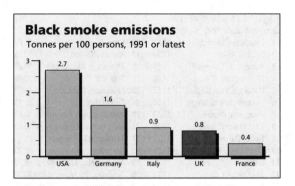

Black smoke emissions

Tonnes per 100 persons, 1991 or latest

USA	Germany	Italy	UK	France
2.7	1.6	0.9	0.8	0.4

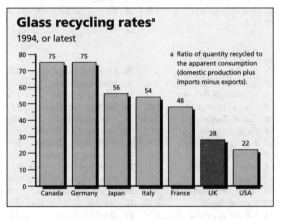

Glass recycling rates[a]

1994, or latest

a Ratio of quantity recycled to the apparent consumption (domestic production plus imports minus exports).

Canada	Germany	Japan	Italy	France	UK	USA
75	75	56	54	48	28	22

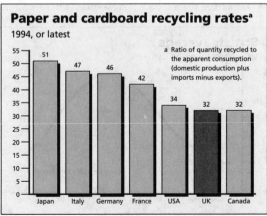

Paper and cardboard recycling rates[a]

1994, or latest

a Ratio of quantity recycled to the apparent consumption (domestic production plus imports minus exports).

Japan	Italy	Germany	France	USA	UK	Canada
51	47	46	42	34	32	32

Temperature

Highest yearly average
July 1994–June 1995, °C

1	Heathrow, London	11.88	16	Hurn, Dorset	11.02
2	Bristol, Avon	11.82	17	Torquay, Devon	10.89
3	Penzance, Cornwall	11.69	18	Rhoose, S. Glamorgan	10.88
4	Cheltenham, Glos.	11.58	19	Tenby, Dyfed	10.78
5	Hastings, East Sussex	11.57	20	Lowestoft, Suffolk	10.74
6	Ventnor, Isle of Wight	11.56	21	Cambridge	10.73
7	Plymouth, Devon	11.53	22	Waddington, Lincolnshire	10.63
8	East Malling, Kent	11.28	23	Long Sutton, Lincolnshire	10.63
9	Bude, Cornwall	11.27	24	Terrington St Clement, Norfolk	10.39
10	Clacton-on-Sea, Essex	11.23	25	Morecambe, Lancashire	10.32
11	Oxford	11.22	26	Ringway, Gtr. Manchester	10.23
12	St Mawgan, Cornwall	11.22	27	Ronaldsway, Isle of Man	10.23
13	Rustington, West Sussex	11.19	28	Skegness, Lincolnshire	10.22
14	Manston, Dorset	11.12			
15	Valley, Gwynedd	11.04			

Lowest yearly average
July 1994–June 1995, °C

1	Braemar, Grampian	6.77	15	Aspatria, Cumbria	9.35
2	Lerwick, Shetland Islands	6.92	16	Presteigne, Powys	9.39
3	Eskdalemuir, Dumfries	7.48	17	Aldergrove, Antrim	9.47
4	Stornaway, Western Isles	8.15	18	Bradford, Yorkshire	9.53
5	Buxton, Derbyshire	8.42	19	Tiree, Strathclyde	9.68
6	Dyce, Grampian	8.51	20	Leeming, North Yorkshire	9.72
7	Boulmer, Northumbria	8.92	21	Whitby, North Yorkshire	9.76
8	Durham	9.03	22	Shawbury, Shropshire	9.95
9	Inverness, Highland	9.08	23	Cleethorpes, Humberside	10.12
10	Bala, Gwynedd	9.10	24	Watnall, Nottinghamshire	10.15
11	Abbotsinch, Strathclyde	9.15	25	Elmdon, Warwickshire	10.16
12	Dundee, Tayside	9.19	26	Sheffield, South Yorkshire	10.18
13	Edinburgh, Lothian	9.22	27	Aberporth, Dyfed	10.21
14	Auchincruive, Ayrshire	9.28	28	Skegness, Lincolnshire	10.22

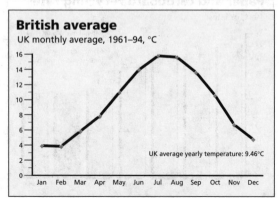

British average
UK monthly average, 1961–94, °C

UK average yearly temperature: 9.46°C

Highest monthly average
July 1994–June 1995, °C

1	Heathrow, London	July 1994	20.7
2	Cheltenham, Gloucestershire	July 1994	19.9
3	Manston, Dorset	July 1994	19.5
4	Cambridge	July 1994	19.5
5	Oxford	July 1994	19.3
6	East Malling, Kent	July 1994	19.3
7	Bristol, Avon	July 1994	19.1
8	Terrington St Clement, Norfolk	July 1994	18.9
9	Clacton-on-Sea, Essex	July 1994	18.8
10	Hastings, East Sussex	July 1994	18.7
11	Lowestoft, Suffolk	July 1994	18.7
12	Hastings, East Sussex	July 1994	18.7
13	Waddington, Lincolnshire	July 1994	18.6
14	Watnall, Nottinghamshire	July 1994	18.5
15	Long Sutton, Lincolnshire	July 1994	18.5
16	Ventnor, Isle of Wight	July 1994	18.3
17	Heathrow, London	August 1994	18.3
18	Hurn, Dorset	July 1994	18.1
19	Rustington, West Sussex	July 1994	18.1
20	Sheffield, South Yorkshire	July 1994	18.1

Lowest monthly average
July 1994–June 1995, °C

1	Braemar, Grampian	January 1995	0.9
2	Braemar, Grampian	March 1995	1.3
3	Eskdalemuir, Dumfries	January 1995	1.5
4	Braemar, Grampian	February 1995	1.7
5	Eskdalemuir, Dumfries	March 1995	2.1
6	Lerwick, Shetland Islands	February 1995	2.5
7	Buxton, Derbyshire	January 1995	2.7
8	Dyce, Grampian	January 1995	2.9
9	Lerwick, Shetland Islands	January 1995	2.9
10	Lerwick, Shetland Islands	March 1995	2.9
11	Braemar, Grampian	December 1994	3.1
12	Dundee, Tayside	January 1995	3.2
13	Durham	January 1995	3.3
14	Eskdalemuir, Dumfries	February 1995	3.3
15	Buxton, Derbyshire	March 1995	3.5
16	Edinburgh, Lothian	January 1995	3.5
17	Leeming, North Yorkshire	January 1995	3.7
18	Stornaway, Western Isles	March 1995	3.7
19	Eskdalemuir, Dumfries	December 1994	3.8
20	Inverness, Highland	January 1995	3.8

Rainfall

Highest yearly average
July 1994–June 1995, mm

1	Eskdalemuir, Dumfries	1,796
2	Buxton, Derbyshire	1,429
3	Bala, Gwynedd	1,334
4	Stornaway, Western Isles	1,314
5	Lerwick, Shetland Islands	1,281
6	Torquay, Devon	1,216
7	Morecambe, Lancashire	1,213
8	Abbotsinch, Strathclyde	1,209
9	Penzance, Cornwall	1,184
10	St Mawgan, Cornwall	1,141
11	Tiree, Strathclyde	1,125
12	Tenby, Dyfed	1,124
13	Bude, Cornwall	1,083
14	Rhoose, South Glamorgan	1,083
15	Plymouth, Devon	1,066
16	Presteigne, Powys	1,050
17	Auchincruive, Ayrshire	1,044
18	Bristol, Avon	1,032
19	Aspatria, Cumbria	1,031
20	Aberporth, Dyfed	1,010
21	Bradford, Yorkshire	973
22	Ringway, Gtr. Manchester	956

Lowest yearly average
July 1994–June 1995, mm

1	Cambridge	527
2	Dundee, Tayside	558
3	Manston, Dorset	563
4	Skegness, Lincolnshire	570
5	Cleethorpes, Humberside	572
6	Edinburgh, Lothian	596
7	Durham	600
8	Lowestoft, Suffolk	601
9	Whitby, North Yorkshire	606
10	Terrington St Clem. Norfolk	609
11	Heathrow, London	610
12	Boulmer, Northumbria	613
13	Waddington, Lincolnshire	615
14	Leeming, North Yorkshire	650
15	Clacton-on-Sea, Essex	653
16	Oxford	679
17	Braemar, Grampian	690
18	East Malling, Kent	703
19	Watnall, Nottinghamshire	711
20	Inverness, Highland	719
21	Elmdon, Warwickshire	720
22	Shawbury, Shropshire	723

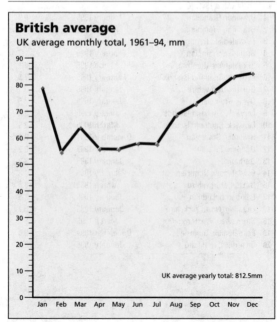

British average
UK average monthly total, 1961–94, mm

UK average yearly total: 812.5mm

Highest monthly total
July 1994–June 1995, mm

1	Eskdalemuir, Dumfries	December 1994	318
2	Eskdalemuir, Dumfries	January 1995	258
3	Buxton, Derbyshire	January 1995	257
4	Abbotsinch, Strathclyde	December 1994	237
4	Bala, Gwynedd	January 1995	237
6	Eskdalemuir, Dumfries	November 1994	224
7	Eskdalemuir, Dumfries	February 1995	221
8	Stornaway, Western Isles	January 1995	212
9	Bala, Gwynedd	December 1994	211
10	Lerwick, Shetland Islands	December 1994	210
11	Penzance, Cornwall	January 1995	208
12	Tenby, Dyfed	December 1994	206
13	Tiree, Strathclyde	December 1994	205
14	Bala, Gwynedd	February 1995	204
15	Aspatria, Cumbria	December 1994	195
16	Auchincruive, Ayrshire	December 1994	190
16	Stornaway, Western Isles	December 1994	190
18	Torquay, Devon	January 1995	187
19	Presteigne, Powys	December 1994	186
19	St Mawgan, Cornwall	January 1995	186

Lowest monthly total
July 1994–June 1995, mm

1	Valley, Gwynedd	June 1995	6
2	Hurn, Dorset	June 1995	7
2	Long Sutton, Lincolnshire	June 1995	7
2	Oxford	June 1995	7
2	Presteigne, Powys	June 1995	7
6	East Malling, Kent	April 1995	8
7	Elmdon, Warwickshire	June 1995	9
8	Cambridge	April 1995	10
8	Cleethorpes, Humberside	June 1995	10
10	Bradford, Yorkshire	June 1995	11
10	Heathrow, London	June 1995	11
10	Sheffield, South Yorkshire	June 1995	11
10	Waddington, Lincolnshire	June 1995	11
14	Bristol, Avon	June 1995	12
14	Long Sutton, Lincolnshire	July 1994	12
14	Rustington, West Sussex	April 1995	12
14	Tenby, Dyfed	June 1995	12
14	Tiree, Strathclyde	April 1995	12
14	Watnall, Nottinghamshire	April 1995	12

Sunshine and daylight

Sun patterns

Total amount of sunlight from sunrise to sunset, taken on the first day of each month, hrs.mins

	London	Bristol	Birmingham	Manchester	Newcastle	Glasgow	Belfast
January	7.56	7.56	7.46	7.35	7.18	7.07	7.23
February	9.10	9.11	9.04	8.57	8.45	8.42	8.49
March	10.56	10.54	10.51	10.49	10.45	10.42	10.45
April	12.57	12.57	12.58	13.01	13.04	13.06	13.03
May	14.50	14.50	14.57	15.03	15.14	15.21	15.11
June	16.19	16.19	16.29	16.40	16.59	17.10	16.54
July	16.34	16.33	16.44	16.52	17.16	17.29	17.11
August	15.25	15.25	15.33	15.41	15.55	16.03	15.50
September	13.35	13.35	13.38	13.41	13.48	13.51	13.46
October	11.39	11.39	11.38	11.36	11.35	11.34	11.36
November	9.41	9.41	9.36	9.30	9.20	9.14	9.22
December	8.12	8.12	8.03	7.53	7.37	7.26	7.41

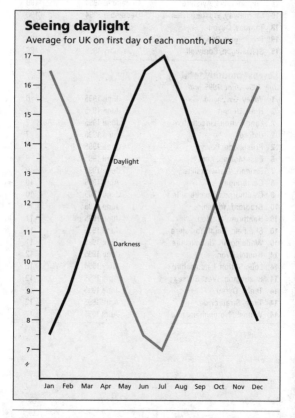

Seeing daylight
Average for UK on first day of each month, hours

Regions compared

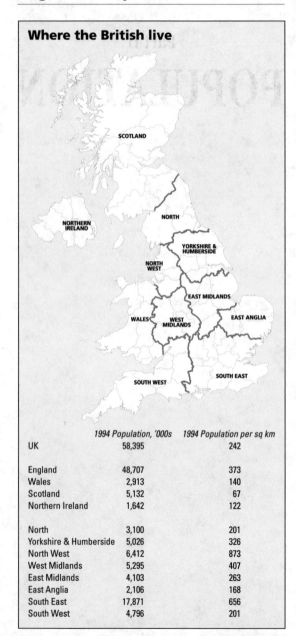

Where the British live

	1994 Population, '000s	1994 Population per sq km
UK	58,395	242
England	48,707	373
Wales	2,913	140
Scotland	5,132	67
Northern Ireland	1,642	122
North	3,100	201
Yorkshire & Humberside	5,026	326
North West	6,412	873
West Midlands	5,295	407
East Midlands	4,103	263
East Anglia	2,106	168
South East	17,871	656
South West	4,796	201

Regional trends
'000s

	1891	1911	1931	1951
UK	34,264	42,082	46,037	50,225
England	27,231	33,649	37,358	41,159
Wales	1,771	2,421	2,593	2,599
Scotland	4,026	4,761	4,843	5,096
Northern Ireland	1,236	1,251	1,243	1,371
North	2,122	2,729	2,938	3,009
Yorkshire & Humberside	3,138	3,896	4,319	4,567
North West	4,585	5,658	6,062	6,305
West Midlands	2,664	3,277	3,743	4,423
East Midlands	1,975	2,467	2,732	3,118
East Anglia	1,105	1,191	1,231	1,381
South East	9,096	11,613	13,349	14,877
South West	2,546	2,818	2,984	3,479

	1961	1971	1981	1991
UK	52,709	55,515	56,353	57,648
England	43,561	46,411	46,821	48,209
Wales	2,644	2,731	2,814	2,886
Scotland	5,179	5,229	5,180	5,100
Northern Ireland	1,425	1,536	1,538	1,594
North	3,120	3,142	3,117	3,019
Yorkshire & Humberside	4,681	4,856	4,918	4,797
North West	6,429	6,597	6,459	6,147
West Midlands	4,758	5,110	5,187	5,089
East Midlands	3,321	3,633	3,853	3,919
East Anglia	1,469	1,669	1,864	2,019
South East	15,994	16,931	16,732	16,794
South West	3,689	4,081	4,327	4,600

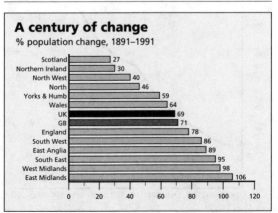

A century of change
% population change, 1891–1991

Scotland	27
Northern Ireland	30
North West	40
North	46
Yorks & Humb	59
Wales	64
UK	69
GB	71
England	78
South West	86
East Anglia	89
South East	95
West Midlands	98
East Midlands	106

Growth

UK population
m

	Total	Male	Female
1801	12.07	5.93	6.32
1811	13.76	6.75	7.18
1821	15.47	7.50	7.97
1831	17.84	8.65	9.19
1841	20.18	9.82	10.36
1851	22.26	10.86	11.40
1861	24.52	11.89	12.63
1871	27.43	13.31	14.12
1881	31.02	15.06	15.96
1891	34.26	16.59	17.67
1901	38.24	18.49	19.75
1911	42.08	20.36	21.73
1921	44.03	21.03	22.99
1931	46.04	22.06	23.98
1941	48.22	23.22	24.95
1951	50.23	24.12	26.11
1961	52.81	25.48	27.23
1971	55.93	26.95	28.56
1981	56.35	27.10	28.74
1991	57.80	27.34	29.12
2001	59.72	29.34	30.38
2011	61.11	30.16	30.95
2021	61.98	30.66	31.32
2031	62.10	30.68	31.42

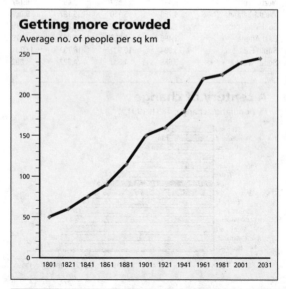

Getting more crowded
Average no. of people per sq km

England and Wales
'000

	Total	Male	Female
1821	12,000	5,850	6,150
1841	15,914	7,778	8,137
1861	20,066	9,776	10,290
1881	25,974	12,640	13,335
1901	32,528	15,729	16,799
1921	37,887	18,075	19,811
1931	39,952	19,133	20,819
1951	43,758	21,016	22,742
1961	46,196	22,347	23,849
1971	49,151	23,897	25,254
1981	49,635	24,160	25,475
1991	51,101	24,995	26,106
2001	52,526	25,819	26,708

Scotland
'000

	Total	Male	Female
1821	2,092	983	1,109
1841	2,620	1,242	1,378
1861	3,062	1,450	1,612
1881	3,736	1,799	1,936
1901	4,472	2,174	2,298
1921	4,882	2,348	2,535
1931	4,843	2,326	2,517
1951	5,096	2,434	2,662
1961	5,184	2,485	2,699
1971	5,236	2,516	2,720
1981	5,180	2,495	2,685
1991	5,107	2,470	2,638
2001	5,026	2,449	2,577

Northern Ireland
'000

	Total	Male	Female
1821	1,380	665	715
1841	1,649	800	849
1861	1,396	668	728
1881	1,305	621	684
1901	1,237	590	647
1921	1,258	610	648
1931	1,243	601	642
1951	1,371	668	703
1961	1,427	696	731
1971	1,540	755	786
1981	1,538	754	784
1991	1,594	777	817
2001	1,686	828	859

Age and sex

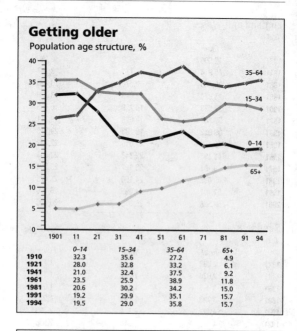

Getting older
Population age structure, %

	0–14	15–34	35–64	65+
1910	32.3	35.6	27.2	4.9
1921	28.0	32.8	33.2	6.1
1941	21.0	32.4	37.5	9.2
1961	23.5	25.9	38.9	11.8
1981	20.6	30.2	34.2	15.0
1991	19.2	29.9	35.1	15.7
1994	19.5	29.0	35.8	15.7

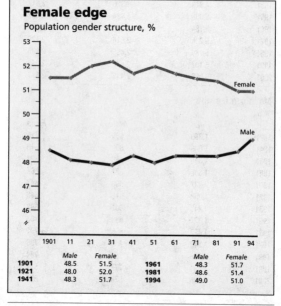

Female edge
Population gender structure, %

	Male	Female		Male	Female
1901	48.5	51.5	**1961**	48.3	51.7
1921	48.0	52.0	**1981**	48.6	51.4
1941	48.3	51.7	**1994**	49.0	51.0

Growth and urbanisation

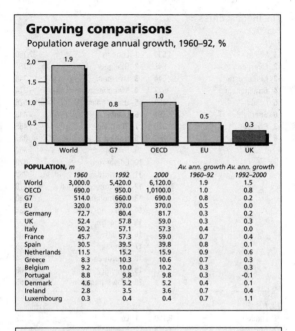

Growing comparisons

Population average annual growth, 1960–92, %

POPULATION, m				Av. ann. growth	Av. ann. growth
	1960	1992	2000	1960–92	1992–2000
World	3,000.0	5,420.0	6,120.0	1.9	1.5
OECD	690.0	950.0	1,0100.0	1.0	0.8
G7	514.0	660.0	690.0	0.8	0.2
EU	320.0	370.0	370.0	0.5	0.0
Germany	72.7	80.4	81.7	0.3	0.2
UK	52.4	57.8	59.0	0.3	0.3
Italy	50.2	57.1	57.3	0.4	0.0
France	45.7	57.3	59.0	0.7	0.4
Spain	30.5	39.5	39.8	0.8	0.1
Netherlands	11.5	15.2	15.9	0.9	0.6
Greece	8.3	10.3	10.6	0.7	0.3
Belgium	9.2	10.0	10.2	0.3	0.3
Portugal	8.8	9.8	9.8	0.3	-0.1
Denmark	4.6	5.2	5.2	0.4	0.1
Ireland	2.8	3.5	3.6	0.7	0.4
Luxembourg	0.3	0.4	0.4	0.7	1.1

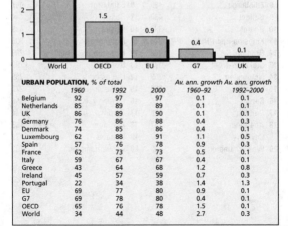

The move to the cities

Urban population as % of total population, average annual growth, 1960–92, %

URBAN POPULATION, % of total				Av. ann. growth	Av. ann. growth
	1960	1992	2000	1960–92	1992–2000
Belgium	92	97	97	0.1	0.1
Netherlands	85	89	89	0.1	0.1
UK	86	89	90	0.1	0.1
Germany	76	86	88	0.4	0.3
Denmark	74	85	86	0.4	0.1
Luxembourg	62	88	91	1.1	0.5
Spain	57	76	78	0.9	0.3
France	62	73	73	0.5	0.1
Italy	59	67	67	0.4	0.1
Greece	43	64	68	1.2	0.8
Ireland	45	57	59	0.7	0.3
Portugal	22	34	38	1.4	1.3
EU	69	77	80	0.9	0.1
G7	69	78	80	0.4	0.1
OECD	65	76	78	1.5	0.1
World	34	44	48	2.7	0.3

City living

The biggest cities
Pop. '000

1901	
1 London	4,536
2 Liverpool	648
3 Manchester	544
4 Birmingham	522
5 Leeds	429
6 Sheffield	381
7 Bristol	329
8 Bradford	280

1911	
1 London	7,160
2 Glasgow	784
3 Liverpool	746
4 Manchester	714
5 Birmingham	526
6 Leeds	446
7 Sheffield	455
8 Belfast	387
9 Bristol	357
10 Edinburgh	320
11 Bradford	288
12 Kingston-upon-Hull	278
13 Nottingham	260
14 Stoke-on-Trent	235
15 Leicester	227
16 Cardiff	182
17 Dundee	165
18 Aberdeen	164
19 Coventry	106
20 Wolverhampton	95

1931	
1 London	8,100
2 Glasgow	1,088
3 Birmingham	1,003
4 Liverpool	856
5 Manchester	766
6 Sheffield	512
7 Leeds	483
8 Edinburgh	439
9 Belfast	438
10 Bristol	397
11 Kingston-upon-Hull	314
12 Bradford	298
13 Stoke-on-Trent	277
14 Nottingham	269
15 Leicester	239
16 Cardiff	224
17 Dundee	176
18 Aberdeen	167
Coventry	167
20 Wolverhampton	133

1951	
1 London	8,197
2 Birmingham	1,113
3 Glasgow	1,090
4 Liverpool	789
5 Manchester	703
6 Sheffield	513
7 Leeds	505
8 Edinburgh	467
9 Belfast	444
10 Bristol	443
11 Nottingham	306
12 Kingston-upon-Hull	299
13 Bradford	292
14 Leicester	285
15 Stoke-on-Trent	275
16 Coventry	258
17 Cardiff	244
18 Aberdeen	183
19 Dundee	177
20 Wolverhampton	163

1961			*1971*		
1	London	7,992	1	London	7,454
2	Birmingham	1,107	2	Birmingham	1,015
3	Glasgow	1,055	3	Glasgow	897
4	Liverpool	746	4	Liverpool	610
5	Manchester	662	5	Manchester	544
6	Leeds	511	6	Sheffield	520
7	Sheffield	494	7	Leeds	496
8	Edinburgh	468	8	Edinburgh	454
9	Bristol	437	9	Bristol	427
10	Belfast	416	10	Belfast	362
11	Nottingham	312	11	Coventry	335
12	Coventry	306	12	Nottingham	301
13	Kingston-upon-Hull	303	13	Bradford	294
14	Bradford	296	14	Kingston-upon-Hull	286
15	Leicester	273	15	Leicester	284
16	Stoke-on-Trent	265	16	Cardiff	279
17	Cardiff	257	17	Wolverhampton	269
18	Aberdeen	185	18	Stoke-on-Trent	265
19	Dundee	183	19	Aberdeen	182
20	Wolverhampton	151		Dundee	182

1981			*1991*		
1	London	6,696	1	London	6,890
2	Birmingham	1,007	2	Birmingham	938
3	Glasgow	766	3	Leeds	677
4	Leeds	705	4	Glasgow	654
5	Sheffield	538	5	Sheffield	503
6	Liverpool	510	6	Bradford	451
7	Bradford	457	7	Liverpool	450
8	Manchester	449	8	Edinburgh	422
9	Edinburgh	437	9	Manchester	400
10	Bristol	391	10	Bristol	372
11	Belfast	314	11	Coventry	295
	Coventry	314	12	Belfast	279
13	Leicester	280	13	Cardiff	277
14	Cardiff	274	14	Leicester	272
15	Nottingham	272	15	Nottingham	262
16	Kingston-upon-Hull	270	16	Kingston-upon-Hull	253
17	Wolverhampton	255	17	Stoke-on-Trent	244
18	Stoke-on-Trent	253	18	Wolverhampton	241
19	Aberdeen	204	19	Aberdeen	201
20	Dundee	180	20	Dundee	166

Immigration and race

Ethnic breakdown
% of population

	White		Black		Indian	
	1983	1994	1983	1994	1983	1994
Great Britain	94.2	94.2	1.0	1.5	1.4	1.6
Wales	97.4	98.8	0.1	0.0	0.3	0.0
Scotland	98.2	99.0	0.0	0.0	0.1	0.0
North	97.6	98.6	0.0	0.0	0.2	0.0
Yorkshire & Humberside	94.9	95.4	0.5	0.6	0.8	1.1
North West	94.9	95.4	0.4	0.7	1.0	1.1
West Midlands	91.0	91.6	1.5	1.4	3.2	3.3
East Midlands	94.4	95.1	0.6	0.8	2.3	2.8
East Anglia	97.2	98.2	0.3	0.5	0.2	0.0
South East	91.0	89.5	2.1	3.6	2.2	2.5
South West	97.4	98.8	0.3	0.3	0.2	0.2

Immigration and emigration
Immigration, '000s
British citizens country of last/next residence

	All countries	EU	Commonwealth countries		
			Australia, Canada, New Zealand	South Africa	Bangladesh, India Sri Lanka
1976	191	32	40	9	15
1981	153	25	20	3	18
1986	250	69	30	18	16
1987	212	55	31	7	14
1988	216	52	36	7	12
1989	250	55	48	12	16
1990	267	66	57	6	13
1991	267	72	47	8	12
1992	216	69	34	7	9
1993	209	51	35	9	13
1994ª	253	76	34	8	10

Emigration, '000s

	All countries	EU	Commonwealth countries		
			Australia, Canada, New Zealand	South Africa	Bangladesh, India Sri Lanka
1976	210	38	63	21	4
1981	233	32	79	23	2
1986	213	58	50	2	4
1987	210	59	59	3	3
1988	237	59	62	5	5
1989	205	45	55	6	5
1990	231	59	59	9	2
1991	239	70	53	6	5
1992	227	57	44	5	3
1993	213	62	48	3	4
1994ª	191	52	38	4	2

a Provisional.

Pakistani/Bangladeshi		Mixed/other		Total pop., '000s	
1983	1994	1983	1994	1983	1994
1.0	1.3	1.1	1.3	54,118	55,893
0.3	0.4	0.6	0.4	2,777	2,888
0.4	0.4	0.3	0.3	5,056	4,988
0.4	0.4	0.6	0.6	3,057	3,052
1.7	2.2	0.6	0.7	4,846	4,948
1.0	1.7	0.9	1.2	6,321	6,322
2.2	2.7	0.7	1.0	5,126	5,239
0.3	0.4	0.7	0.8	3,833	4,066
0.3	0.0	0.7	0.8	1,912	2,125
0.9	1.8	2.1	2.6	16,825	17,524
0.1	0.0	0.5	0.5	4,365	4,740

Pakistan	Caribbean	Other	Other foreign countries	
			USA	Other
12	4	36	16	27
9	3	26	17	32
10	5	29	26	47
10	3	26	28	38
9	3	26	23	48
10	3	30	31	45
9	7	30	29	50
12	3	39	25	49
8	2	29	18	40
7	2	25	23	44
6	1	36	30	52

Pakistan	Caribbean	Other	Other foreign countries	
			USA	Other
2	3	21	21	37
1	3	23	25	45
2	2	19	34	42
1	3	15	34	33
3	4	26	30	43
4	3	22	30	35
3	4	19	42	34
3	2	27	32	41
2	3	21	37	55
2	3	23	33	35
3	3	21	24	44

Births and deaths

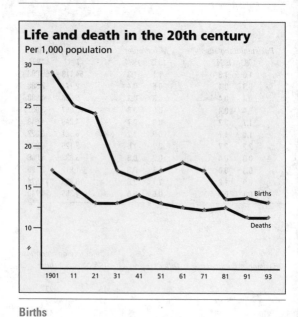

Life and death in the 20th century
Per 1,000 population

Births

Per 1,000 population

	1961	1971	1981	1991	1993
Wales	17.0	15.8	12.7	13.2	12.6
Scotland	19.5	16.6	13.3	13.1	12.4
North	18.7	16.7	12.8	13.3	12.4
Yorkshire & Humberside	17.8	16.4	12.7	13.8	13.0
North-West	18.3	16.9	13.1	14.3	13.2
West Midlands	18.6	17.2	13.0	14.1	13.2
East Midlands	17.6	15.5	12.8	13.4	12.7
East Anglia	16.5	15.8	12.5	12.6	12.2
South East	16.6	15.4	13.0	14.0	13.7
South West	16.3	13.9	11.5	12.2	11.9

Deaths

Per 1,000 population

	1961	1971	1981	1991	1993
Wales	12.8	12.7	12.4	11.8	12.3
Scotland	12.3	11.8	12.4	12.0	12.5
North	11.9	11.9	12.3	12.3	12.2
Yorkshire & Humberside	12.5	12.0	12.0	11.5	11.4
North-West	13.3	12.4	12.4	12.0	12.1
West Midlands	10.9	10.4	10.9	10.8	11.0
East Midlands	11.2	11.0	11.2	10.9	11.1
East Anglia	11.6	11.2	11.1	10.9	11.1
South East	11.9	11.2	11.1	10.3	10.4
South West	12.4	12.3	12.5	11.9	11.9

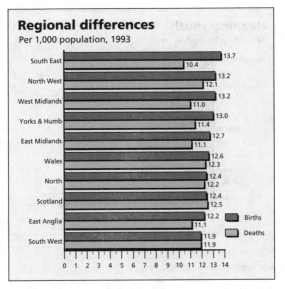

Regional differences
Per 1,000 population, 1993

Region	Births	Deaths
South East	13.7	10.4
North West	13.2	12.1
West Midlands	13.2	11.0
Yorks & Humb	13.0	11.4
East Midlands	12.7	11.1
Wales	12.6	12.3
North	12.4	12.2
Scotland	12.4	12.5
East Anglia	12.2	11.1
South West	11.9	11.9

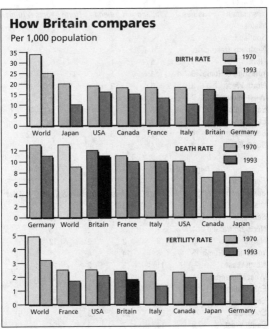

How Britain compares
Per 1,000 population

BIRTH RATE — 1970, 1993
World, Japan, USA, Canada, France, Italy, Britain, Germany

DEATH RATE — 1970, 1993
Germany, World, Britain, France, Italy, USA, Canada, Japan

FERTILITY RATE — 1970, 1993
World, France, USA, Britain, Italy, Canada, Japan, Germany

Internal migration

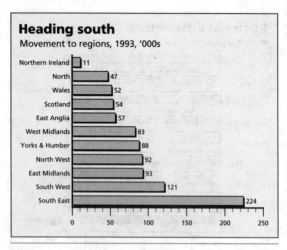

Heading south
Movement to regions, 1993, '000s

Northern Ireland	11
North	47
Wales	52
Scotland	54
East Anglia	57
West Midlands	83
Yorks & Humber	88
North West	92
East Midlands	93
South West	121
South East	224

Moving around
Inter-regional movements, 1993, '000s

Region of destination	Region of origin				
	Wales	Scotland	N Ireland	North	Yorks & Humb
Wales	–	2	…	1	3
Scotland	2	–	2	6	5
Northern Ireland	…	1	–	…	1
North	1	5	1	–	9
Yorkshire & Humb	3	4	1	11	–
North West	8	6	2	8	14
West Midlands	7	3	1	3	7
East Midlands	3	3	1	4	16
East Anglia	1	2	…	2	4
South East	14	17	3	12	22
South West	9	4	1	3	6

Region of destination	Region of origin					
	N West	W Mids	E Mids	E Anglia	S East	S West
Wales	9	8	3	1	16	8
Scotland	7	3	3	2	19	4
Northern Ireland	1	1	…	…	5	1
North	8	3	3	2	12	3
Yorkshire & Humb	15	8	14	4	24	6
North West	–	11	8	3	26	7
West Midlands	11	–	11	3	26	11
East Midlands	9	13	–	7	30	7
East Anglia	3	3	7	–	31	4
South East	27	28	26	23	–	51
South West	9	14	7	4	64	–

Gross domestic product

National trends
GDP, £bn

	UK[a]	England	Wales	Scotland	N.Ireland
1975	98.1	82.8	4.2	8.9	2.2
1976	114.6	96.5	4.9	10.6	2.6
1977	133.3	112.7	5.6	12.1	2.9
1978	152.2	129.1	6.4	13.4	3.3
1979	175.7	149.4	7.3	15.3	3.7
1980	203.3	173.5	8.2	17.4	4.2
1981	220.9	188.4	8.8	19.1	4.6
1982	237.7	203.1	9.6	20.1	4.9
1983	261.2	208.0	10.4	22.0	5.3
1984	280.7	221.4	11.1	22.8	5.8
1985	307.9	246.3	12.0	25.2	6.3
1986	328.3	272.1	13.5	27.3	7.0
1987	360.7	298.8	15.1	29.8	7.5
1988	401.4	336.2	17.2	33.0	8.4
1989	441.8	371.1	18.9	36.2	9.2
1990	478.9	401.5	20.3	40.1	10.2
1991	495.9	415.8	20.9	42.1	11.1
1992	516.5	432.8	21.3	44.4	11.6
1993	546.7	457.5	22.3	46.9	12.3
1994	578.7	483.4	23.8	50.0	13.2

Regional trends
GDP, £bn

	North	Yorkshire & Humberside	North West	West Midlands
1975	5.1	8.0	11.0	8.8
1976	6.1	9.3	12.8	10.0
1977	7.0	10.9	14.7	11.4
1978	7.7	12.4	16.9	13.2
1979	8.7	14.0	18.9	14.7
1980	10.0	15.5	21.4	16.3
1981	10.9	16.9	22.4	17.1
1982	11.7	18.4	24.4	18.6
1983	12.6	20.0	26.4	20.4
1984	13.3	21.3	27.9	21.8
1985	14.7	23.7	30.8	24.5
1986	15.6	26.1	33.7	26.7
1987	17.2	28.3	36.5	29.3
1988	19.0	31.2	40.9	33.3
1989	20.8	34.5	44.3	36.8
1990	22.2	37.1	47.3	40.2
1991	23.3	38.7	48.6	41.4
1992	24.4	39.9	50.6	43.3
1993	25.5	41.8	53.5	45.6
1994	26.9	43.9	56.5	47.9

a Including Continental Shelf.

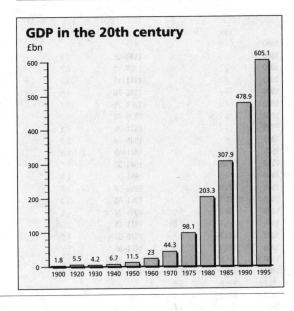

GDP in the 20th century
£bn

Year	GDP
1900	1.8
1920	5.5
1930	4.2
1940	6.7
1950	11.5
1960	23
1970	44.3
1975	98.1
1980	203.3
1985	307.9
1990	478.9
1995	605.1

East Midlands	East Anglia	Greater London	Rest of South East	South West
6.2	2.9	16.3	17.6	6.7
7.2	3.5	18.5	20.6	7.9
8.4	4.1	21.0	24.0	9.2
9.4	4.6	23.9	28.3	10.3
10.9	5.2	27.1	32.7	11.9
12.7	6.2	30.7	37.8	13.9
13.8	6.7	32.9	41.0	15.1
15.0	7.5	33.5	44.1	16.6
16.3	8.2	36.5	49.3	18.3
17.8	9.2	37.8	52.8	19.5
19.8	10.2	42.4	58.5	21.7
21.7	11.4	47.3	65.3	24.2
23.8	12.4	52.4	72.0	26.8
26.6	14.1	58.2	82.6	30.3
29.8	15.7	64.3	91.4	33.4
32.0	17.2	70.0	99.1	36.4
33.5	17.8	72.4	102.2	37.9
34.7	18.8	75.6	105.5	39.9
36.6	19.6	81.2	111.5	42.2
38.5	21.0	85.5	118.4	44.8

Economic growth

GDP[a], total		
	£bn	% world GDP
1900	1.8	…
1905	1.9	…
1910	2.1	…
1915	3.2	…
1920	5.5	…
1925	4.2	…
1930	4.2	…
1935	4.2	…
1940	6.7	…
1945	8.7	…
1950	11.5	…
1955	17.0	…
1960	23.0	…
1965	31.7	…
1970	44.3	3.9
1975	98.1	3.8
1980	203.3	4.7
1985	307.9	3.6
1990	478.9	3.8
1991	495.9	3.8
1992	516.5	3.9
1993	546.7	3.4
1994	578.7	3.4
1995	605.1	3.3

GDP real average annual growth	
%	
1901–05	1.8
1906–10	0.7
1911–15	4.9
1916–20	-4.5
1921–25	1.7
1926–30	1.2
1931–35	1.3
1936–40	5.7
1941–45	-0.5
1946–50	1.1
1951–55	2.9
1956–60	2.7
1961–65	3.2
1966–70	2.5
1971–75	2.0
1976–80	1.9
1981–85	1.9
1986–90	3.2
1991–95	1.2

G7 members compared

GDP, real % change on a year earlier

	UK	USA	Japan	Germany[b]	France	Italy	Canada
1980	-2.2	-0.3	3.6	1.0	1.6	4.1	1.5
1981	-1.3	2.5	3.6	0.1	1.2	0.6	3.7
1982	1.7	-2.1	3.2	-0.9	2.5	0.2	-3.2
1983	3.7	4.0	2.7	1.8	0.7	1.0	3.2
1984	2.3	6.8	4.3	2.8	1.3	2.7	6.3
1985	3.8	3.7	5.0	2.0	1.9	2.6	4.7
1986	4.3	3.0	2.6	2.3	2.5	2.9	3.3
1987	4.8	2.9	4.1	1.5	2.3	3.1	4.2
1988	5.0	3.8	6.2	3.7	4.5	4.1	5.0
1989	2.2	3.4	4.7	3.6	4.3	2.9	2.4
1990	0.4	1.3	4.8	5.7	2.5	2.1	-0.2
1991	-2.0	-1.0	4.3	5.0	0.8	1.1	-1.8
1992	-0.5	2.7	1.1	2.2	1.2	0.6	0.8
1993	2.3	2.2	0.1	-1.2	-1.3	-1.2	2.2
1994	4.0	3.5	0.6	3.0	2.8	2.1	4.6
1995	2.5	2.0	0.7	2.1	2.2	3.0	2.2

a Factor cost, current prices.
b Western Germany only to 1991.

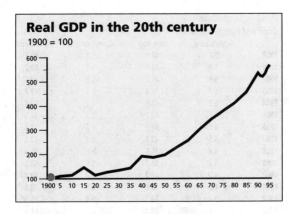

Real GDP in the 20th century

1900 = 100

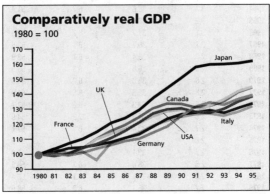

Comparatively real GDP

1980 = 100

North-south divide

GDP at current prices, average annual growth, %

	1971–80	1981–90	1991–94
UK	14.6	8.9	4.9
Wales	14.0	9.3	4.1
Scotland	14.3	8.6	5.7
Northern Ireland	14.1	9.1	6.6
North	14.2	8.3	4.9
North West	13.5	8.3	4.6
Yorkshire & Humberside	14.0	9.1	4.3
West Midlands	12.9	9.4	4.5
East Midlands	15.3	9.6	4.7
East Anglia	15.4	10.7	5.1
Greater London	13.5	8.7	5.1
Rest of South East	14.7	10.2	4.5
South West	15.1	10.1	5.3

GDP by sector

Post-war change
Origins of GDP, % of total

	Agriculture	Industry	Construction	Services
1950	5.7	40.4	5.3	48.6
1951	5.5	41.1	5.3	48.2
1952	5.6	40.7	5.5	48.1
1953	5.4	41.4	5.7	47.4
1954	5.0	41.9	5.7	47.4
1955	4.7	42.1	5.7	47.5
1956	4.5	41.9	6.0	47.6
1957	4.5	42.1	5.9	47.5
1958	4.4	41.6	6.0	48.0
1959	4.2	41.7	5.9	48.2
1960	4.0	41.7	6.0	48.4
1961	4.0	40.6	6.3	49.1
1962	3.8	38.7	6.4	51.0
1963	3.5	38.3	6.4	51.8
1964	3.3	38.6	6.7	51.4
1965	3.2	38.4	6.7	51.7
1966	3.1	37.7	6.7	52.5
1967	3.1	36.7	6.7	53.5
1968	2.9	36.4	6.7	53.9
1969	2.9	36.6	6.6	53.9
1970	2.8	35.9	6.7	54.6
1971	2.8	35.5	6.8	54.9
1972	2.5	33.3	6.5	57.7
1973	2.9	34.9	7.3	54.9
1974	2.7	33.4	6.7	57.1
1975	2.6	33.0	6.6	57.8
1976	2.7	33.1	6.4	57.8
1977	2.5	35.0	6.1	56.5
1978	2.3	35.1	6.1	56.4
1979	2.2	35.1	6.2	56.5
1980	2.1	34.9	6.0	57.0
1981	2.0	33.9	5.7	58.4
1982	2.3	34.9	5.7	57.1
1983	2.0	34.4	5.8	57.8
1984	2.3	33.5	5.9	58.3
1985	1.9	33.8	5.7	58.5
1986	1.9	30.2	5.8	62.1
1987	1.9	29.5	6.2	62.4
1988	1.7	28.0	6.7	63.6
1989	1.8	27.9	7.1	63.2
1990	1.8	26.7	6.9	64.7
1991	1.8	26.5	6.4	65.3
1992	1.9	26.0	5.8	66.3
1993	2.0	25.8	5.3	66.9
1994	2.0	25.9	5.4	66.7

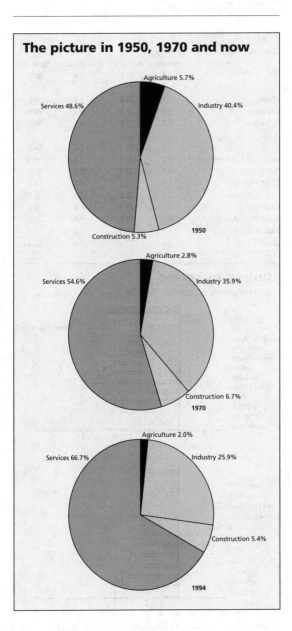

The picture in 1950, 1970 and now

Agriculture 5.7%
Industry 40.4%
Services 48.6%
Construction 5.3%
1950

Agriculture 2.8%
Industry 35.9%
Services 54.6%
Construction 6.7%
1970

Agriculture 2.0%
Industry 25.9%
Services 66.7%
Construction 5.4%
1994

Regional trends

Origins of GDP, 1986
% of total

	Agriculture	Industry	Construction	Services
UK[a]	1.8	31.1	6.8	60.2
Wales	2.7	34.9	5.7	56.8
Scotland	3.0	28.8	7.3	60.9
N. Ireland	4.0	22.8	6.1	67.1
North	1.9	35.1	6.4	56.6
Yorkshire & Humberside	2.1	35.1	5.9	56.9
North West	0.8	36.0	12.0	51.2
West Midlands	1.8	38.1	5.9	54.2
East Midlands	2.9	38.8	5.9	52.5
East Anglia	6.7	27.0	7.4	59.0
Greater London	0.1	18.1	4.5	77.2
Rest of South East	1.4	25.3	7.5	65.9
South West	2.8	25.9	7.5	63.8

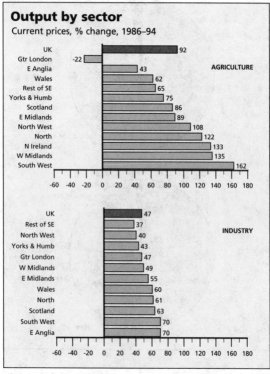

Output by sector
Current prices, % change, 1986–94

AGRICULTURE

UK	92
Gtr London	-22
E Anglia	43
Wales	62
Rest of SE	65
Yorks & Humb	75
Scotland	86
E Midlands	89
North West	108
North	122
N Ireland	133
W Midlands	135
South West	162

INDUSTRY

UK	47
Rest of SE	37
North West	40
Yorks & Humb	43
Gtr London	47
W Midlands	49
E Midlands	55
Wales	60
North	61
Scotland	63
South West	70
E Anglia	70

a Includes the Continental Shelf.

Origins of GDP, 1994
% of total

	Agriculture	Industry	Construction	Services
UK[a]	2.0	25.8	5.2	67
Wales	2.4	30.8	5.3	61.5
Scotland	3.1	25.8	6.5	64.7
N. Ireland	4.9	21.9	5.5	67.7
North	2.3	31.8	2.0	63.9
Yorkshire & Humberside	2.2	29.2	5.9	62.7
North West	1.0	30.0	5.4	63.5
West Midlands	2.3	31.4	5.3	61.0
East Midlands	3	33.1	6.1	57.7
East Anglia	5.1	24.6	5.4	64.8
Greater London	0.0	14.9	3.9	81.2
Rest of South East	1.3	19.3	5.6	73.8
South West	3.9	23.6	5.7	66.8

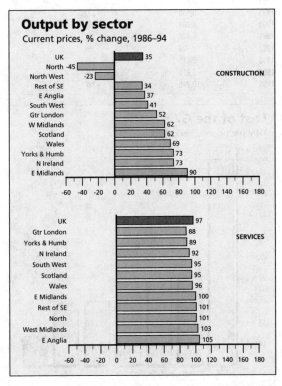

Output by sector
Current prices, % change, 1986–94

CONSTRUCTION

UK	35
North	-45
North West	-23
Rest of SE	34
E Anglia	37
South West	41
Gtr London	52
W Midlands	62
Scotland	62
Wales	69
Yorks & Humb	73
N Ireland	73
E Midlands	90

-60 -40 -20 0 20 40 60 80 100 120 140 160 180

SERVICES

UK	97
Gtr London	88
Yorks & Humb	89
N Ireland	92
South West	95
Scotland	95
Wales	96
E Midlands	100
Rest of SE	101
North	101
West Midlands	103
E Anglia	105

-60 -40 -20 0 20 40 60 80 100 120 140 160 180

Living standards

GDP per person

	£	real GDP per person, 1900 = 100
1900	44	100
1905	44	105
1910	47	104
1915	69	128
1920	126	108
1925	93	114
1930	92	119
1935	90	124
1940	139	158
1945	177	152
1950	227	156
1955	334	178
1960	439	197
1965	583	222
1970	796	246
1975	1,745	269
1980	3,609	294
1985	5,438	322
1990	8,201	372
1991	8,475	361
1992	8,928	358
1993	9,415	365
1994	9,910	378
1995	10,315	386

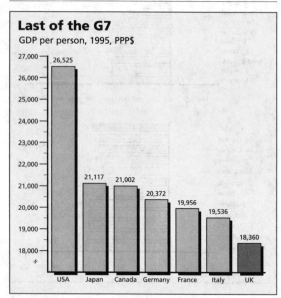

Last of the G7
GDP per person, 1995, PPP$

USA	Japan	Canada	Germany	France	Italy	UK
26,525	21,117	21,002	20,372	19,956	19,536	18,360

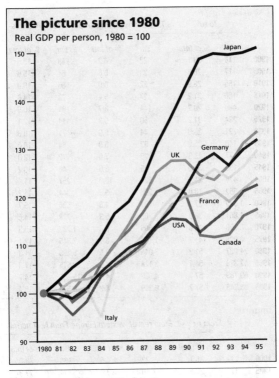

The picture since 1980
Real GDP per person, 1980 = 100

Japan, Germany, UK, France, USA, Canada, Italy (chart lines, 1980–95, indexed 90–150)

GDP per person, current prices
$

	1960	1970	1980	1990	1995
Japan	477	1,964	9,069	23,801	39,540
Germany	1,300	3,042	13,154	23,658	29,585
France	1,333	2,814	12,335	21,014	26,596
USA	2,849	4,933	11,891	21,866	26,520
Italy	791	2,003	8,023	18,991	19,079
Canada	2,257	3,960	10,934	21,273	18,998
UK	1,382	2,226	9,540	16,968	18,782

Regional growth rankings
GDP per head 1994, UK = 100

Greater London	125.7	West Midlands	92.6
Rest of South East	111.2	North West	90.2
East Anglia	102.0	Yorkshire & Humberside	89.4
England	101.6	North	88.8
Scotland	99.7	Wales	83.7
East Midlands	96.1	Northern Ireland	82.2
South West	95.7		

Trade: partners and products

Exports

	To EU[a]		To rest of western Europe		To N. America	
	£m	% of total	£m	% of total	£m	% of total
1900	118	33.1	22	6.2	48	13.5
1905	117	28.6	23	5.6	64	15.6
1910	155	28.9	32	6.0	86	16.0
1915	156	31.2	27	5.4	73	14.6
1920	486	29.2	144	8.7	181	10.9
1925	294	31.2	50	5.3	114	12.1
1930	221	33.0	44	6.6	71	10.6
1935	140	25.9	32	5.9	54	10.0
1940	77	19.3	28	7.0	72	18.0
1945	139	30.9	25	5.6	46	10.2
1950	476	21.1	227	10.0	257	11.4
1955	552	18.0	296	9.6	344	11.2
1960	1,049	27.7	181	4.8	596	15.7
1965	1,801	36.5	263	5.3	728	14.8
1970	3,228	40.0	505	6.3	1,232	15.3
1975	8,098	41.7	1,194	6.1	2,345	12.1
1980	24,087	51.2	3,046	6.5	5,299	11.3
1985	42,329	54.1	3,128	4.0	13,515	17.3
1990	59,789	57.7	4,580	4.4	15,235	14.7
1995	88,348	57.7	6,399	4.2	20,574	13.4

Imports

	From EU[a]		From rest of western Europe		From N. America	
	£m	% of total	£m	% of total	£m	% of total
1900	178	36.7	22	4.5	163	33.6
1905	172	32.6	40	7.6	144	27.3
1910	188	29.7	44	7.0	149	23.6
1915	116	13.8	51	6.1	282	33.6
1920	287	15.8	135	7.5	666	36.8
1925	336	27.8	73	6.0	321	26.6
1930	327	34.3	67	7.0	196	20.6
1935	165	22.8	53	7.3	146	20.2
1940	...	...	...	...	364	36.4
1945	...	...	...	...	527	75.3
1950	546	23.6	168	7.3	392	17.0
1955	776	22.9	322	9.5	764	22.6
1960	1,311	28.2	158	3.4	950	20.4
1965	1,861	32.3	221	3.8	1,131	19.6
1970	3,319	36.5	547	6.0	1,877	20.7
1975	10,868	45.5	1,390	5.8	3,223	13.5
1980	24,267	49.6	3,528	7.2	7,383	15.1
1985	46,059	54.2	7,544	8.9	11,931	14.1
1990	72,802	57.7	9,388	7.4	16,924	13.4
1995	92,104	55.1	10,686	6.4	23,048	13.8

a EU12 up to 1955. EU15 from 1960.

To Japan	
£m	*% of total*
10	2.8
10	2.4
10	1.9
5	1.0
28	1.7
17	1.8
8	1.2
4	0.7
…	…
…	…
3	0.1
14	0.5
29	0.8
53	1.1
149	1.8
310	1.6
596	1.3
1,011	1.3
2,632	2.5
2,786	1.8

From Japan	
£m	*% of total*
2	0.4
2	0.4
4	0.6
9	1.1
30	1.7
7	0.6
8	0.8
8	1.1
6	0.6
…	…
8	0.3
24	0.7
42	0.9
78	1.4
135	1.5
673	2.8
1,709	3.5
4,115	4.8
6,760	5.4
9,630	5.8

What Britain trades

EXPORTS 1950

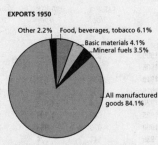

Other 2.2%
Food, beverages, tobacco 6.1%
Basic materials 4.1%
Mineral fuels 3.5%
All manufactured goods 84.1%

EXPORTS 1995

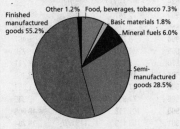

Other 1.2%
Food, beverages, tobacco 7.3%
Finished manufactured goods 55.2%
Basic materials 1.8%
Mineral fuels 6.0%
Semi-manufactured goods 28.5%

IMPORTS 1950

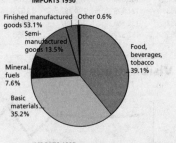

Finished manufactured goods 53.1%
Other 0.6%
Semi-manufactured goods 13.5%
Mineral fuels 7.6%
Basic materials 35.2%
Food, beverages, tobacco 39.1%

IMPORTS 1995

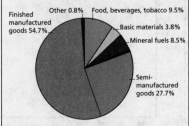

Other 0.8%
Food, beverages, tobacco 9.5%
Finished manufactured goods 54.7%
Basic materials 3.8%
Mineral fuels 8.5%
Semi-manufactured goods 27.7%

Trade: balances

Balance of payments
£m

	Exports (fob)	Imports (fob)	Visible-trade balance	Invisible-trade balance	of which services balance
1900	356	485	-129	163	61
1905	409	527	-118	206	86
1910	536	632	-96	270	104
1915	500	840	-340	285	120
1920	1,664	1,812	-148	485	240
1925	943	1,208	-265	317	66
1930	670	953	-283	319	67
1935	541	724	-183	206	25
1940	400	1,000	-600	-200	-350
1945	450	700	-250	-620	-650
1950	2,261	2,312	-51	358	-30
1955	3,073	3,386	-313	158	9
1960	3,737	4,138	-401	164	-1
1965	4,913	5,173	-260	183	-98
1970	8,130	8,141	-11	832	421
1975	19,185	22,441	-3,256	1,732	1,315
1980	47,149	45,792	1,357	1,486	3,653
1985	77,991	81,336	-3,345	5,583	6,398
1990	101,718	120,527	-18,809	-484	3,689
1991	103,413	113,697	-10,284	1,751	3,708
1992	107,343	120,447	-13,104	3,636	5,051
1993	121,409	134,787	-13,378	2,336	5,685
1994	134,666	145,497	-10,831	8,751	4,679
1995	152,671	164,221	-11,550	4,890	…

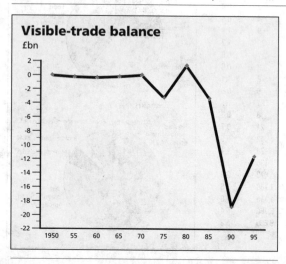

Visible-trade balance
£bn

Current-account balance	Current-account balance as % of GDP	**Trade share** Exports as % of world exports	
		1950	10.4
		1951	9.6
		1952	9.8
		1953	9.3
34	1.8	**1954**	9.2
88	4.2	**1955**	9.3
174	7.8	**1956**	9.4
-55	-1.6	**1957**	9.0
337	5.8	**1958**	9.1
52	1.1	**1959**	8.7
36	0.8	**1960**	8.1
23	0.5	**1961**	8.2
-800	-10.6	**1962**	7.9
-870	-8.8	**1963**	7.8
307	2.4	**1964**	7.4
-155	-0.8	**1965**	7.4
-237	-0.9	**1966**	7.2
-77	-0.2	**1967**	6.7
821	1.6	**1968**	6.5
-1,524	-1.4	**1969**	6.4
2,843	1.2	**1970**	6.3
2,238	0.6	**1971**	6.3
-19,293	-3.5	**1972**	5.7
-8,533	-1.5	**1973**	5.1
-9,468	-1.6	**1974**	4.6
-11,042	-1.8	**1975**	4.9
-2,080	-0.3	**1976**	4.6
-6,670	-1.0	**1977**	4.9
		1978	5.2
		1979	5.3
		1980	5.4
		1981	5.1
		1982	5.1
		1983	5.0
		1984	4.8
		1985	5.2
		1986	5.0
		1987	5.2
		1988	5.0
		1989	4.9
		1990	5.3
		1991	5.2
		1992	5.0
		1993	4.7
		1994	4.7
		1995	4.6

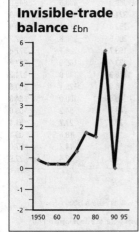

Invisible-trade balance £bn

The pound in your pocket

Internal purchasing power of the pound
Year in which purchasing power was 100p

	1900	1905	1910	1915	1920
1900	100.0	94.9	106.3	146.8	341.8
1905	105.3	100.0	112.0	154.7	360.0
1910	94.0	89.3	100.0	138.1	321.4
1915	68.1	64.7	72.4	100.0	232.8
1920	29.3	27.8	31.1	43.0	100.0
1925	54.1	51.4	57.5	79.5	184.9
1930	76.0	72.1	80.8	111.5	259.6
1935	76.7	72.8	81.6	112.6	262.1
1940	52.0	49.3	55.3	76.3	177.6
1945	41.4	39.3	44.0	60.7	141.4
1950	33.8	32.1	35.9	49.6	115.4
1955	27.5	26.1	29.3	40.4	94.1
1960	24.5	23.3	26.1	36.0	83.9
1965	20.6	19.6	21.9	30.3	70.5
1970	16.5	15.7	17.5	24.2	56.4
1975	8.9	8.5	9.5	13.1	30.6
1980	4.6	4.3	4.9	6.7	15.6
1985	3.2	3.1	3.4	4.7	11.0
1990	2.4	2.3	2.6	3.6	8.3
1995	2.1	2.0	2.2	3.0	7.0

	1955	1960	1965	1970	1975
1900	363.3	407.6	484.8	606.3	1,117.7
1905	382.7	429.3	510.7	638.7	1,177.3
1910	341.7	383.3	456.0	570.2	1,051.2
1915	247.4	277.6	330.2	412.9	761.2
1920	106.3	119.3	141.9	177.4	327.0
1925	196.6	220.5	262.3	328.1	604.8
1930	276.0	309.6	368.3	460.6	849.0
1935	278.6	312.6	371.8	465.0	857.3
1940	188.8	211.8	252.0	315.1	580.9
1945	150.3	168.6	200.5	250.8	462.3
1950	122.6	137.6	163.7	204.7	377.4
1955	100.0	112.2	133.4	166.9	307.7
1960	89.1	100.0	118.9	148.8	274.2
1965	74.9	84.1	100.0	125.1	230.5
1970	59.9	67.2	80.0	100.0	184.3
1975	32.5	36.5	43.4	54.2	100.0
1980	16.6	18.6	22.2	27.7	51.1
1985	11.7	13.2	15.7	19.6	36.1
1990	8.8	9.9	11.7	14.7	27.0
1995	7.4	8.4	9.9	12.4	22.9

For help with using the table, note that:
- in 1995 the pound was worth 2.1p compared with its value in 1900 and 8.4p compared with its value in 1960;
- compared with its value in 1995, the pound was worth 48.8 times more in 1900 and 12.0 times more in 1960.

1925	1930	1935	1940	1945	1950
184.8	131.6	130.4	192.4	241.8	296.2
194.7	138.7	137.3	202.7	254.7	312.0
173.8	123.8	122.6	181.0	227.4	278.6
125.9	89.7	88.8	131.0	164.7	201.7
54.1	38.5	38.1	56.3	70.7	86.7
100.0	71.2	70.5	104.1	130.8	160.3
140.4	100.0	99.0	146.2	183.7	225.0
141.7	101.0	100.0	147.6	185.4	227.2
96.1	68.4	67.8	100.0	125.7	153.9
76.4	54.5	53.9	79.6	100.0	122.5
62.4	44.4	44.0	65.0	81.6	100.0
50.9	36.2	35.9	53.0	66.6	81.5
45.3	32.3	32.0	47.2	59.3	72.7
38.1	27.2	26.9	39.7	49.9	61.1
30.5	21.7	21.5	31.7	39.9	48.9
16.5	11.8	11.7	17.2	21.6	26.5
8.4	6.0	6.0	8.8	11.1	13.5
6.0	4.3	4.2	6.2	7.8	9.6
4.5	3.2	3.2	4.7	5.8	7.2
3.8	2.7	2.7	3.9	5.0	6.1

1980	1985	1990	1995
2,187.3	3,097.5	4,132.9	4,878.9
2,304.0	3,262.7	4,353.3	5,139.0
2,057.1	2,913.1	3,886.9	4,588.5
1,489.7	2,109.5	2,814.7	3,322.7
640.0	906.3	1,209.3	1,427.6
1,183.6	1,676.0	2,236.3	2,639.9
1,661.5	2,352.9	3,139.4	3,706.1
1,677.7	2,375.7	3,169.9	3,742.1
1,136.8	1,609.9	2,148.0	2,535.7
904.7	1,281.2	1,709.4	2,018.0
738.5	1,045.7	1,395.3	1,647.2
602.1	852.6	1,137.6	1,342.9
536.6	759.9	1,014.0	1,197.0
451.2	638.9	852.5	1,006.4
360.8	510.9	681.6	804.7
195.7	277.1	369.8	436.5
100.0	141.6	188.9	223.0
70.6	100.0	133.4	157.5
52.9	74.9	100.0	118.1
44.8	63.5	84.7	100.0

The value of the pound: abroad

Annual average exchange rates to the £

	US dollar	French franc[a]	D-mark[b]	Yen
1900	4.872	25.38	20.72	9.9
1905	4.866	25.31	20.62	9.8
1910	4.868	25.45	20.71	9.9
1915	4.748	26.51	...	...
1920	3.661	52.47	404.59	7.6
1925	4.829	102.54	20.41	11.9
1930	4.862	123.88	20.38	9.9
1935	4.903	74.27	12.18	17.1
1940	4.030	176.62	...	16.8
1945	4.030	203.89	...	60.5
1950	2.800	980.00	...	1010.2
1955	2.800	978.10	11.74	1011.4
1960	2.808	13.77	11.71·	1008.2
1965	2.796	13.7	11.17	1013.0
1970	2.396	13.24	8.74	857.8
1975	2.220	9.50	5.45	658.1

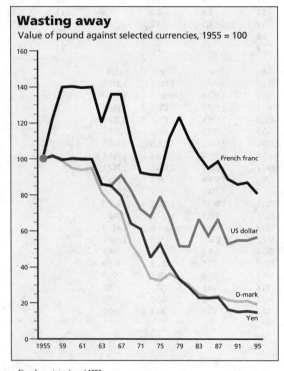

Wasting away

Value of pound against selected currencies, 1955 = 100

a New franc introduced 1959.
b Reichsmark 1900–1929.

	US dollar	French franc	D-mark	Yen
1980	2.328	9.82	4.23	525.6
1981	2.028	11.02	4.58	444.6
1982	1.751	11.50	4.25	435.2
1983	1.517	11.56	3.87	359.9
1984	1.336	11.68	3.80	316.8
1985	1.298	11.55	3.78	307.1
1986	1.467	10.16	3.19	246.8
1987	1.639	9.85	2.95	236.5
1988	1.781	10.61	3.13	228.0
1989	1.640	10.46	3.08	226.2
1990	1.785	9.72	2.88	258.4
1991	1.769	9.95	2.93	237.6
1992	1.766	9.32	2.75	223.7
1993	1.502	8.51	2.48	166.7
1994	1.533	8.49	2.48	156.4
1995	1.578	7.87	2.26	148.4

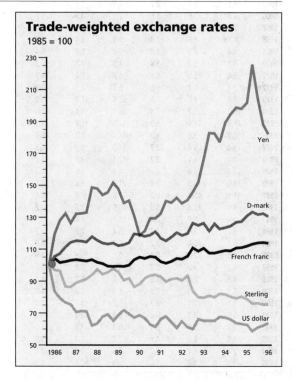

Trade-weighted exchange rates
1985 = 100

For an explanation of trade-weighted exchange rates, see page 12.

Inflation's ups and downs

Consumer price changes compared
% change on a year earlier

	UK	France	Germany[a]	Italy	Japan	USA
1950	3.1	8.0	-6.2	-1.0	-7.1	-1.4
1951	7.3	17.7	7.7	12.5	16.5	8.0
1952	7.2	12.0	2.1	1.9	5.0	2.2
1953	1.5	-1.9	-1.9	1.4	6.6	0.8
1954	1.1	0.4	0.2	2.9	6.5	0.4
1955	4.0	1.0	1.7	2.3	-1.0	-0.3
1956	4.9	4.3	2.6	3.4	0.0	1.5
1957	3.7	-0.8	2.1	1.2	3.3	3.5
1958	2.2	15.3	2.1	2.9	-0.3	2.8
1959	0.0	5.7	1.0	-0.5	1.0	0.8
1960	0.9	4.2	1.5	2.4	3.8	1.6
1961	3.4	2.4	2.3	2.1	5.4	1.1
1962	4.2	5.2	2.9	4.6	6.6	1.1
1963	2.0	5.1	3.0	7.6	7.8	1.2
1964	3.4	3.2	2.4	5.9	3.7	1.3
1965	4.6	2.7	3.2	4.5	6.7	1.6
1966	3.9	2.6	3.6	2.4	4.9	3.1
1967	2.5	2.8	1.6	3.7	4.1	2.8
1968	4.7	4.6	1.6	1.4	5.4	4.2
1969	5.4	6.1	1.9	2.7	5.3	5.4
1970	6.4	5.9	3.4	4.9	7.6	5.9
1971	9.4	5.5	5.2	4.8	6.2	4.3
1972	7.1	6.2	5.5	5.7	4.5	3.3
1973	9.3	7.3	7.0	10.8	11.7	6.2
1974	16.0	13.7	7.0	19.1	24.4	11.0
1975	24.2	11.8	5.9	17.0	11.8	9.1
1976	16.7	9.6	4.3	16.8	9.3	5.8
1977	15.8	9.4	3.7	17.0	8.0	6.5
1978	8.3	9.1	2.7	12.1	3.8	7.6
1979	13.4	10.8	4.1	14.8	3.6	11.3
1980	18.0	13.3	5.4	21.2	8.0	13.5
1981	11.9	13.4	6.3	17.8	4.9	10.4
1982	8.6	11.8	5.3	16.5	2.6	6.2
1983	4.6	9.6	3.3	14.7	1.8	3.2
1984	5.0	7.4	2.4	10.8	2.3	4.3
1985	6.1	5.8	2.2	9.2	2.0	3.6
1986	3.4	2.5	-0.1	5.9	0.6	1.9
1987	4.2	3.3	0.2	4.7	0.0	3.7
1988	4.9	2.7	1.3	5.0	0.7	4.0
1989	7.8	3.5	2.8	6.2	2.3	4.8
1990	9.5	3.4	2.7	6.3	3.1	5.4
1991	5.9	3.2	3.6	6.4	3.3	4.2
1992	3.7	2.4	5.1	5.3	1.7	3.1
1993	1.6	2.1	4.5	4.2	1.3	3.0
1994	2.4	1.7	2.7	3.9	0.7	2.5
1995	3.5	1.8	1.8	5.4	-0.1	2.9

a Western 1991, all Germany from 1992.

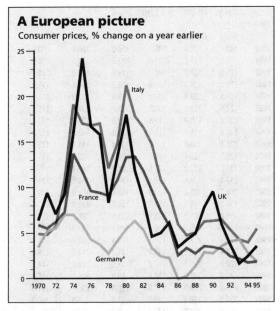

A European picture
Consumer prices, % change on a year earlier

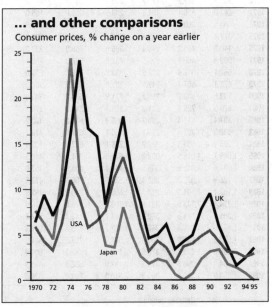

... and other comparisons
Consumer prices, % change on a year earlier

Consumer price indices compared
1950=100

	UK	France	Germany[a]	Italy	Japan	USA
1950	100.0	100.0	100.0	100.0	100.0	100.0
1951	107.3	117.7	107.7	112.5	116.5	108.0
1952	115.0	131.8	110.0	114.6	122.3	110.4
1953	116.7	129.3	107.9	116.2	130.4	111.3
1954	117.9	129.8	108.1	119.6	138.9	111.7
1955	122.6	131.1	109.9	122.4	137.5	111.4
1956	128.6	136.8	112.8	126.5	137.5	113.0
1957	133.3	135.7	115.2	128.0	142.0	117.0
1958	136.3	156.4	117.6	131.8	141.6	120.3
1959	136.3	165.4	118.7	131.1	143.0	121.2
1960	137.6	172.3	120.5	134.2	148.4	123.2
1961	142.3	176.4	123.3	137.1	156.5	124.5
1962	148.3	185.6	126.9	143.4	166.8	125.9
1963	151.3	195.1	130.7	154.3	179.8	127.4
1964	156.4	201.3	133.8	163.4	186.5	129.1
1965	163.7	206.8	138.1	170.7	198.9	131.1
1966	170.1	212.1	143.1	174.8	208.7	135.2
1967	174.4	218.1	145.4	181.3	217.2	139.0
1968	182.5	228.1	147.7	183.8	229.0	144.8
1969	192.3	242.0	150.5	188.8	241.1	152.6
1970	204.7	256.3	155.6	198.0	259.4	161.6
1971	223.9	270.4	163.7	207.5	275.5	168.6
1972	239.7	287.2	172.7	219.4	287.9	174.2
1973	262.0	308.1	184.8	243.1	321.6	185.0
1974	303.8	350.3	197.7	289.5	400.1	205.3
1975	377.4	391.7	209.4	338.7	447.3	224.0
1976	440.2	429.3	218.4	395.6	488.9	237.0
1977	509.8	469.6	226.5	462.9	528.0	252.4
1978	552.1	512.4	232.6	518.9	548.1	271.6
1979	626.1	567.7	242.1	595.6	567.8	302.2
1980	738.5	643.2	255.2	721.9	613.2	343.0
1981	826.5	729.4	271.3	850.4	643.3	378.7
1982	897.4	815.4	285.7	990.7	660.0	402.2
1983	938.9	893.7	295.1	1,136.4	671.9	415.1
1984	985.9	959.9	302.2	1,259.1	687.3	432.9
1985	1,045.7	1,015.5	308.8	1,375.0	701.1	448.5
1986	1,081.6	1,040.9	308.5	1,456.1	705.3	457.0
1987	1,126.9	1,075.3	309.1	1,524.5	705.3	473.9
1988	1,182.1	1,104.3	313.1	1,600.7	710.2	492.9
1989	1,274.4	1,143.0	321.9	1,700.0	726.6	516.6
1990	1,395.3	1,181.8	330.6	1,807.1	749.1	544.5
1991	1,477.8	1,219.6	342.5	1,922.7	773.8	567.3
1992	1,532.5	1,248.9	360.0	2,024.6	787.0	584.3
1993	1,556.8	1,275.1	376.2	2,109.7	797.2	601.9
1994	1,594.2	1,296.8	386.3	2,192.0	802.8	616.9
1995	1,650.0	1,320.1	393.3	2,310.3	802.0	634.8

a Western to 1990, all Germany from 1991.

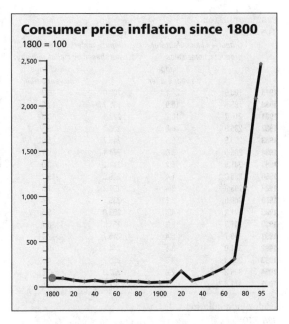

Consumer price inflation since 1800

1800 = 100

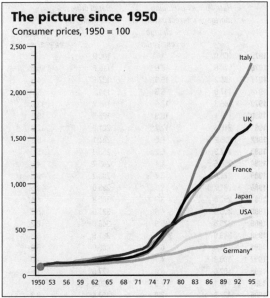

The picture since 1950

Consumer prices, 1950 = 100

Italy

UK

France

Japan

USA

Germany[a]

Producer prices
1975 = 100

| | Output – all manufactured products: home sales | | Input – materials and fuels purchased by manuf. industry | |
		% change on year earlier		% change on year earlier
1975	100.0	23.1	100.0	10.3
1980	195.9	15.9	196.7	17.5
1981	216.7	10.7	222.9	13.3
1982	235.5	8.6	236.7	6.3
1983	250.5	6.5	249.7	5.5
1984	265.5	6.0	274.1	9.7
1985	281.9	6.2	274.1	0.0
1986	286.0	1.4	229.9	-16.2
1987	295.9	3.4	234.2	1.9
1988	306.5	3.7	239.7	2.4
1989	321.2	4.8	253.0	5.5
1990	341.3	6.2	251.3	-0.7
1991	359.7	5.4	245.7	-2.1
1992	371.0	3.1	244.7	-0.4
1993	385.3	3.9	255.7	4.5
1994	395.2	2.6	262.3	2.6
1995	411.6	4.1	287.2	9.5

Underlying inflation
1975 = 100

| | Retail prices excluding mortgage interest payments | | Retail prices excluding food | |
		% change on year earlier		% change on year earlier
1975	100.0		100.0	
1976	116.6	16.6	115.6	15.6
1977	135.2	15.9	132.8	14.9
1978	147.0	8.6	144.3	8.7
1979	165.3	12.5	164.2	13.8
1980	193.1	16.9	196.5	19.6
1981	216.6	12.2	221.6	12.8
1982	235.2	8.5	241.1	8.8
1983	247.3	5.2	253.0	5.0
1984	258.5	4.4	265.2	4.8
1985	271.6	5.2	283.2	6.8
1986	281.7	3.6	293.0	3.5
1987	292.0	3.7	305.8	4.4
1988	305.4	4.6	321.5	5.2
1989	323.5	5.9	348.0	8.2
1990	349.6	8.1	381.9	9.8
1991	373.4	6.7	405.0	6.0
1992	390.9	4.7	421.2	4.0
1993	402.6	3.0	427.5	1.5
1994	412.1	2.3	439.2	2.7
1995	423.8	2.9	453.8	3.3

Revenue and spending

Raising it
£bn

	Personal taxes	Corporate taxes	Customs & excise	Social security	Total receipts
1885	0.02	...	0.05	...	0.09
1890	0.01	...	0.05	...	0.10
1895	0.02	...	0.05	...	0.11
1900	0.03	...	0.07	...	0.14
1905	0.03	...	0.07	...	0.15
1910	0.06	...	0.07	...	0.20
1915	0.13	0.14	0.12	...	0.34
1920	0.39	0.22	0.33	...	1.43
1925	0.33	0.01	0.24	...	0.81
1930	0.32	0.00	0.25	...	0.86
1935	0.29	0.00	0.30	...	0.85
1940	0.55	0.07	0.51	...	1.28
1945	1.43	0.47	1.21	...	3.27
1950	1.42	0.26	1.58	0.44	5.02
1955	1.96	0.20	1.99	0.59	6.30
1960	2.29	0.26	2.37	0.91	8.10
1965	3.37	0.47	3.43	1.68	12.22
1970	5.49	1.67	5.13	2.66	21.21
1975	14.32	2.32	9.08	6.85	42.96
1980	24.31	4.84	22.56	13.94	91.71
1985	35.17	9.05	38.61	24.19	147.14
1990	53.74	22.06	54.79	32.50	191.79
1995	66.88	22.76	76.36	42.38	240.54

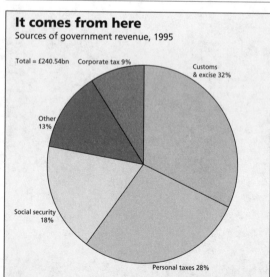

It comes from here
Sources of government revenue, 1995

Total = £240.54bn

Corporate tax 9%

Customs & excise 32%

Other 13%

Social security 18%

Personal taxes 28%

Spending it
£bn

	Defence	Education	Health & social services	Debt interest	Total spending
1885	...	...	...	...	...
1890	0.03	0.03	...	0.02	0.13
1895	0.04	0.04	...	0.02	0.16
1900	0.13	0.05	...	0.02	0.28
1905	0.06	0.07	...	0.02	0.24
1910	0.07	0.09	...	0.02	0.27
1915	0.72	0.09	...	0.06	0.96
1920	0.52	0.10	0.26	0.32	1.59
1925	0.13	0.10	0.24	0.30	1.07
1930	0.12	0.11	0.32	0.29	1.15
1935	0.14	0.12	0.35	0.21	1.12
1940	...	...	...	...	...
1945	...	...	...	0.53	4.59
1950	0.86	0.37	1.21	0.55	4.50
1955	1.54	0.55	1.69	0.77	6.26
1960	1.63	0.92	2.49	1.02	8.34
1965	2.11	1.59	3.91	1.35	12.38
1970	2.46	2.53	6.33	2.03	20.91
1975	5.17	6.63	15.43	4.13	51.48
1980	11.44	12.75	37.07	10.87	104.20
1985	18.21	17.28	64.14	17.59	157.76
1990	22.91	26.72	91.69	18.75	215.59
1995	22.26	40.17	...	25.39	276.12

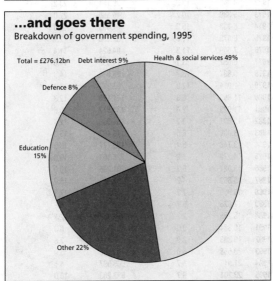

...and goes there
Breakdown of government spending, 1995

Total = £276.12bn — Debt interest 9% — Health & social services 49%

Defence 8%

Education 15%

Other 22%

Reserves, rates and money supply

Official reserves
End year

	$bn		$bn		$bn
1945	2.48	**1962**	2.81	**1979**	22.54
1946	2.70	**1963**	0.95	**1980**	27.48
1947	2.08	**1964**	0.83	**1981**	23.35
1948	1.86	**1965**	1.07	**1982**	17.00
1949	1.69	**1966**	1.11	**1983**	17.82
1950	3.30	**1967**	1.12	**1984**	15.69
1951	2.34	**1968**	1.01	**1985**	15.54
1952	1.85	**1969**	1.05	**1986**	21.92
1953	2.52	**1970**	1.18	**1987**	44.33
1954	2.76	**1971**	2.53	**1988**	51.69
1955	2.12	**1972**	2.17	**1989**	38.65
1956	2.13	**1973**	2.24	**1990**	38.46
1957	2.27	**1974**	6.79	**1991**	44.13
1958	3.07	**1975**	5.43	**1992**	41.65
1959	2.74	**1976**	4.13	**1993**	42.93
1960	3.23	**1977**	20.56	**1994**	43.90
1961	3.32	**1978**	15.69	**1995**	49.99

Money supply
Amount outstanding, end period

	M0 £bn	% increase on year earlier	M4 £bn	% increase on year earlier
1970	4.099		26.644	
1971	4.289	4.6	30.973	16.2
1972	4.845	13.0	38.161	23.2
1973	5.339	10.2	46.556	22.0
1974	6.158	15.3	51.669	11.0
1975	6.873	11.6	57.938	12.1
1976	7.649	11.3	64.524	11.4
1977	8.652	13.1	74.092	14.8
1978	9.837	13.7	85.098	14.9
1979	11.014	12.0	97.317	14.4
1980	11.650	5.8	114.128	17.3
1981	11.925	2.4	137.812	20.8
1982	12.301	3.2	154.909	12.4
1983	13.038	6.0	175.462	13.3
1984	13.746	5.4	199.177	13.5
1985	14.278	3.9	225.109	13.0
1986	15.027	5.2	261.235	16.0
1987	15.663	4.2	303.007	16.0
1988	16.869	7.7	355.424	17.3
1989	17.826	5.7	422.337	18.8
1990	18.299	2.7	473.561	12.1
1991	18.854	3.0	503.427	6.3
1992	19.393	2.9	517.299	2.8
1993	20.558	6.0	543.280	5.0
1994	21.945	6.7	565.597	4.1
1995	23.201	5.7	622.203	10.0

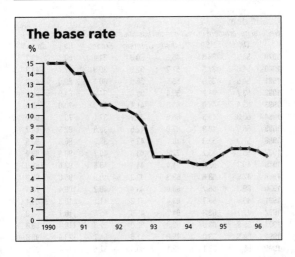

The base rate

%

Interest rates

End year	Base rate	Inter-bank 3-month	Government bonds 5-year	20-year
1971	4.50	4.75	6.69	8.90
1972	7.50	9.06	7.55	8.90
1973	13.00	16.31	10.41	10.71
1974	12.00	12.83	12.51	14.77
1975	11.00	11.19	10.57	14.39
1976	14.00	14.63	12.06	14.43
1977	7.50	6.75	10.08	12.73
1978	12.50	12.63	11.32	12.47
1979	17.00	17.06	11.73	12.99
1980	14.00	14.88	13.84	13.79
1981	14.50	15.75	14.65	14.74
1982	10.25	10.63	12.79	12.88
1983	9.00	9.41	11.19	10.81
1984	9.75	10.13	11.29	10.69
1985	11.50	11.94	11.13	10.62
1986	11.00	11.13	10.01	9.87
1987	8.50	9.00	9.36	9.48
1988	13.00	13.19	9.66	9.36
1989	15.00	15.16	10.73	9.58
1990	14.00	14.00	12.08	11.08
1991	10.50	11.00	9.67	9.65
1992	7.00	7.25	7.25	9.31
1993	5.50	5.31	5.77	6.64
1994	6.25	6.56	8.69	8.39
1995	6.50	6.50	6.86	7.94

For definitions of money supply and reserves, see page 12.

Public debt

Public debt
General government gross financial liabilities as % of GDP

	UK	USA	Japan	Germany[a]	France	Italy	Canada
1979	54.3	36.8	45.6	30.8	31.4	60.3	43.7
1980	54.0	37.3	51.2	32.8	30.9	57.7	44.3
1981	54.5	36.6	55.5	36.5	30.1	59.9	45.0
1982	53.2	41.2	59.4	39.6	34.2	64.9	50.1
1983	53.4	44.0	63.8	41.1	35.3	70.0	55.5
1984	60.3	45.3	65.8	41.7	37.1	75.2	59.2
1985	58.9	48.9	67.0	42.5	38.6	82.3	64.7
1986	57.9	52.3	70.7	42.5	39.3	86.3	68.5
1987	55.6	53.2	72.8	43.8	40.7	90.5	69.2
1988	49.3	52.9	71.4	44.4	40.6	92.6	68.9
1989	42.9	53.6	69.3	43.2	40.6	95.6	69.9
1990	39.3	55.7	66.0	43.4	40.2	106.4	73.1
1991	40.6	59.7	63.4	41.2	41.1	110.3	80.4
1992	47.7	62.3	64.7	45.6	45.4	116.7	88.0
1993	56.9	63.9	69.3	52.0	52.6	118.4	93.8
1994	54.5	63.0	75.6	51.5	54.7	123.9	95.6
1995[b]	56.8	63.1	83.1	60.0	57.5	124.4	97.3

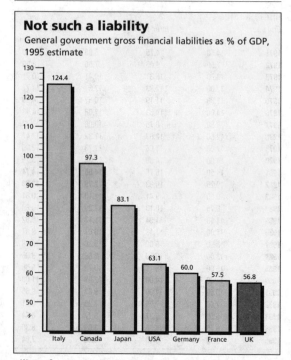

Not such a liability
General government gross financial liabilities as % of GDP, 1995 estimate

Italy	Canada	Japan	USA	Germany	France	UK
124.4	97.3	83.1	63.1	60.0	57.5	56.8

a Western Germany up to 1990.

The interest burden

General government net debt interest payments as % of total outlays

	UK	USA	Japan	Germany[a]	France	Italy	Canada
1979	6.8	3.7	2.6	2.3	1.8	10.6	4.6
1980	7.2	3.8	3.1	2.7	1.7	11.2	4.9
1981	7.5	4.7	3.7	3.3	2.5	12.0	5.8
1982	7.2	5.0	4.2	4.1	2.4	13.9	6.5
1983	6.9	5.0	4.8	4.8	3.3	14.4	6.4
1984	7.3	6.1	5.3	4.9	3.7	15.2	7.8
1985	7.7	6.3	5.4	5.5	4.0	14.5	8.8
1986	7.3	5.9	5.0	5.6	4.1	15.4	9.4
1987	7.4	6.0	4.3	5.1	4.3	14.7	9.7
1988	7.1	5.8	3.5	5.6	4.2	15.1	10.1
1989	6.4	6.2	2.9	4.9	4.5	16.4	11.1
1990	5.8	6.3	2.2	4.4	4.8	17.1	11.5
1991	5.2	6.5	1.3	4.2	5.0	18.1	10.6
1992	4.9	6.0	0.9	5.4	5.4	20.3	9.6
1993	5.0	5.5	0.9	5.2	5.5	20.4	9.5
1994	6.0	5.7	1.1	5.5	5.7	19.0	9.8
1995[b]	6.9	6.3	1.3	6.7	6.0	19.6	10.8

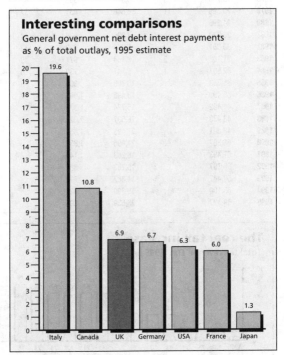

Interesting comparisons

General government net debt interest payments
as % of total outlays, 1995 estimate

b Estimates.

Taxes

The tax take
Financial years beginning April, £m

	Income tax	Surtax	Corporation tax	Capital gains tax	Estate duty
1908	34	...	...	...	18
1918	258	36	...	...	31
1928	327	56	...	...	81
1938	336	63	...	...	77
1948	1,360	100	...	...	178
1958	2,318	168	...	...	187
1968	4,349	225	1,344	47	382
1970	5,731	248	1,583	139	357
1971	6,432	348	1,554	155	451
1972	6,477	341	1,533	208	459
1973	7,137	307	2,262	324	412
1974	10,271	186	2,859	382	339
1975	15,041	109	1,996	387	212
1976	17,014	62	2,655	323	124
1977	17,420	30	3,343	340	87
1978	18,748	15	3,940	353	46
1979	20,599	11	4,646	431	32
1980	24,295	5	4,645	508	27
1981	28,720	4	4,930	526	17
1982	30,361	2	5,677	632	12
1983	31,108	2	8,184	671	9
1984	32,507	1	8,341	730	6
1985	35,353	...	10,708	908	6
1986	38,499	...	13,495	1,064	7
1987	41,402	...	15,734	1,379	...
1988	43,433	...	18,537	2,323	...
1989	48,801	...	21,495	1,854	...
1990	55,287	...	21,495	1,852	...
1991	57,493	...	18,263	1,140	...
1992	56,797	...	15,783	982	...
1993	58,442	...	14,887	710	...
1994	63,100	...	19,390	926	...
1995	68,127	...	23,539	806	...

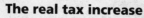

The real tax increase
Total tax revenue £bn, 1995 prices

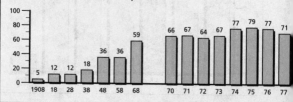

1908	18	28	38	48	58	68	70	71	72	73	74	75	76	77
5	12	12	18	36	36	59	66	67	64	67	77	79	77	71

Inheritance & capital transfer tax	Stamp duty	Development land tax	Other taxes	Total
...	8	...	36	96
...	12	...	287	624
...	30	...	3	407
...	21	...	24	521
...	57	...	360	2,055
...	66	...	275	3,012
...	124	...	75	6,546
...	117	...	5	8,180
...	166	...	4	9,110
...	228	...	2	9,248
...	190	...	2	10,634
...	198	...	1	14,236
118	281	...	1	18,143
259	272	1	...	20,711
311	376	7	...	21,914
323	433	13	183	24,055
401	620	26	1,435	28,201
425	641	27	3,410	32,983
480	797	38	4,770	40,282
499	873	65	5,669	43,790
599	1,138	68	6,017	45,796
658	911	81	7,177	50,412
881	1,226	62	6,375	55,520
988	1,860	55	1,188	57,156
1,078	2,440	28	2,296	64,357
1,071	2,255	15	1,371	69,005
1,232	2,117	10	1,050	76,559
1,262	1,703	4	860	82,464
1,300	1,697	...	-216	79,676
1,211	1,268	...	68	76,105
1,335	1,736	...	359	77,468
1,409	1,799	...	711	87,335
1,558	2,022	...	948	96,997

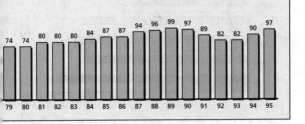

Tax comparisons

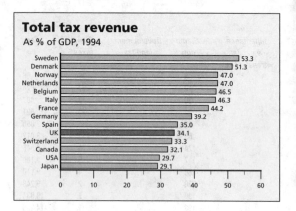

Total tax revenue
As % of GDP, 1994

Sweden	53.3
Denmark	51.3
Norway	47.0
Netherlands	47.0
Belgium	46.5
Italy	46.3
France	44.2
Germany	39.2
Spain	35.0
UK	34.1
Switzerland	33.3
Canada	32.1
USA	29.7
Japan	29.1

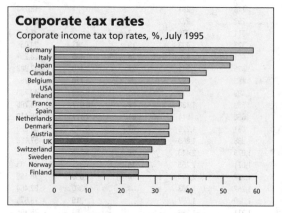

Corporate tax rates
Corporate income tax top rates, %, July 1995

Germany
Italy
Japan
Canada
Belgium
USA
Ireland
France
Spain
Netherlands
Denmark
Austria
UK
Switzerland
Sweden
Norway
Finland

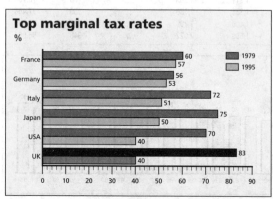

Top marginal tax rates
%

1979
1995

	1979	1995
France	60	57
Germany	56	53
Italy	72	51
Japan	75	50
USA	70	40
UK	83	40

Part V
LABOUR

Employment

Breakdown of employed workforce
'000

	Total	Agriculture, forestry & fishing	Mining & quarrying	Manufac- turing	Construction
1900	18,020	2,420	1,020	5,990	1,090
1905	18,400	...	...	...	...
1910	19,280	2,400	1,290	6,550	1,030
1915	20,890	...	...	...	...
1920	20,297	1,741	1,325	7,208	927
1925	18,588	1,576	1,205	6,227	924
1930	19,115	1,460	1,034	6,066	1,035
1935	20,037	1,370	870	6,387	1,141
1940	23,100	...	...	...	...
1945	24,200	...	...	...	...
1950	23,257	806	857	8,520	1,325
1955	24,298	692	867	9,222	1,385
1960	24,183	743	740	8,418	1,426
1965	25,204	605	597	8,561	1,621
1970	24,753	466	410	8,342	1,339
1975	25,050	397	352	7,490	1,314
1980	25,327	361	a	6,940	1,252
1985	24,539	341	a	5,365	1,022
1990	26,881	277	a	4,993	1,060
1995	25,097	295	a	3,863	823

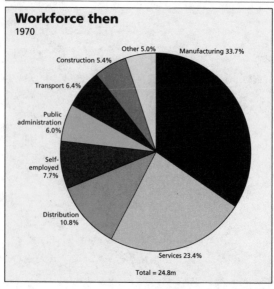

Workforce then
1970

Other 5.0%
Manufacturing 33.7%
Construction 5.4%
Transport 6.4%
Public administration 6.0%
Self-employed 7.7%
Distribution 10.8%
Services 23.4%

Total = 24.8m

a Included with gas, electricity and water under new heading of energy and water supply.

Gas, electricity & water	Transport & communication	Distributive trades	Other services	Public administration & defence	Self-employed
100	1,450	1,990	3,590	880	...
...	...	...	...	...	...
120	1,580	2,460	3,890	840	...
...	...	...	...	...	...
185	1,641	2,352	3,521	637	...
199	1,558	2,320	3,630	599	...
230	1,595	2,724	3,980	664	...
263	1,579	2,965	4,411	718	...
...	...	...	...	...	...
...	...	...	...	...	...
360	1,769	2,130	3,573	1,402	1,802
384	1,708	2,378	3,755	1,331	1,787
380	1,652	2,737	4,490	1,287	1,766
419	1,648	2,909	5,327	1,374	1,696
391	1,572	2,675	5,802	1,481	1,902
353	1,518	2,763	6,861	1,657	1,993
726	1,483	3,090	7,451	1,669	2,013
589	1,345	3,001	8,229	1,613	2,610
441	1,361	3,499	9,014	1,942	3,259
226	1,259	3,586	9,819	1,313	3,252

Workforce now

1995

Construction 3.3%
Transport 5.0%
Public administration 5.2%
Services 39.1%
Self-employed 13.0%
Distribution 14.3%
Other 4.7%
Manufacturing 15.4%

Total = 25.1m

Unemployment

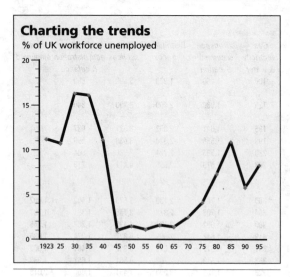

Charting the trends
% of UK workforce unemployed

Regional trends
% of workforce unemployed

	North	North East	North West	Midlands
1923	...	11.5	14.2	9.9
1925	...	14.6	10.9	8.5
1930	...	20.8	23.9	14.9
1935	...	21.8	20.4	11.1
1939	18.7	11.8	15.4	8.1
1945	0.5	0.5	0.5	0.6

	North	Yorkshire & Humberside	North West	West Midlands
1950	2.6	...	1.7	0.6
1955	1.8	...	1.4	0.5
1960	2.9	...	1.9	1.0
1965	2.4	1.0	1.5	0.6
1970	4.6	2.8	2.6	1.9
1975	4.1	2.8	3.8	2.9
1980	7.7	5.0	6.2	5.2
1985	15.3	11.9	13.6	12.7
1990	8.7	6.6	7.6	5.7
1993	11.9	10.2	10.7	10.8
1994	11.6	9.6	10.0	9.9
1995	10.6	8.8	8.8	8.4

National trends
% of workforce unemployed

	Total	Wales	Scotland	N. Ireland
1923	11.2	6.3	13.8	16.4
1925	10.7	16.9	14.7	22.8
1930	16.3	26.7	18.7	22.6
1935	16.1	33.3	23.2	25.3
1939	11.1	22.0	16.1	26.2
1945	1.0	4.0	2.0	5.6
1950	1.5	4.0	3.0	6.5
1955	1.1	1.8	2.4	6.8
1960	1.6	2.7	3.6	6.7
1965	1.4	2.6	3.0	6.1
1970	2.5	3.8	4.2	6.8
1975	4.1	5.6	5.2	7.9
1980	7.3	10.3	10.0	13.7
1985	10.9	13.6	12.9	16.0
1990	5.8	6.6	8.0	13.3
1993	10.3	10.3	9.7	13.8
1994	9.4	9.3	9.3	12.6
1995	8.3	8.3	8.2	11.4

South East	South West
9.2	10.4
5.5	8.0
8.0	10.5
8.5	12.3
8.6	7.2
0.7	0.7

East Midlands	East Anglia	South East	South West
0.7	...	1.1	1.4
0.6	...	0.7	1.1
1.1	...	1.0	1.7
0.8	1.2	0.8	1.5
2.2	2.0	1.6	2.7
2.5	2.5	2.0	3.2
4.2	3.6	2.9	4.2
9.8	8.1	8.0	9.1
5.0	3.6	3.8	4.1
9.5	8.1	10.2	9.5
8.7	7.1	9.0	8.1
7.7	6.4	7.9	7.0

Earnings

Pay norms
Average weekly earnings in manufacturing, manual employees, £

	Men	% increase on previous year	Women	% increase on previous year
1949	7.40	6.8	3.95	7.6
1950	7.83	5.8	4.14	4.8
1951	8.60	9.8	4.50	8.7
1952	9.24	7.4	4.77	6.0
1953	9.83	6.4	5.15	8.0
1954	10.61	7.9	5.43	5.4
1955	11.55	8.9	5.78	6.4
1956	12.28	6.3	6.17	6.7
1957	13.06	6.4	6.49	5.2
1958	13.27	1.6	6.70	3.2
1959	14.21	7.1	7.07	5.5
1960	15.11	6.3	7.41	4.8
1961	15.89	5.2	7.71	4.0
1962	16.34	2.8	8.03	4.2
1963	17.29	5.8	8.41	4.7
1964	18.67	8.0	8.95	6.4
1965	20.16	8.0	9.60	7.3
1966	20.78	3.1	10.06	4.8
1967	21.89	5.3	10.54	4.8
1968	23.62	7.9	11.31	7.3
1969	25.54	8.1	11.87	5.0
1970	28.91	13.2	14.34	20.8
1971	31.37	8.5	15.80	10.2
1972	36.20	15.4	19.40	22.8
1973	41.23	13.9	22.68	16.9
1974	48.77	18.3	27.05	19.3
1975	59.32	21.6	34.23	26.5
1976	67.35	13.5	40.71	18.9
1977	73.04	8.4	44.46	9.2
1978	84.17	15.2	50.10	12.7
1979	97.59	15.9	58.46	16.7
1980	110.85	13.6	68.42	17.0
1981	122.36	10.4	75.73	10.7
1982	133.31	8.9	83.20	9.9
1983	146.19	9.7	90.32	8.6
1984	157.50	7.7	96.30	6.6
1985	172.60	9.6	104.50	8.5
1986	183.40	6.3	111.60	6.8
1987	195.90	6.8	119.60	7.2
1988	212.30	8.4	127.90	6.9
1989	230.60	8.6	138.20	8.1
1990	251.40	9.0	152.80	10.6
1991	261.80	4.1	162.10	6.1
1992	279.70	6.8	174.40	7.6
1993	287.90	2.9	182.40	4.6
1994	297.70	3.1	186.70	2.2
1995	313.40	5.3	198.50	6.3

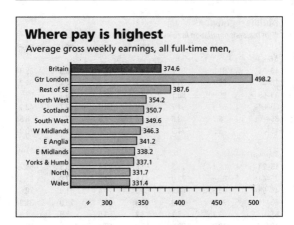

Where pay is highest
Average gross weekly earnings, all full-time men,

Britain	374.6
Gtr London	498.2
Rest of SE	387.6
North West	354.2
Scotland	350.7
South West	349.6
W Midlands	346.3
E Anglia	341.2
E Midlands	338.2
Yorks & Humb	337.1
North	331.7
Wales	331.4

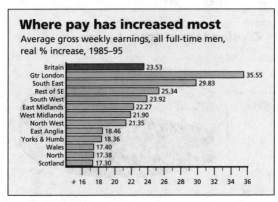

Where pay has increased most
Average gross weekly earnings, all full-time men,
real % increase, 1985–95

Britain	23.53
Gtr London	35.55
South East	29.83
Rest of SE	25.34
South West	23.92
East Midlands	22.27
West Midlands	21.90
North West	21.35
East Anglia	18.46
Yorks & Humb	18.36
Wales	17.40
North	17.38
Scotland	17.30

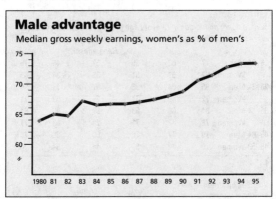

Male advantage
Median gross weekly earnings, women's as % of men's

Sex, age and race

Middle-aged peak
% of resident population in relevant age group in civilian labour force

	1984	1991	1994	1996	2001	2006
Men						
16–24	81.8	81.2	75.1	72.4	70.3	69.3
25–44	96.1	95.7	94.1	94.2	94.4	94.2
45–59	90.0	88.1	86.1	86.4	85.3	83.7
60–64	57.5	54.2	51.0	50.4	49.7	49.1
65+	8.7	8.6	7.6	7.5	7.0	6.8
16+	75.9	74.9	72.6	72.2	71.5	70.0
Women						
16–24	69.1	71.3	64.6	63.6	63.3	63.2
25–44	65.6	73.0	73.5	74.8	77.8	81.3
45–59	63.3	66.9	69.3	70.4	71.9	72.6
60–64	21.8	23.9	25.3	26.6	29.0	31.9
65+	3.1	3.1	3.2	3.0	2.8	2.9
16+	49.2	53.1	53.0	53.7	55.5	56.7

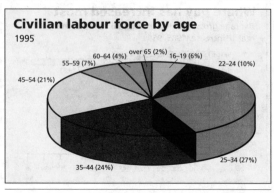

Civilian labour force by age
1995

60–64 (4%)
over 65 (2%)
16–19 (6%)
22–24 (10%)
55–59 (7%)
45–54 (21%)
25–34 (27%)
35–44 (24%)

Ethnic factors
% of resident population in relevant age group in civilian labour force

		White	Black[a]	Indian	Pakistani/ Bangladeshi	Other[b]	All ethnic groups
16–24	Men	77	62	55	57	45	75
	Women	67	51	51	35	34	65
25–34	Men	95	84	93	97	75	95
	Women	72	49	67	25	52	71
35–44	Men	94	89	93	87	90	94
	Women	78	73	71	23	63	77
45–64	Men	79	77	76	63	80	79
45–59	Women	70	72	53	na	54	70

a Caribbean, African.
b Includes Chinese.

Women at work

Now almost equal in numbers
Employees in employment, '000s

	Male	Female	Women as % of all employees
1923	8,493	2,993	26.1
1925	8,717	3,175	26.7
1930	8,932	3,474	28.0
1935	10,055	3,527	26.0
1945	8,602	5,398	38.6
1950	13,937	7,118	33.8
1955	14,224	7,689	35.1
1960	14,719	8,098	35.5
1965	15,243	8,677	36.3
1970	14,604	8,842	37.7
1970	13,952	8,450	37.7
1975	13,443	9,170	40.6
1980	12,929	9,456	42.2
1985	11,910	9,503	44.4
1990	12,051	10,858	47.4
1991	11,538	10,713	48.1
1992	11,226	10,677	48.7
1993	10,951	10,636	49.3
1994	10,921	10,717	49.5
1995	11,047	10,842	49.5

But room for more at the top
Women's % of top positions

	1992	1993	1994	1995
Chairmen	0.4	0.3	0.1	0.1
Chief executive/ managing directors	0.5	0.7	0.6	0.6
Finance directors	0.9	1.3	1.5	1.5
Finance controllers/ chief accountants	3.0	6.1	10.8	5.9
Investor relations officers	11.2	12.9	13.7	15.4
Company secretaries	5.3	6.6	7.0	7.3
Other senior positions	1.3	1.3	2.0	1.8
Total	2.1	2.6	2.8	2.9

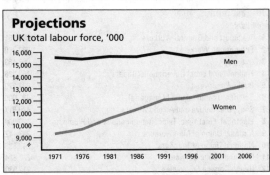

Projections
UK total labour force, '000

Unions

The rise and fall of union appeal
Total union members, '000s

Year	Members	Year	Members	Year	Members
1893	1,559	1927	4,919	1961	9,916
1894	1,530	1928	4,806	1962	10,014
1895	1,504	1929	4,858	1963	10,067
1896	1,608	1930	4,842	1964	10,218
1897	1,731	1931	4,624	1965	10,325
1898	1,752	1932	4,444	1966	10,259
1899	1,911	1933	4,392	1967	10,194
1900	2,022	1934	4,590	1968	10,200
1901	2,025	1935	4,867	1969	10,471
1902	2,013	1936	5,295	1970	11,187
1903	1,994	1937	5,842	1971	11,135
1904	1,967	1938	6,053	1972	11,359
1905	1,997	1939	6,298	1973	11,456
1906	2,210	1940	6,613	1974	11,764
1907	2,513	1941	7,165	1975	12,026
1908	2,485	1942	7,867	1976	12,386
1909	2,477	1943	8,174	1977	12,846
1910	2,565	1944	8,087	1978	13,112
1911	3,139	1945	7,875	1979	13,289
1912	3,416	1946	8,803	1980	12,947
1913	4,135	1947	9,145	1981	12,106
1914	4,145	1948	9,362	1982	11,593
1915	4,359	1949	9,318	1983	11,236
1916	4,644	1950	9,289	1984	10,994
1917	5,499	1951	9,535	1985	10,821
1918	6,533	1952	9,588	1986	10,539
1919	7,926	1953	9,527	1987	10,475
1920	8,348	1954	9,566	1988	10,376
1921	6,633	1955	9,741	1989	10,158
1922	5,625	1956	9,778	1990	9,947
1923	5,429	1957	9,829	1991	9,585
1924	5,544	1958	9,639	1992	9,048
1925	5,506	1959	9,623	1993	8,700
1926	5,219	1960	9,835	1994	8,278

Biggest unions, 1980
Members

1	Transport and General Workers	2,086,261
2	Engineering Workers	1,032,760
3	GMB	967,153
4	National and Local Government Officers	753,226
5	Public Employees	691,770
6	Science, Technical and Managerial	491,000
7	Shop, Distributive and Allied Workers	470,017
8	Electrical, Electronic, Telecommunications and Plumbing	420,000
9	National Union of Mineworkers	253,142
10	National Union of Teachers	248,896
11	Civil and Public Services	223,884
12	Health Service Employees	212,930

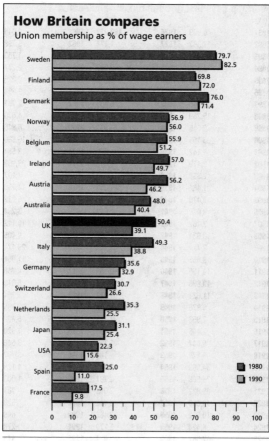

How Britain compares
Union membership as % of wage earners

Country	1980	1990
Sweden	79.7	82.5
Finland	69.8	72.0
Denmark	76.0	71.4
Norway	56.9	56.0
Belgium	55.9	51.2
Ireland	57.0	49.7
Austria	56.2	46.2
Australia	48.0	40.4
UK	50.4	39.1
Italy	49.3	38.8
Germany	35.6	32.9
Switzerland	30.7	26.6
Netherlands	35.3	25.5
Japan	31.1	25.4
USA	22.3	15.6
Spain	25.0	11.0
France	17.5	9.8

■ 1980
□ 1990

Biggest unions, 1995
Members

1	UNISON	1,368,796
2	Transport and General Workers	918,923
3	GMB	789,672
4	Amalgamated Engineering and Electrical	781,137
5	Manufacturing Science Finance	482,000
6	Shop, Distributive and Allied Workers	282,816
7	Communication Workers	266,486
8	Graphical, Paper and Media	208,458
9	National Union of Teachers	175,323
10	Public Services, Tax and Commerce Union	164,789
11	Schoolmasters Union of Women Teachers	146,266
12	Banking, Insurance and Finance	134,012

Strikes

Working days lost through industrial disputes[a]
'000s

1891	6,809	1926	162,233	1961	3,046
1892	17,382	1927	1,174	1962	5,798
1893	30,468	1928	1,388	1963	1,755
1894	9,529	1929	8,287	1964	2,277
1895	5,725	1930	4,399	1965	2,925
1896	3,746	1931	6,983	1966	2,398
1897	10,346	1932	6,488	1967	2,787
1898	15,289	1933	1,072	1968	4,690
1899	2,516	1934	959	1969	6,846
1900	3,153	1935	1,955	1970	10,980
1901	4,142	1936	1,829	1971	13,551
1902	3,479	1937	3,413	1972	23,909
1903	2,339	1938	1,334	1973	7,197
1904	1,484	1939	1,356	1974	14,750
1905	2,470	1940	940	1975	6,012
1906	3,029	1941	1,079	1976	3,284
1907	2,162	1942	1,527	1977	10,142
1908	10,834	1943	1,808	1978	9,405
1909	2,774	1944	3,714	1979	29,474
1910	9,867	1945	2,835	1980	11,964
1911	10,155	1946	2,158	1981	4,266
1912	40,890	1947	2,433	1982	5,313
1913	11,631	1948	1,944	1983	3,754
1914	9,878	1949	1,807	1984	27,135
1915	2,953	1950	1,389	1985	6,402
1916	2,446	1951	1,694	1986	1,920
1917	5,647	1952	1,792	1987	3,546
1918	5,875	1953	2,184	1988	3,702
1919	34,969	1954	2,457	1989	4,128
1920	26,568	1955	3,781	1990	1,903
1921	85,872	1956	2,083	1991	761
1922	19,850	1957	8,412	1992	528
1923	10,672	1958	3,462	1993	649
1924	8,424	1959	5,270	1994	278
1925	7,952	1960	3,024	1995	415

How Britain compares

Working days lost per 1,000 employees, average 1990–94

Greece	3,500	Sweden	57
Spain	492	Belgium	57
Turkey	253	United States	43
Italy	240	Portugal	39
Canada	231	Denmark	37
Finland	218	UK	37
Australia	157	France	30
Ireland	135	Germany	23
New Zealand	105	Netherlands	16
Norway	72	Austria	7

a 1891–1909 is Great Britain and Ireland; 1910 onwards is Great Britain and N. Ireland.

Part VI

BUSINESS AND FINANCE

Leading companies

The big thirty
By market capitalisation, £bn

1971

1	Shell	2.30	16	Prudential Assurance	0.36
2	British Petroleum	1.91	17	Guest Keen Nettlefolds	0.34
3	ICI	1.31	18	Nat. Westminster Bank	0.34
4	British American Tobacco	0.82	19	Commercial Union	0.34
5	Marks and Spencer	0.75	20	F.W. Woolworth UK	0.34
6	General Electric	0.60	21	Allied Breweries	0.31
7	RTZ	0.56	22	Barclays Bank	0.31
8	Great Universal Stores	0.56	23	Bass Charrington	0.31
9	Distillers	0.53	24	Plessey	0.29
10	Burmah Oil	0.48	25	Boots	0.29
11	Unilever	0.48	26	Glaxo	0.27
12	Imperial Group	0.46	27	Lloyds Bank	0.24
13	Courtaulds	0.39	28	Reed International	0.22
14	Beecham	0.36	29	Midland Bank	0.22
15	Royal Insurance	0.36	30	Thorn Electrical	0.22

1976

1	British Petroleum	2.55	16	Royal Insurance	0.52
2	Shell	2.37	17	Boots	0.51
3	ICI	1.87	18	Commercial Union	0.49
4	British American Tobacco	1.03	19	Courtaulds	0.46
5	Unilever	0.89	20	Midland Bank	0.44
6	General Electric	0.87	21	Allied Breweries	0.41
7	De Beers	0.75	22	Prudential Assurance	0.39
8	Marks and Spencer	0.71	23	Guest Keen Nettlefolds	0.38
9	Imperial	0.65	24	Glaxo Holdings	0.38
10	Barclays Bank	0.65	25	Lloyds Bank	0.34
11	Distillers	0.59	26	Standard Chartered Bank	0.33
12	Great Universal Stores	0.58	27	Thorn Electrical	0.32
13	Beecham	0.57	28	Land Securities	0.32
14	RTZ	0.53	29	F.W. Woolworth	0.31
15	Nat. Westminster Bank	0.52	30	Bass Charrington	0.30

1981

1	British Petroleum	8.56	16	Unilever	1.03
2	Shell	6.43	17	Grand Metropolitan	0.97
3	General Electric	4.12	18	Distillers	0.85
4	ICI	2.38	19	Bass	0.82
5	Marks and Spencer	1.88	20	Plessey	0.81
6	De Beers	1.85	21	Prudential Corporation	0.81
7	Barclays Bank	1.51	22	J. Sainsbury	0.76
8	Great Universal Stores	1.46	23	Lloyds Bank	0.71
9	Beecham	1.41	24	Commercial Union	0.70
10	RTZ	1.26	25	Standard Chartered Bank	0.70
11	Land Securities	1.23	26	Thorn-EMI	0.69
12	B.A.T Industries	1.17	27	Midland Bank	0.67
13	Nat. Westminster Bank	1.12	28	Burmah Oil	0.66
14	Racal Electronics	1.08	29	Royal Insurance	0.65
15	Boots	1.06	30	Imperial Group	0.64

1986

1	British Telecom	11.51	16	Unilever	2.53
2	British Petroleum	10.19	17	Nat. Westminster Bank	2.50
3	Shell	7.32	18	Prudential Corporation	2.36
4	Glaxo	5.70	19	Bass	2.15
5	ICI	5.00	20	Great Universal Stores	2.03
6	BTR	4.97	21	Imperial Group	1.93
7	Marks and Spencer	4.69	22	Boots	1.90
8	B.A.T Industries	4.65	23	Royal Insurance	1.88
9	General Electric	4.38	24	Allied-Lyons	1.87
10	Barclays Bank	3.27	25	Distillers	1.80
11	Grand Metropolitan	3.09	26	Lloyds Bank	1.74
12	Cable & Wireless	2.94	27	Burton	1.65
13	Hanson Trust	2.87	28	Sears	1.65
14	Beecham	2.72	29	Asda-MFI	1.63
15	J. Sainsbury	2.60	30	RTZ	1.61

1991

1	British Petroleum	19.76	16	J. Sainsbury	5.11
2	British Telecom	19.24	17	General Electric	5.06
3	Shell	16.75	18	RTZ	4.90
4	Glaxo	13.98	19	Nat. Westminster Bank	4.70
5	British Gas	10.58	20	SmithKline Beecham	4.70
6	Hanson Trust	9.79	21	De Beers	4.25
7	B.A.T Industries	9.46	22	Allied-Lyons	4.14
8	Guinness	7.54	23	Lloyds Bank	4.12
9	Grand Metropolitan	7.36	24	Bass	4.10
10	ICI	6.73	25	Wellcome	4.09
11	Marks and Spencer	6.66	26	Prudential	4.02
12	Barclays	6.34	27	Tesco	3.96
13	BTR	6.16	28	Boots	3.47
14	Unilever	6.00	29	Reuters	3.34
15	Cable & Wireless	5.23	30	Abbey National	3.32

1996

1	British Petroleum	31.14	16	Cable & Wireless	9.88
2	Shell Transport & Trading	30.43	17	Hanson	9.73
3	Glaxo Wellcome	29.61	18	Grand Metropolitan	9.13
4	BT	22.37	19	Guinness	8.97
5	SmithKline Beecham	18.01	20	HSBC Holdings	8.46
6	B.A.T Industries	16.07	21	British Gas	8.40
7	Lloyds TSB	15.96	22	Vodaphone	7.81
8	Marks and Spencer	13.02	23	BSkyB	7.73
9	Zeneca	12.98	24	Abbey National	7.31
10	Reuters	12.59	25	J. Sainsbury	7.27
11	Barclays Bank	11.90	26	Bass	7.18
12	Nat. Westminster Bank	11.07	27	Granada	7.00
13	BTR	10.94	28	Great Universal Stores	6.84
14	RTZ	10.76	29	Tesco	6.50
15	GEC	10.30	30	Reed	6.33

Leading sectors

From services to investment trusts
Market value of listed UK equities, end March 1996, £bn

	1994	1995	1996
Services	**164.3**	**168.1**	**221.1**
Distributors	8.7	7.5	9.2
Leisure & hotels	19.7	21.3	22.2
Media	31.5	35.6	58.6
Retailers, food	19.9	23.0	22.8
Retailers, general	38.9	38.6	48.3
Breweries, pubs & restaurants	13.1	12.0	20.8
Support services	10.9	10.3	17.9
Transport	21.6	19.8	21.2
General industrials	**164.7**	**153.2**	**170.5**
Building & construction	8.0	6.5	8.0
Building materials & merchants	24.9	21.3	21.3
Chemicals	16.9	16.4	20.2
Diversified industrials	44.2	39.4	37.2
Electronic & electrical equipment	17.2	17.4	21.5
Engineering	28.4	26.9	38.0
Engineering, vehicles	6.1	6.8	8.1
Paper, packaging & printing	13.7	14.2	11.6
Textiles & apparel	5.3	4.3	4.6
Financials	**123.2**	**128.7**	**154.5**
Banks, retail	62.6	67.6	85.2
Banks, merchant	5.0	5.6	3.8
Insurance	16.5	15.8	17.8
Life assurance	14.9	14.7	18.7
Other financial	8.3	9.5	12.2
Property	16.0	15.5	16.8
Consumer goods	**116.1**	**137.1**	**141.3**
Alcoholic beverages	24.9	24.7	24.4
Food products	26.1	28.4	28.1
Household goods	3.9	4.3	4.8
Health care	4.8	5.3	5.6
Pharmaceuticals	42.3	58.1	63.4
Tobacco	14.1	16.3	15.0
Utilities	**98.1**	**92.9**	**100.3**
Electricity	30.0	25.1	27.8
Gas distribution	13.7	13.0	10.6
Telecommunications	41.1	42.0	46.6
Water	13.4	12.8	15.3
Mineral extraction	**57.7**	**65.3**	**82.2**
Extractive industries	10.8	10.8	12.6
Oil, integrated	42.4	48.9	62.9
Oil exploration and production	4.5	5.6	6.7
Investment trusts	**31.0**	**32.3**	**40.2**
Other funds	**8.4**	**9.9**	**8.2**
Off-shore investment co's & funds	7.7	8.6	6.6
Currency funds	0.2	0.4	0.5
Other investment trusts	0.6	0.9	1.2
Total	**763.6**	**787.5**	**918.2**

Banking

Leading banks

Assets, £bn

1970			*1980*		
1	Barclays	6.60	**1**	Barclays	37.10
2	National Westminster	5.39	**2**	National Westminster	34.57
3	Midland	3.69	**3**	Midland	25.34
4	Lloyds	3.19	**4**	Lloyds	19.87
5	Standard & Chartered	2.36	**5**	Standard Chartered	15.42
6	Australia & New Zealand Banking Group	1.62	**6**	Royal Bank of Scotland	6.15
7	National & Commercial Banking Group	1.23	**7**	Grindlays Holdings	3.83
8	Bank of London & South America	0.89	**8**	Bank of Scotland	3.30
9	National & Grindlays	0.87	**9**	Kleinwort, Benson, Lonsdale	2.71
10	Bank of Scotland	0.59	**10**	Schroder Wagg	1.84

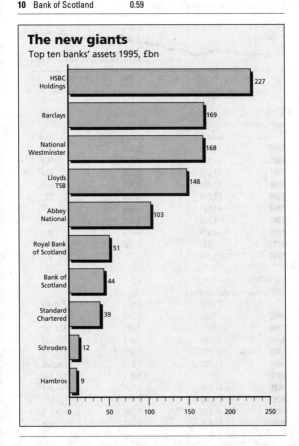

The new giants

Top ten banks' assets 1995, £bn

Bank	Assets
HSBC Holdings	227
Barclays	169
National Westminster	168
Lloyds TSB	148
Abbey National	103
Royal Bank of Scotland	51
Bank of Scotland	44
Standard Chartered	39
Schroders	12
Hambros	9

Agriculture

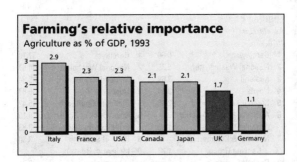

Farming's relative importance
Agriculture as % of GDP, 1993

Italy	France	USA	Canada	Japan	UK	Germany
2.9	2.3	2.3	2.1	2.1	1.7	1.1

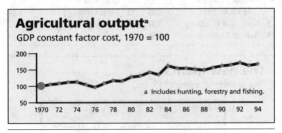

Agricultural output[a]
GDP constant factor cost, 1970 = 100

a Includes hunting, forestry and fishing.

Crops

'000 tonnes harvested

	Wheat	Barley	Oats
1985	12,046	10,954	614
1986	13,911	10,014	503
1987	11,940	9,229	454
1988	11,751	8,778	548
1989	14,033	8,073	529
1990	14,035	7,904	528
1991	14,362	7,625	521
1992	14,095	7,365	502
1993	12,890	6,038	479
1994	13,314	5,945	597

Livestock

'000 on agricultural holdings

	Cattle	Pigs	Poultry
1985	12,933	7,867	119,474
1986	12,554	7,939	120,760
1987	12,189	7,945	128,825
1988	11,902	7,983	131,018
1989	11,993	7,510	120,366
1990	12,079	7,450	124,636
1991	11,885	7,597	127,241
1992	11,804	7,609	124,013
1993	11,729	7,754	130,175
1994	11,834	7,797	125,718

Manufacturing

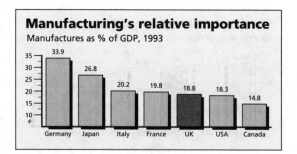

Manufacturing's relative importance
Manufactures as % of GDP, 1993

Germany 33.9 · Japan 26.8 · Italy 20.2 · France 19.8 · UK 18.8 · USA 18.3 · Canada 14.8

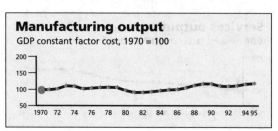

Manufacturing output
GDP constant factor cost, 1970 = 100

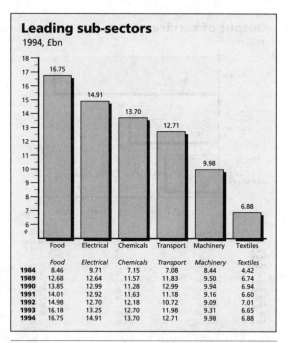

Leading sub-sectors
1994, £bn

Food 16.75 · Electrical 14.91 · Chemicals 13.70 · Transport 12.71 · Machinery 9.98 · Textiles 6.88

	Food	Electrical	Chemicals	Transport	Machinery	Textiles
1984	8.46	9.71	7.15	7.08	8.44	4.42
1989	12.68	12.64	11.57	11.83	9.50	6.74
1990	13.85	12.99	11.28	12.99	9.94	6.94
1991	14.01	12.92	11.63	11.18	9.16	6.60
1992	14.98	12.70	12.18	10.72	9.09	7.01
1993	16.18	13.25	12.70	11.98	9.31	6.65
1994	16.75	14.91	13.70	12.71	9.98	6.88

Services

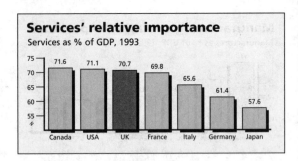

Services' relative importance

Services as % of GDP, 1993

Country	%
Canada	71.6
USA	71.1
UK	70.7
France	69.8
Italy	65.6
Germany	61.4
Japan	57.6

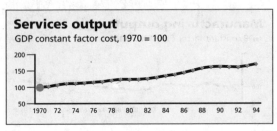

Services output

GDP constant factor cost, 1970 = 100

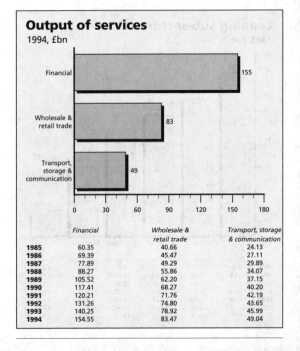

Output of services

1994, £bn

	Financial	Wholesale & retail trade	Transport, storage & communication
Financial	155		
Wholesale & retail trade	83		
Transport, storage & communication	49		

	Financial	Wholesale & retail trade	Transport, storage & communication
1985	60.35	40.66	24.13
1986	69.39	45.47	27.11
1987	77.89	49.29	29.89
1988	88.27	55.86	34.07
1989	105.52	62.20	37.15
1990	117.41	68.27	40.20
1991	120.21	71.76	42.19
1992	131.26	74.80	43.65
1993	140.25	78.92	45.99
1994	154.55	83.47	49.04

Financing business

How money is raised
Money raised by UK and Irish listed companies, £m

	Equities	Conver-tibles	Debentures & loans	Prefer-ence	Euro-bonds	Total
1981	2,493	253	43	120	...	2,909
1982	1,776	73	891	280	100	3,120
1983	2,569	99	461	1,382	70	4,581
1984	6,899	173	490	919	520	9,001
1985	4,775	795	597	440	7,239	13,846
1986	14,019	320	1,243	561	7,107	23,250
1987	18,648	982	1,275	141	5,611	26,657
1988	9,935	2,166	1,207	427	6,124	19,858
1989	12,626	1,309	2,421	780	9,446	26,581
1990	12,035	667	814	364	13,975	27,854
1991	18,312	1,502	1,023	925	13,370	35,131
1992	7,119	1,828	1,151	779	13,357	24,234
1993	17,712	3,251	1,981	1,549	24,642	49,135
1994	20,391	3,041	1,324	96	32,671	57,524
1995	8,941	3,480	860	400	23,893	37,573

Issues

	No. of issues	Money raised £m	Of which new companies No. of issues	Of which new companies Money raised £m
1981	2,267	2,909	63	631
1982	1,890	3,120	59	1,169
1983	2,519	4,581	79	1,592
1984	3,094	9,001	87	5,950
1985	3,242	13,846	80	1,462
1986	4,111	23,250	136	8,874
1987	4,883	26,657	155	5,002
1988	4,072	19,858	129	3,790
1989	3,956	26,581	110	7,578
1990	3,205	27,854	120	7,095
1991	3,319	35,131	101	7,474
1992	2,876	24,234	82	2,937
1993	2,655	49,135	180	5,966
1994	3,168	57,524	256	11,519
1995	2,803	37,573	190	2,962

The value of privatisation

	No. of issues	Money raised £m		No. of issues	Money raised £m
1981	2	374	**1989**	10	5,239
1982	2	620	**1990**	12	5,183
1983	2	297	**1991**	4	5,035
1984	4	4,654	**1992**	...	...
1985	1	363	**1993**	1	362
1986	2	6,930	**1994**	...	...
1987	3	3,488	**1995**	1	...
1988	1	2,500			

Stockmarkets

Indices compared

end year	London	Tokyo	New York	Frankfurt
1980	647.4	7,063.13	963.98	480.92
1981	684.3	7,681.84	875.00	490.39
1982	834.3	8,016.67	1,046.55	552.77
1983	1,000.0	9,893.82	1,258.64	773.95
1984	1,232.2	11,542.60	1,211.57	820.91
1985	1,412.6	13,083.18	1,546.67	1,366.23
1986	1,679.0	18,820.64	1,895.95	1,432.25
1987	1,712.7	21,564.00	1,938.83	1,000.00
1988	1,793.1	30,159.00	2,168.57	1,327.87
1989	2,422.7	38,915.87	2,753.20	1,790.37
1990	2,143.5	23,848.71	2,633.66	1,398.23
1991	2,493.1	22,983.77	3,168.83	1,577.98
1992	2,846.5	16,924.95	3,301.11	1,545.05
1993	3,418.4	17,417.24	3,754.09	2,266.68
1994ª	3,065.5	19,723.06	3,834.44	2,106.58
1995	3,689.3	19,868.15	5,117.12	2,253.88
1996ª	3,747.8	21,956.19	5,643.18	2,542.80

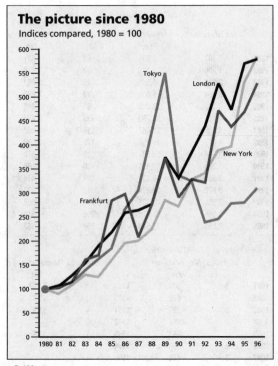

The picture since 1980
Indices compared, 1980 = 100

Tokyo · London · New York · Frankfurt

a End May.

Value traded
$bn

	UK	USA	Japan	Germany
1984	48.86	786.20	286.18	29.76
1985	68.42	997.19	329.97	71.57
1986	132.91	1,796.00	1,145.62	135.70
1987	389.83	2,423.07	2,047.22	373.43
1988	579.17	1,719.73	2,597.64	350.27
1989	320.27	2,015.54	2,800.70	628.63
1990	278.74	1,815.48	1,602.39	501.81
1991	315.28	2,254.98	995.94	379.38
1992	383.00	2,678.52	635.26	446.02
1993	423.53	3,507.22	954.34	302.99
1994	928.17	3,564.32	1,121.44	460.62
1995	1,020.26	5,108.59	1,231.55	1,147.10

Market capitalisation
$bn

	UK	USA	Japan	Germany
1984	242.70	1,862.95	667.05	78.40
1985	328.00	2,324.65	978.66	183.77
1986	439.50	2,636.60	1,841.79	257.68
1987	680.72	2,588.89	2,802.95	213.17
1988	771.21	2,793.82	3,906.68	251.78
1989	826.60	3,505.69	4,392.60	365.18
1990	848.87	3,089.65	2,917.68	355.07
1991	987.95	4,087.66	3,130.86	393.45
1992	927.13	4,485.00	2,399.00	348.14
1993	1,151.65	5,136.20	2,999.76	463.48
1994	1,210.25	5,067.02	3,719.91	470.52
1995	1,407.74	6,857.62	3,667.29	577.37

Number of companies listed

	UK	USA	Japan	Germany
1984	2,171	7,977	1,802	449
1985	2,116	8,022	1,829	472
1986	2,106	8,403	1,866	492
1987	2,135	7,181	1,912	507
1988	2,054	6,680	1,967	609
1989	2,015	6,727	2,019	628
1990	1,701	6,599	2,071	413
1991	1,623	6,742	2,107	428
1992	1,874	6,699	2,118	665
1993	1,646	7,246	2,155	426
1994	2,070	7,692	2,205	417
1995	2,078	7,671	2,263	678

Confidence and failure

Business confidence

	ONS longer leading indicator, trend=100	Gallup consumer confidence survey	CBI optimism balance[a]
1965	95.55	...	-20
1966	95.83	...	-64
1967	103.73	...	5
1968	100.89	...	27
1969	97.15	...	8
1970	95.82	...	-1
1971	102.08	...	16
1972	105.18	...	29
1973	98.62	...	12
1974	92.95	-17.07	-56
1975	100.77	-25.19	-18
1976	101.35	-15.73	-9
1977	103.02	-7.17	0
1978	103.60	6.95	6
1979	97.08	-2.92	-40
1980	92.18	-18.12	-54
1981	99.17	-20.54	-9
1982	101.05	-10.77	-28
1983	105.57	-2.02	7
1984	101.81	-5.00	-5
1985	96.03	-10.16	-6
1986	98.97	-6.64	0
1987	105.11	4.51	23
1988	104.60	1.92	6
1989	95.12	-17.25	-26
1990	93.14	-25.37	-47
1991	98.39	-17.02	2
1992	97.71	-15.92	-23
1993	105.22	-12.58	1
1994	107.49	-12.17	16
1995	98.17	-10.50	-11
1996[b]	95.07	-7.33	-3

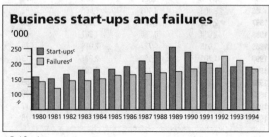

Business start-ups and failures

'000

- Start-ups[c]
- Failures[d]

1980 1981 1982 1983 1984 1985 1986 1987 1988 1989 1990 1991 1992 1993 1994

a End October.
b End April
c VAT registrations.
d VAT deregistrations.
For an explanation of confiidence indices, see page 11

Tourism

No. of visitors and receipts

	No. of foreign visitors to UK, '000s	Tourism receipts, £m	Tourist receipts, 1993 prices £m
1948	504	33	549
1949	563	43	690
1950	618	61	950
1951	712	75	1,089
1952	733	80	1,083
1953	819	88	1,174
1954	902	95	1,254
1955	1,037	111	1,409
1956	1,107	121	1,464
1957	1,180	129	1,506
1958	1,259	134	1,530
1959	1,395	143	1,633
1960	1,669	169	1,912
1961	1,824	176	1,925
1962	1,955	183	1,921
1963	2,159	188	1,935
1964	2,595	190	1,891
1965	2,895	193	1,836
1966	3,270	219	2,005
1967	3,557	236	2,107
1968	4,045	282	2,406
1969	5,057	359	2,906
1970	5,949	432	3,286
1971	6,410	500	3,476
1972	6,808	576	3,740
1973	7,439	726	4,315
1974	7,814	898	4,601
1975	8,787	1,218	5,025
1976	10,105	1,768	6,253
1977	11,518	2,352	7,182
1978	11,734	2,507	7,069
1979	11,563	2,797	6,955
1980	11,465	2,961	6,242
1981	10,578	2,970	5,594
1982	10,724	3,188	5,530
1983	11,556	4,003	6,638
1984	12,735	4,614	7,286
1985	14,449	5,442	8,102
1986	13,897	5,553	7,993
1987	15,566	6,260	8,648
1988	15,799	6,184	8,145
1989	17,338	6,945	8,484
1990	18,013	7,748	8,645
1991	17,125	7,386	7,781
1992	18,535	7,891	8,016
1993	19,863	9,487	9,487
1994	21,034	9,919	9,685
1995	23,746	11,885	11,215

How Britain compares

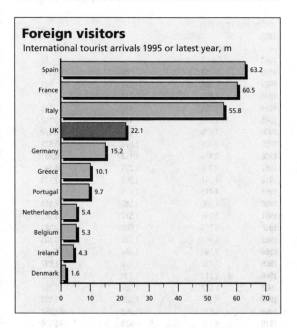

Foreign visitors
International tourist arrivals 1995 or latest year, m

Spain	63.2
France	60.5
Italy	55.8
UK	22.1
Germany	15.2
Greece	10.1
Portugal	9.7
Netherlands	5.4
Belgium	5.3
Ireland	4.3
Denmark	1.6

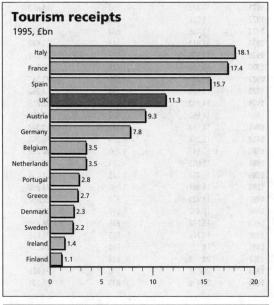

Tourism receipts
1995, £bn

Italy	18.1
France	17.4
Spain	15.7
UK	11.3
Austria	9.3
Germany	7.8
Belgium	3.5
Netherlands	3.5
Portugal	2.8
Greece	2.7
Denmark	2.3
Sweden	2.2
Ireland	1.4
Finland	1.1

Roads and vehicles

Vehicles registered
'000s

	Motor cars	Motor cycles	All vehicles
1903	8		17
1909	53	36	143
1920	187	228	591
1930	1,056	712	2,272
1939	2,034	418	3,148
1946	1,770	449	3,107
1950	1,979	643	3,970
1955	3,109	1,076	5,822
1956	3,437	1,137	6,287
1957	3,707	1,261	6,743
1958	4,047	1,300	7,175
1959	4,416	1,479	7,809
1960	4,900	1,583	8,512
1961	5,296	1,577	8,989
1962	5,776	1,567	9,532
1963	6,462	1,546	10,336
1964	7,190	1,534	11,176
1965	7,732	1,420	11,697
1966	8,210	1,239	12,022
1967	8,882	1,190	12,760
1968	9,285	1,082	13,082
1969	9,672	993	13,362
1970	9,971	923	13,548
1971	10,443	899	14,030
1972	11,006	866	14,584
1973	11,738	887	15,427
1974	11,917	918	15,642
1975	12,526	1,077	16,511
1976	13,184	1,175	17,318
1977	13,220	1,190	17,345
1978	13,626	1,194	17,758
1979	14,162	1,292	18,616
1980	14,660	1,372	19,199
1981	14,867	1,371	19,347
1982	15,264	1,370	19,762
1983	15,543	1,290	20,209
1984	16,055	1,225	20,765
1985	16,454	1,148	21,159
1986	16,981	1,065	21,699
1987	17,421	978	22,152
1988	18,432	912	23,301
1989	19,248	875	24,196
1990	19,742	833	24,672
1991	19,737	750	24,511
1992	20,116	688	24,851
1993	20,102	650	24,826
1994	20,479	630	25,231

A history of Britain's roads
Km of road

	Total	of which motorways are
1909	282,380	
1951	297,466	
1959	309,406	13
1970	322,484	1,057
1980	339,633	2,556
1990	358,034	3,070
1994	364,967	3,168

Road accidents

	Accidents, '000s	Deaths		Accidents, '000s	Deaths
1926	124	4,886	**1962**	264	6,709
1928	148	6,138	**1964**	292	7,820
1930	157	7,305	**1966**	292	7,985
1932	184	6,667	**1968**	264	6,810
1934	205	7,343	**1970**	267	7,499
1936	199	6,561	**1972**	265	7,763
1938	196	6,648	**1974**	244	6,876
1940	…	8,609	**1976**	259	6,570
1942	…	6,926	**1978**	265	6,813
1944	…	6,416	**1980**	252	6,010
1946	…	5,062	**1982**	256	5,934
1948	…	4,513	**1984**	253	5,599
1950	167	5,012	**1986**	248	5,382
1952	172	4,706	**1988**	247	5,052
1954	196	5,010	**1990**	258	5,217
1956	216	5,367	**1992**	233	4,229
1958	237	5,970	**1993**	229	3,814
1960	272	6,970	**1994**	234	3,650

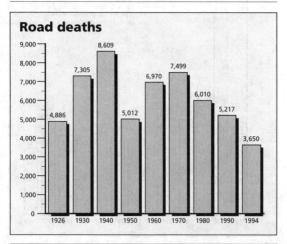

Road deaths

Rail

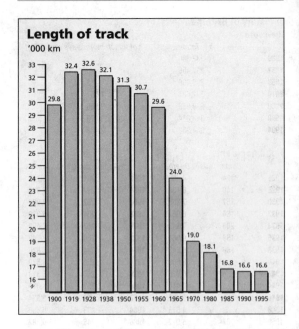

Length of track
'000 km

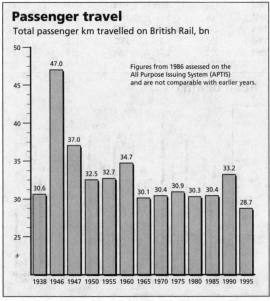

Passenger travel
Total passenger km travelled on British Rail, bn

Figures from 1986 assessed on the
All Purpose Issuing System (APTIS)
and are not comparable with earlier years.

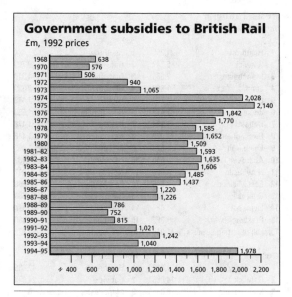

Government subsidies to British Rail

£m, 1992 prices

Year	£m
1968	638
1970	576
1971	506
1972	940
1973	1,065
1974	2,028
1975	2,140
1976	1,842
1977	1,770
1978	1,585
1979	1,652
1980	1,509
1981–82	1,593
1982–83	1,635
1983–84	1,606
1984–85	1,485
1985–86	1,437
1986–87	1,220
1987–88	1,226
1988–89	786
1989–90	752
1990–91	815
1991–92	1,021
1992–93	1,242
1993–94	1,040
1994–95	1,978

Rail buffs: who trains most

Rail km travelled per year per person

	1970	1975	1980	1985	1990	1993
Japan	2,770	2,869	2,697	2,648	2,995	3,223
Switzerland	1,293	1,576	1,424	1,855	1,937	1,914[a]
Austria	804	924	1,060	926	1,167	1,207
France	808	968	1,021	1,124	1,128	1,013
Netherlands	614	659	636	621	736	991
Denmark	812	593	781	976	973	890
Italy	650	649	709	683	798	850
Hungary	1,548	1,519	1,400	1,127	1,042	819
Germany	627	615	666	721	720	714
Sweden	622	732	842	838	700	683
Belgium	829	817	711	710	702	666
Finland	434	637	628	612	602	593
Portugal	442	550	614	606	608	577
Norway	516	499	489	482	471	537
Great Britain	539	622	533	636	575	524
Spain	444	506	400	416	436	419
Ireland	236	315	294	281	285	303
Greece	227	221	207	201	198	167
USA	83	74	79	75	84	81

a 1992.

Air

Busiest airports
Terminal passengers, '000

1975			1980		
1	Heathrow	21,295	1	Heathrow	27,484
2	Gatwick	5,342	2	Gatwick	9,703
3	Manchester	2,580	3	Manchester	4,316
4	Luton	1,869	4	Glasgow	2,339
5	Glasgow	1,763	5	Luton	2,088
6	Jersey	1,418	6	Birmingham	1,563
7	Belfast	1,184	7	Belfast	1,478
8	Birmingham	1,082	8	Aberdeen	1,448
9	Edinburgh	874	9	Jersey	1,353
10	Aberdeen	645	10	Edinburgh	1,162
11	Newcastle	605	11	Newcastle	917
12	East Midlands	545	12	East Midlands	668
13	Guernsey	525	13	Guernsey	534
14	Liverpool	437	14	Prestwick	394
15	Prestwick	395	15	Liverpool	380
Total all reporting airports		41,846	Total all reporting airports		57,822

1985			1990		
1	Heathrow	31,310	1	Heathrow	42,635
2	Gatwick	14,885	2	Gatwick	21,043
3	Manchester	6,054	3	Manchester	10,146
4	Glasgow	2,695	4	Glasgow	4,286
5	Aberdeen	1,697	5	Birmingham	3,492
6	Belfast	1,646	6	Luton	2,679
7	Birmingham	1,634	7	Edinburgh	2,492
8	Luton	1,586	8	Belfast	2,294
9	Edinburgh	1,574	9	Aberdeen	1,947
10	Jersey	1,552	10	Jersey	1,867
11	Newcastle	1,028	11	Newcastle	1,555
12	East Midlands	925	12	East Midlands	1,280
13	Guernsey	656	13	Stansted	1,156
14	Stansted	515	14	Guernsey	862
15	Leeds/Bradford	463	15	Leeds/Bradford	834
Total all reporting airports		70,434	Total all reporting airports		102,418

1995					
1	Heathrow	54,132	12	Luton	1,810
2	Gatwick	22,383	13	Bristol	1,431
3	Manchester	14,533	14	Belfast City	1,280
4	Glasgow	5,423	15	Cardiff	1,038
5	Birmingham	5,193	16	Leeds/Bradford	925
6	Stansted	3,890	17	London City	554
7	Edinburgh	3,275	18	Isle of Man	533
8	Newcastle	2,486	19	Southampton	511
9	Belfast International	2,346	20	Liverpool	503
10	Aberdeen	2,243	21	Sumburgh	478
11	East Midlands	1,879	Total all reporting airports		129,586

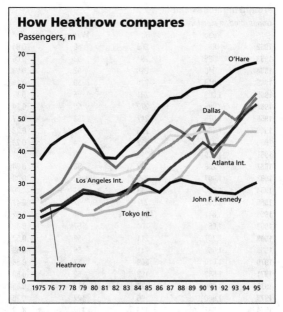

How Heathrow compares
Passengers, m

O'Hare
Dallas
Atlanta Int.
Los Angeles Int.
John F. Kennedy
Tokyo Int.
Heathrow

1975 76 77 78 79 80 81 82 83 84 85 86 87 88 89 90 91 92 93 94 95

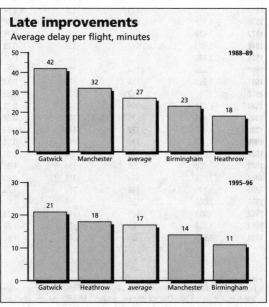

Late improvements
Average delay per flight, minutes

1988–89

Gatwick	Manchester	average	Birmingham	Heathrow
42	32	27	23	18

1995–96

Gatwick	Heathrow	average	Manchester	Birmingham
21	18	17	14	11

Freight: rail decline

Freight methods used
Goods lifted, million tonnes

	Road[a]	Rail[b]	Water[c]	Air[d]
1952	861	289	50	0.04
1953	889	294	52	0.06
1954	940	288	52	0.08
1955	1,013	279	50	0.11
1956	1,009	281	55	0.12
1957	985	279	55	0.14
1958	1,078	247	53	0.17
1959	1,164	238	53	0.23
1960	1,211	252	54	0.28
1961	1,260	242	56	0.31
1962	1,268	232	58	0.34
1963	1,407	239	60	0.36
1964	1,560	243	61	0.40
1965	1,590	232	62	0.42
1966	1,641	217	61	0.52
1967	1,651	204	57	0.49
1968	1,707	211	59	0.52
1969	1,658	211	59	0.59
1970	1,610	209	57	0.58
1971	1,582	198	52	0.53
1972	1,629	177	117	0.65
1973	1,660	196	122	0.70
1974	1,537	176	117	0.72
1975	1,511	175	108	0.64
1976	1,515	176	113	0.66
1977	1,429	171	122	0.71
1978	1,503	171	133	0.75
1979	1,499	169	140	0.80
1980	1,395	154	137	0.74
1981	1,299	154	129	0.72
1982	1,389	142	137	0.69
1983	1,358	145	143	0.73
1984	1,400	79	140	0.86
1985	1,452	122	142	0.85
1986	1,473	140	144	0.88
1987	1,542	141	142	0.98
1988	1,758	150	156	1.09
1989	1,812	146	155	1.15
1990	1,749	140	152	1.19
1991	1,600	135	144	1.12
1992	1,555	125	140	1.24
1993	1,615	109	134	1.38
1994	1,689	97	140	1.61

a All goods vehicles, including those up to 3.5 tonnes gross vehicle weight.
b Figures up to 1962 include free-hauled (i.e. departmental) traffic on revenue-earning trains. Figures for rail from 1991 are for fiinancial years 1991/92 etc

Freight methods used
Goods lifted, % of total carried

	Road	Rail	Water & air
1952	71.7	24.1	4.2
1953	72.0	23.8	4.2
1954	73.4	22.5	4.1
1955	75.5	20.8	3.7
1956	75.0	20.9	4.1
1957	74.7	21.2	4.1
1958	78.2	17.9	3.9
1959	80.0	16.4	3.6
1960	79.8	16.6	3.6
1961	80.9	15.5	3.6
1962	81.4	14.9	3.7
1963	82.5	14.0	3.5
1964	83.7	13.0	3.3
1965	84.4	12.3	3.3
1966	85.5	11.3	3.2
1967	86.3	10.7	3.0
1968	86.3	10.7	3.0
1969	86.0	10.9	3.1
1970	85.8	11.1	3.1
1971	86.3	10.8	2.9
1972	84.7	9.2	6.1
1973	83.9	9.9	6.2
1974	84.0	9.6	6.4
1975	84.2	9.8	6.0
1976	83.9	9.8	6.3
1977	83.0	9.9	7.1
1978	83.1	9.5	7.4
1979	82.9	9.3	7.8
1980	82.7	9.1	8.2
1981	82.1	9.7	8.2
1982	83.2	8.5	8.3
1983	82.5	8.8	8.7
1984	86.4	4.9	8.7
1985	84.6	7.1	8.3
1986	83.8	8.0	8.2
1987	84.4	7.7	7.9
1988	85.1	7.3	7.6
1989	85.7	6.9	7.4
1990	85.6	6.9	7.5
1991	85.1	7.2	7.7
1992	85.4	6.8	7.8
1993	86.9	5.9	7.2
1994	87.6	5.0	7.4

c Figures from 1972 onwards are not comparable with earlier years. From 1972, water includes all UK coastwise and one-port freight movements by sea and inland waterway traffic. Earlier years include only GB coastwise traffic and internal traffic on BWB waterways.

d Goods uplifted plus good landed. Excludes mail (0.2m tonnes in 1994).

Sea

Largest ports

Total cargo traffic, 1994, '000 tonnes

1	London	51,593	11	Orkneys	14,097
2	Forth estuary	44,359	12	Dover	14,089
3	Tees and Hartlepool	42,994	13	Port Talbot	11,092
4	Grimsby-Immingham	40,920	14	Hull	10,205
5	Sullom Voe	38,592	15	Belfast	9,898
6	Milford Haven	34,421	16	Manchester	7,687
7	Southampton	31,537	17	Bristol	7,074
8	Liverpool	29,265	18	Clyde	6,781
9	Felixstowe	22,116	19	River Hull and Humber	6,326
10	Medway	14,660	20	Glasgow	5,253

Cross-Channel traffic

Car arrivals at, and departures from, UK ports, by overseas country

By ship	1981	1986	1991	1993	1994
France	1,402	1,944	3,329	4,058	4,575
Irish Republic	378	345	611	621	634
Belgium	591	478	514	413	404
Netherlands	259	325	399	410	328
Spain & Portugal	20	27	47	70	79
Germany	22	21	34	44	48
Scandinavia & Baltic	62	67	56	53	42
Denmark	50	45	44	32	39
By hovercraft					
France	287	218	189	158	181
Total	3,071	3,470	5,223	5,859	6,330

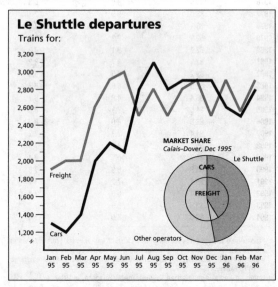

Le Shuttle departures

Trains for:

MARKET SHARE
Calais–Dover, Dec 1995

Le Shuttle

CARS

FREIGHT

Other operators

Freight

Cars

=== **Part VIII** ===

HOUSING

Household size and spending

Households by size
UK

	Total m	Average size[a]	Distribution by size, %					
			1	2	3	4	5	6 or more
1951	14.5	3.2	11	27	25	19	10	8
1961	16.2	3.1	14	30	23	18	9	7
1971	18.2	2.9	18	32	19	17	8	6
1981	19.5	2.7	22	32	17	18	7	4
1991	22.4	2.5	27	34	16	16	5	2
1994–95	23.1	2.4	27	34	16	15	6	2

Regional variations in households

	1985		1993	
	Average size[a]	% lone parents	Average size[a]	% lone parents
UK	2.62	…	2.48	…
England	2.60	8.9	…	9.0
Wales	2.68	8.9	2.53	9.0
Scotland	2.64	…	2.42	11.0
Northern Ireland	3.07	…	2.85	…
North	2.61	9.6	2.42	12.0
Yorkshire & Humberside	2.59	8.9	2.43	8.0
North West	2.64	9.9	2.47	11.0
West Midlands	2.66	9.0	2.51	10.0
East Midlands	2.62	8.4	2.46	8.0
East Anglia	2.61	7.4	2.42	7.0
South East	2.57	9.0	2.41	10.0
South West	2.56	7.7	2.40	7.0

Spending on housing
% of average weekly spending, 1994–95

UK	16.4
England	16.7
Wales	14.8
Scotland	14.7
Northern Ireland	11.5
North	14.8
Yorkshire & Humberside	15.0
North West	15.4
West Midlands	15.5
East Midlands	14.6
East Anglia	17.1
South East	18.4
Greater London	19.0
Rest of South East	18.1
South West	17.8

a Number of people.

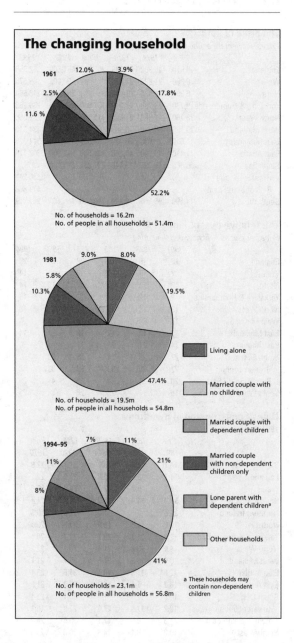

The changing household

1961

12.0% 3.9%
2.5% 17.8%
11.6 %
52.2%

No. of households = 16.2m
No. of people in all households = 51.4m

1981

9.0% 8.0%
5.8%
10.3% 19.5%

47.4%

No. of households = 19.5m
No. of people in all households = 54.8m

1994–95

7% 11%
11% 21%
8%

41%

No. of households = 23.1m
No. of people in all households = 56.8m

Living alone

Married couple with
no children

Married couple with
dependent children

Married couple
with non-dependent
children only

Lone parent with
dependent children[a]

Other households

a These households may
contain non-dependent
children

Land and housing stock

The price of land
Prices per hectare of housing land, £

	1969	1974	1979	1984	1989	1993
England	19,510	48,899	73,149	202,900	451,600	342,359
Wales	8,390	21,820	31,020	...	180,000	169,575
North	6,300	26,530	61,240	...	284,800	243,564
Yorkshire & Humberside	9,730	28,280	41,210	107,900	250,900	239,263
North West	13,760	40,960	51,880	111,600	382,000	269,655
West Midlands	23,130	55,480	79,960	165,000	457,500	434,040
East Midlands	11,640	28,630	35,720	92,300	413,700	314,265
East Anglia	11,410	29,000	44,860	131,500	541,900	302,176
South East	36,960	117,398	119,145	397,800	895,000	...
Greater London	...	...	...	...	...	1,330,243
Rest of South East	...	...	...	...	...	477,868
South West	14,190	55,290	78,490	190,300	460,800	267,322

The relative cost of land
Price per plot as % of new dwelling price

	1981	1983	1985	1987	1990	1994
England	16	19	19	29	23	23
Wales	7	10[a]	11[a]	12[a]	22	14
North	12	15[a]	11[a]	19[a]	15	14
Yorkshire & Humberside	9	12	13	12	16	16
North West	13	13	15	17	21	18
West Midlands	17	20	23	26	25	24
East Midlands	11	13	12	18	27	14
East Anglia	14	11	21	17	45	30
South East	22	23	34	39	39	...
Greater London	27	29	33	53	33	58
Rest of South East	20	21	34	35	44	28
South West	15	17	23	26	13	23

Date of construction of dwellings
1993, %

	Pre 1891	1891 –1918	1919 –1944	1945 –1970	Post 1970
UK	14.1	12.6	19.1	31.4	22.8
England	14.1	12.2	19.8	31.2	22.7
Wales	20.4	16.2	12.7	28.7	22.0
Scotland	10.0	14.4	16.0	34.8	24.4
Northern Ireland	20.6[b]		1.0	22.0	46.3
North	11.0	14.5	19.0	34.8	20.7
Yorkshire & Humberside	12.8	14.7	20.7	31.7	20.1
North West	14.4	13.8	21.4	30.1	22.1
West Midlands	10.9	10.8	21.5	35.2	21.7
East Midlands	12.6	11.5	18.1	31.6	26.1
East Anglia	18.7	7.4	12.7	29.7	31.6
South East	14.3	12.3	21.2	30.1	22.1
Greater London	18.2	17.5	27.2	22.0	15.1
Rest of South East	11.8	8.9	17.1	35.5	26.7
South West	19.2	9.4	14.9	30.0	26.5

Housing stock
No. of houses at censuses, '000s

	England & Wales	Scotland	Northern Ireland
1851	3,432	...	267
1861	3,924	...	269
1871	4,520	...	267
1881	5,218	799	273
1891	5,824	869	274
1901	6,710	986	291
1911	7,550	1,102	291
1921	7,979	1,109	...
1926	...	...	285
1931	9,400	1,197	...
1936–37	...	...	322
1951	12,389	1,442	346
1961	14,646	1,627	387
1966	15,449	1,691	419
1971	16,455	1,717	455
1981	19,108	1,970	502
1991	20,971	2,158	573
1993	21,273	2,193	590

	Apr 1966	Dec 1976	Dec 1981	Dec 1986	Dec 1991	Dec 1993
UK	17,865	20,599	21,581	22,601	23,702	24,056
England	14,885	17,168	18,021	18,883	19,787	20,070
Wales	886	1,029	1,089	1,128	1,184	1,203
Scotland	1,697	1,921	1,970	2,050	2,158	2,193
Northern Ireland	397	481	500	540	573	590
North	1,094	1,169	1,214	1,249	1,287	1,301
Yorkshire & Humberside	1,633	1,829	1,900	1,960	2,031	2,058
North West	2,239	2,396	2,466	2,526	2,593	2,622
West Midlands	1,594	1,840	1,941	2,016	2,089	2,117
East Midlands	1,114	1,393	1,484	1,558	1,646	1,676
East Anglia	545	692	755	807	870	890
South East	5,414	6,236	6,531	6,913	7,288	7,391
Greater London	...	2,640	2,676	2,801	2,928	2,959
Rest of South East	...	3,596	3,855	4,112	4,360	4,432
South West	1,252	1,613	1,727	1,853	1,983	2,015

a Estimate.
b Pre 1919.
c Post 1944.

Housebuilding

Public sector decline

No. of house completions in Great Britain, '000s (%)

	Private sector	Housing Associations	Local authorities, new towns & govt. departments	Total
1950	27.4 (13.8)	1.6 (0.8)	169.2 (85.4)	198.2
1951	22.6 (11.6)	1.8 (0.9)	170.5 (87.5)	194.9
1952	34.3 (14.3)	2.2 (0.9)	203.4 (84.8)	239.9
1953	62.9 (19.7)	7.9 (2.5)	247.9 (77.8)	318.7
1954	90.6 (26.0)	14.9 (4.3)	242.3 (69.7)	347.8
1955	113.5 (35.7)	4.6 (1.4)	199.4 (62.8)	317.5
1956	124.2 (41.3)	2.7 (0.9)	173.8 (57.8)	300.7
1957	126.5 (42.0)	2.0 (0.7)	172.6 (57.3)	301.1
1958	128.1 (46.8)	1.2 (0.4)	144.3 (52.7)	273.6
1959	150.7 (54.5)	1.1 (0.4)	124.8 (45.1)	276.6
1960	168.6 (56.6)	1.8 (0.6)	127.4 (42.8)	297.8
1961	177.5 (60.0)	1.6 (0.5)	116.9 (39.5)	296.0
1962	174.8 (57.2)	1.6 (0.5)	129.0 (42.2)	305.4
1963	174.9 (58.5)	2.0 (0.7)	122.1 (40.8)	299.0
1964	218.1 (58.4)	2.9 (0.8)	152.7 (40.9)	373.7
1965	213.8 (55.9)	4.0 (1.0)	164.5 (43.0)	382.3
1966	205.4 (53.3)	4.6 (1.2)	175.6 (45.5)	385.6
1967	200.4 (49.6)	5.0 (1.2)	198.9 (49.2)	404.3
1968	222.0 (53.7)	6.3 (1.5)	185.4 (44.8)	413.7
1969	181.7 (49.5)	7.3 (2.0)	177.8 (48.5)	366.8
1970	170.3 (48.6)	8.5 (2.4)	171.6 (49.0)	350.4
1971	191.6 (54.6)	10.7 (3.1)	148.3 (42.3)	350.6
1972	196.5 (61.5)	7.7 (2.4)	115.2 (36.1)	319.4
1973	186.6 (63.4)	8.9 (3.0)	98.6 (33.5)	294.1
1974	140.9 (52.3)	9.9 (3.7)	118.7 (44.0)	269.5
1975	150.8 (48.2)	14.7 (4.7)	147.6 (47.1)	313.1
1976	152.2 (48.3)	15.8 (5.0)	147.2 (46.7)	315.2
1977	140.8 (46.4)	25.1 (8.3)	137.4 (45.3)	303.3
1978	149.0 (53.3)	22.8 (8.1)	108.0 (38.6)	279.8
1979	140.5 (57.5)	17.8 (7.3)	86.2 (35.3)	244.5
1980	128.4 (54.5)	21.1 (9.0)	86.0 (36.5)	235.5
1981	115.0 (57.6)	19.3 (9.7)	65.5 (32.8)	199.8
1982	125.4 (71.3)	13.1 (7.5)	37.3 (21.2)	175.8
1983	148.1 (78.2)	16.1 (6.8)	35.1 (14.9)	235.3
1984	159.4 (75.9)	16.6 (7.9)	34.1 (16.2)	210.1
1985	156.5 (79.5)	13.1 (6.7)	27.2 (13.8)	196.8
1986	170.4 (82.8)	12.5 (6.1)	22.9 (11.1)	205.8
1987	183.7 (84.9)	12.5 (5.8)	20.1 (9.3)	216.4
1988	199.8 (86.0)	12.8 (5.5)	19.9 (8.5)	232.5
1989	179.7 (85.1)	13.9 (6.6)	17.5 (8.3)	211.1
1990	160.7 (82.7)	16.9 (8.7)	16.6 (8.6)	194.2
1991	154.1 (83.7)	19.7 (10.7)	10.3 (5.6)	184.1
1992	141.1 (82.5)	25.2 (14.7)	4.7 (2.8)	171.0
1993	140.5 (79.3)	34.1 (19.3)	2.5 (1.4)	177.1
1994	146.0 (80.1)	34.3 (18.8)	1.9 (1.1)	182.2
1995	147.3 (78.4)	38.5 (20.5)	2.0 (1.1)	187.8

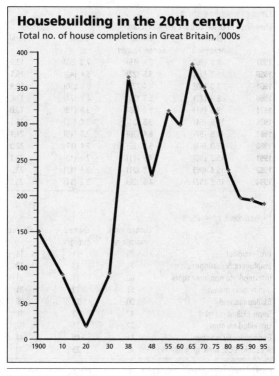

Housebuilding in the 20th century
Total no. of house completions in Great Britain, '000s

Regional variations
New dwellings per '000 pop.

	1968	1970	1975	1980	1985	1990	1993
UK	...	...	5.8	4.3	3.5	3.4	...
England	7.7	6.3	5.6	4.3	3.4	3.4	3.0
Wales	7.1	5.7	6.2	3.7	2.9	3.6	3.3
Scotland	8.1	8.6	6.5	4.0	3.6	3.9	3.7
Northern Ireland	...	...	5.8	4.2	5.6	5.0	4.4
North	7.9	5.9	5.6	3.7	2.9	3.0	2.4
Yorkshire & Humberside	7.5	5.8	5.0	4.2	2.7	2.6	2.9
North West	6.9	6.6	5.0	3.8	2.7	2.8	2.9
West Midlands	8.6	6.3	5.0	4.2	3.1	3.1	2.9
East Midlands	8.4	6.8	7.0	4.7	3.5	3.6	3.6
East Anglia	10.3	8.1	8.9	6.5	5.7	6.0	4.7
South East	7.1	6.1	5.5	4.3	3.4	3.4	2.7
Greater London	...	...	...	3.3	1.3	2.6	1.9
Rest of South East	...	...	...	5.0	4.7	4.0	3.3
South West	8.8	6.6	6.2	4.8	5.3	4.2	3.2

Home ownership

Owners and renters
Dwellings in Great Britain, m (% of total)

	Owner-occupied	Public sector rented	Other	Total
1951	4.1 (29)	2.5 (18)	7.3 (53)	13.9
1956	5.2 (34)	3.5 (23)	6.4 (43)	15.1
1961	7.0 (43)	4.4 (27)	5.0 (30)	16.4
1966	8.3 (47)	5.1 (29)	4.2 (24)	17.6
1971	9.6 (51)	5.8 (30)	3.6 (19)	19.0
1976	10.8 (54)	6.3 (31)	3.0 (15)	20.1
1981	11.9 (57)	6.4 (30)	2.8 (13)	21.1
1986	13.8 (63)	5.8 (26)	2.4 (11)	22.0
1991	15.3 (66)	4.9 (21)	2.9 (13)	23.1
1992	15.4 (66)	4.8 (21)	3.1 (13)	23.3
1994	15.8 (67)	4.6 (20)	3.2 (14)	23.6

Class divisions
Great Britain, 1994–95, %

	Owned with mortgage	Owned outright	Rented[a]
Professional	75	11	14
Employers & managers	74	13	13
Intermediate non-managers	68	11	21
Junior non-manual	57	12	31
Skilled manual	60	14	26
Semi-skilled manual	42	12	46
Unskilled manual	32	11	57
Economically inactive	11	45	44
All socio-economic groups	42	25	33

Owner-occupation in Europe
Owner-occupied as % of all homes

Ireland, Spain, Italy, Greece, UK, Portugal, Belgium, Luxembourg, France, Denmark, Netherlands, Germany

Early 1980s
Early 1990s

Owner-occupation by region
% of total

	1969	1976	1981	1986	1989	1993
UK	...	54	57	62	67	67
England	51	56	59	64	68	67
Wales	54	59	63	67	71	72
Scotland	30	34	36	43	49	57
Northern Ireland	...	51	54	61	64	68
North	41	46	49	55	59	61
Yorkshire & Humberside	48	54	57	62	66	66
North West	54	58	61	65	68	68
West Midlands	49	55	59	63	67	68
East Midlands	50	57	61	66	70	71
East Anglia	51	56	60	66	70	69
Greater London	46	47	50	56	61	58
Rest of South East	57	61	65	71	74	74
South West	57	62	65	70	73	73

Sales of local authority dwellings[b]

	Stock at April 1979, '000s	Sales 1979–1993	Stock at end-1993	Total sales as % of stock at April 1979
UK	6,679	1,920	4,748	28.8
England	5,256	1,545	3,700	29.4
Wales	308	96	213	31.0
Scotland	903	223	677	24.8
Northern Ireland	213	57	158	26.6
North	465	119	344	25.6
Yorkshire & Humberside	603	144	459	23.9
North West	690	157	526	22.9
West Midlands	629	162	463	25.9
East Midlands	430	124	305	28.9
East Anglia	200	76	124	38.0
Greater London	911	255	650	28.2
Rest of South East	938	378	570	39.9
South West	388	129	259	33.3

a Includes renting from housing association and those renting with a job or business.
b Includes dwellings transferred to housing associations and private developers.

House prices

National variations

Average dwelling price, all mortgages, £

	UK	Wales	Scotland	N. Ireland
1970	4,975	4,434	5,002	4,387
1975	11,787	10,083	11,139	10,023
1976	12,704	11,129	12,974	12,860
1977	13,650	11,673	14,236	15,722
1978	15,594	13,373	16,147	18,395
1979	19,925	17,061	19,371	21,824
1980	23,596	19,363	21,754	23,656
1981	24,188	20,155	23,014	19,890
1982	23,644	19,662	22,522	20,177
1983	26,469	22,533	23,822	20,878
1984	29,106	23,665	25,865	21,455
1985	31,103	25,005	26,941	23,012
1986	36,276	27,354	28,242	25,743
1987	40,391	29,704	29,591	27,773
1988	49,355	34,244	31,479	29,875
1989	54,846	42,981	35,394	30,280
1990	59,785	46,464	41,744	31,849
1991	62,455	48,989	48,772	35,352
1992	60,821	49,685	49,224	37,775
1993	61,223	52,070	49,553	38,878
1994	63,077	52,144	50,598	38,685
1995*	65,079	54,191	56,743	42,936

Regional variations

Average dwelling price, all mortgages, £

	North	Yorkshire & Humberside	North-West	West Midlands	East Midlands
1970	3,942	3,634	4,184	4,490	3,966
1975	9,601	9,085	9,771	10,866	9,989
1980	17,710	17,689	20,092	21,663	18,928
1981	18,602	19,202	20,554	21,755	19,465
1982	18,071	18,180	20,744	20,992	19,487
1983	20,034	20,870	22,827	23,133	22,034
1984	22,604	22,356	24,410	24,989	24,377
1985	22,786	23,338	25,126	25,855	25,539
1986	24,333	25,607	27,503	28,437	28,483
1987	27,275	27,747	29,527	32,657	31,808
1988	30,193	32,685	34,074	41,700	40,521
1989	37,374	41,817	42,126	49,815	49,421
1990	43,655	47,231	50,005	54,694	52,620
1991	46,005	52,343	53,178	58,659	55,740
1992	48,347	52,278	56,377	57,827	54,599
1993	49,337	54,346	54,890	58,315	53,370
1994	49,380	53,439	56,350	59,128	54,618
1995*	47,134	55,944	55,633	60,438	51,699

a Third quarter.

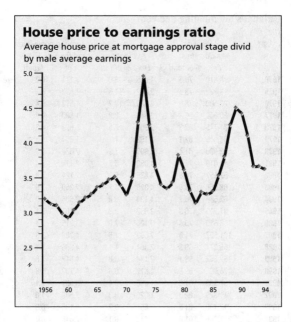

House price to earnings ratio

Average house price at mortgage approval stage divid
by male average earnings

East Anglia	Greater London	South East	South West
4,515	6,882	6,223	4,879
11,528	14,918	14,664	12,096
22,808	30,968	29,832	25,293
23,060	30,757	29,975	25,365
23,358	30,712	29,676	25,514
25,814	34,632	33,753	27,996
28,296	39,346	37,334	30,612
31,661	44,301	40,487	32,948
36,061	54,863	48,544	38,536
42,681	66,024	57,387	44,728
57,295	77,697	72,561	58,457
64,610	82,383	81,635	67,004
61,427	83,821	80,525	65,378
61,141	85,742	79,042	65,346
56,770	78,254	74,347	61,460
58,039	78,399	74,605	60,791
58,458	85,197	77,717	62,903
58,553	83,842	80,802	66,935

Housing purchase loans

Balances outstanding end year
UK

	Building Societies		Local Authorities		Insurance companies and Pension Funds	
	£m	% of total	£m	% of total	£m	% of total
1970	8,810	76.5	1,035	9.0	1,171	10.2
1975	18,882	75.5	2,872	11.5	1,533	6.1
1976	22,500	78.0	2,939	10.2	1,572	5.4
1977	26,600	80.3	2,943	8.9	1,580	4.8
1978	31,715	82.3	2,900	7.5	1,623	4.2
1979	36,986	82.1	3,193	7.1	1,854	4.1
1980	42,696	81.4	3,809	7.3	2,030	3.9
1981	49,019	78.7	4,080	6.6	2,118	3.4
1982	57,152	74.8	4,635	6.1	2,124	2.8
1983	68,056	74.6	4,329	4.7	2,250	2.5
1984	82,586	76.2	4,134	3.8	2,506	2.3
1985	97,213	76.3	3,632	2.9	2,707	2.1
1986	116,640	75.6	3,126	2.0	3,215	2.1
1987	131,557	71.6	2,693	1.5	4,203	2.3
1988	155,277	69.3	2,364	1.1	4,686	2.1
1989	152,542	59.1	2,134	0.8	4,542	1.8
1990	176,682	59.9	1,812	0.6	4,752	1.6
1991	197,609	61.6	1,366	0.4	3,604	1.1
1992	211,329	62.3	1,029	0.3	3,508	1.0
1993	217,736	61.6	651	0.2	3,188	0.9
1994	231,766	61.6	410	0.1	2,618	0.7
1995	223,822	57.3	183	…	2,321	0.6

Mortgage[a] arrears and possessions
UK, '000s

	Total no. of Mortgages	Loans in arrears at end period		Properties taken into possession in period
		By 6–12 months	By over 12 months	
1971	4,506	17.6	…	2.8
1976	5,322	16.0	…	5.0
1981	6,336	21.5	…	4.9
1982	6,518	27.4	5.5	6.9
1983	6,846	29.4	7.5	8.4
1984	7,313	48.3	9.5	12.4
1985	7,717	57.1	13.1	19.3
1986	8,138	52.1	13.0	24.1
1987	8,283	55.5	15.0	26.4
1988	8,564	42.8	10.3	18.5
1989	9,125	66.8	13.8	15.8
1990	9,415	123.1	36.1	43.9
1991	9,815	183.6	91.7	75.5
1992	9,922	205.0	147.0	68.5
1993	10,137	164.6	151.8	58.5
1994	10,410	133.7	117.1	49.2
1995	10,521	126.7	85.2	49.4

Banks		Other specialist Mortgage lenders		Other public sector		Total
£m	% of total	£m	% of total	£m	% of total	£m
415	3.6	...	...	79	0.7	11,510
1,310	5.2	...	...	405	1.6	25,002
1,380	4.8	...	...	465	1.6	28,856
1,520	4.6	...	...	483	1.5	33,126
1,805	4.7	...	...	500	1.3	38,533
2,430	5.4	...	...	572	1.3	45,001
2,880	5.5	...	...	1,026	2.0	52,557
5,673	9.1	...	...	1,379	2.2	62,567
10,751	14.1	...	...	1,737	2.3	76,399
14,845	16.3	...	...	1,778	1.9	91,524
16,888	15.6	480	0.4	1,737	1.6	108,331
21,111	16.6	971	0.8	1,798	1.4	127,432
25,916	16.8	3,539	2.3	1,852	1.2	154,288
35,948	19.6	7,495	4.1	1,901	1.0	183,797
45,335	20.2	14,227	6.4	2,045	0.9	223,934
79,190	30.7	17,416	6.8	2,179	0.8	258,003
85,677	29.0	24,038	8.1	2,077	0.7	295,505
90,371	28.2	26,222	8.2	1,641	0.5	320,813
96,470	28.5	25,115	7.4	1,516	0.4	338,967
108,517	30.7	22,734	6.4	1,467	0.4	354,293
115,890	30.8	24,463	6.5	1,388	0.4	376,535
139,899	35.8	23,491	6.0	1,369	0.4	391,085

County court actions for mortgage possessions[b]
Actions entered, '000s

	1987	1989	1991	1993	1994
England	74.0	86.2	176.4	109.7	83.5
Wales	5.1	5.1	10.2	6.4	4.4
North	4.7	4.5	6.9	4.6	3.7
Yorkshire & Humberside	7.8	7.4	14.1	8.4	7.6
North West	13.0	11.3	21.4	14.1	11.7
West Midlands	9.9	8.5	17.7	10.3	8.6
East Midlands	6.4	6.2	13.5	7.7	6.0
East Anglia	2.3	3.2	6.2	3.9	3.0
South East	24.5	37.9	79.9	48.9	35.5
Greater London	9.0	15.9	35.3	21.3	15.5
Rest of South East	15.6	22.0	44.6	27.7	20.0
South West	5.3	7.2	16.7	11.7	7.4

a Council of Mortgage Lenders estimates covering members of the Council, who account for 95% of all mortgages outstanding.
b Local authority and private.

Building societies

Numbers

	No. of societies	No. of branches	No. of shareholders '000s	No. of depositors '000s	No. of borrowers '000s
1930	1,026	...	1,449	428	720
1940	952	...	2,088	771	1,503
1950	819	...	2,256	654	1,508
1960	726	...	3,910	571	2,349
1970	481	2,016	10,265	618	3,655
1980	273	5,684	30,636	915	5,383
1985	167	6,926	39,996	2,149	6,657
1990	117	6,051	36,948	4,299	6,724
1994	96	5,566	38,150	5,509	7,370

Assets, loans and balances

	Share balances £m	Deposit & loan balances, £m	Mortgage balances £m	Total assets £m	Advances during yr. Number '000s	Advances during yr. Amount £m
1930	303	45	316	371	159	89
1940	552	142	678	756	43	21
1950	962	205	1,060	1,256	302	270
1960	2,721	222	2,647	3,166	387	560
1970	9,788	382	8,752	10,819	624	1,954
1980	48,915	1,762	42,437	53,793	936	9,503
1985	102,332	10,752	96,765	120,763	1,682	26,531
1990	160,538	40,695	175,745	216,848	1,397	43,081
1994	201,182	71,899	23,658	301,011	1,093	36,792

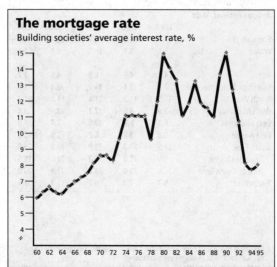

The mortgage rate
Building societies' average interest rate, %

Living longer

Expectation of life at varying ages
Further number of years which a person can expect to live, UK

Males

	1901	1931	1961	1991	1996	2001	2021
at birth	45.5	57.7	67.8	73.2	74.4	75.4	77.6
at age 1 year	54.6	62.4	69.5	73.8	74.8	75.7	77.9
at age 10 years	60.4	65.2	69.9	73.9	75.0	75.9	78.0
at age 20 years	61.7	66.3	70.3	74.2	75.3	76.1	78.2
at age 40 years	66.1	69.3	71.4	75.1	76.3	77.2	79.3
at age 60 years	73.3	74.3	74.9	77.7	78.6	79.5	81.4
at age 80 years	84.9	84.7	85.2	86.4	86.8	87.2	88.8

Females

	1901	1931	1961	1991	1996	2001	2021
at birth	49.0	61.6	73.6	78.7	79.7	80.6	82.6
at age 1 year	56.8	65.3	75.1	79.2	80.1	80.9	82.8
at age 10 years	62.7	67.9	75.4	79.4	80.3	81.1	83.0
at age 20 years	64.1	69.0	75.6	79.5	80.4	81.2	83.1
at age 40 years	68.3	71.9	76.3	80.0	80.9	81.7	83.5
at age 60 years	74.6	76.1	78.8	81.9	82.6	83.3	84.9
at age 80 years	85.3	85.4	86.3	88.3	88.8	89.1	90.0

Expectation of life at birth
Number of years which a person can expect to live

	1961	1971	1981	1990	1993
Males					
UK	67.9	68.8	70.8	72.9	73.8
England & Wales	68.1	69.0	71.0	73.1	74.0
Scotland	66.3	67.3	69.0	71.1	71.7
Northern Ireland	67.6	67.6	69.3	71.8	72.8
Females					
UK	73.8	75.0	76.8	78.5	79.1
England & Wales	74.0	75.2	77.0	78.7	79.3
Scotland	72.0	73.7	75.2	76.7	77.3
Northern Ireland	72.4	73.7	75.7	77.6	78.4

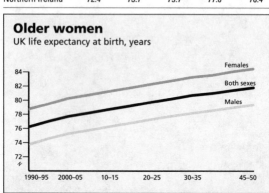

Older women
UK life expectancy at birth, years

Females

Both sexes

Males

1990–95 2000–05 10–15 20–25 30–35 45–50

A hundred up
Number of centenarians

	No. 1991 census	Per million population
England and Wales	6,619	86
Wales	373	85
North	346	72
Yorkshire & Humberside	563	78
North West	726	76
West Midlands	520	68
East Midlands	474	79
East Anglia	322	95
South East	2,463	92
South West	832	117

Octogenarian boom
Growth in proportion of over 80-year olds in total population

	1960	2000	2040
UK	1.92	4.08	5.94
Australia	1.24	2.99	5.95
Belgium	1.94	3.65	8.33
Canada	1.25	3.53	7.95
Finland	0.93	3.34	6.79
Japan	0.72	3.60	8.69
New Zealand	1.51	2.79	5.03
Spain	1.41	3.43	6.47
Switzerland	1.55	3.93	6.61
USA	1.40	3.49	7.63

Outliving most
Life expectancy at birth, years

1950–1955 / 1995–2000

Region	1950–1955	1995–2000
Africa	53.0	54.2
World	64.4	65.8
Asia	64.5	66.2
Latin America	68.5	69.8
Europe	72.9	73.3
Oceania	72.8	73.8
UK	76.1	76.2
North America	76.1	76.9
Australia & New Zealand	77.3	77.9

Dying older

Death rates, UK
Males

	1900-02	1910-12	1920-22	1930-32	1940-42
All ages[a]	340,664	303,703	284,876	284,249	314,643
Per 1,000 pop.	18.4	14.9	13.5	12.9	...
1 year	87,242	63,885	48,044	28,840	24,624
1–4 years	37,834	29,452	19,008	11,276	6,949
5–9 years	8,429	7,091	6,052	4,580	3,400
10–14 years	4,696	4,095	3,953	2,890	2,474
15–19 years	7,047	5,873	5,906	5,076	4,653
20–24 years	8,766	6,817	6,572	6,495	4,246
25–34 years	19,154	16,141	13,663	12,327	11,506
35–44 years	24,739	21,813	19,702	16,326	17,296
45–54 years	30,488	28,981	29,256	29,376	30,082
55–64 years	37,610	37,721	40,583	47,989	57,076
65–74 years	39,765	45,140	49,398	63,804	79,652
75–84 years	28,320	29,397	34,937	45,247	59,733
85 and over	6,563	7,283	7,801	10,022	12,900

Females

	1900-02	1910-12	1920-22	1930-32	1940-42
All ages	322,058	289,608	274,772	275,336	296,646
Per 1,000 pop.	16.3	13.3	11.9	11.5	...
1 year	68,770	49,865	335,356	21,072	17,936
1–4 years	36,164	27,817	17,323	9,995	5,952
5–9 years	8,757	7,113	5,808	3,990	2,743
10–14 years	5,034	4,355	4,133	2,734	2,068
15–19 years	6,818	5,683	5,729	4,721	4,180
20–24 years	8,264	6,531	6753	5,931	5,028
25–34 years	18,702	15,676	14,878	12,699	11,261
35–44 years	21,887	19,647	18,121	15,373	14,255
45–54 years	25,679	24,481	24,347	24,695	23,629
55–64 years	34,521	32,813	34,026	39,471	42,651
65–74 years	42,456	46,453	48,573	59,520	70,907
75–84 years	34,907	37,353	45,521	56,250	71,377
85 and over	10,099	11,828	14,203	18,886	24,658

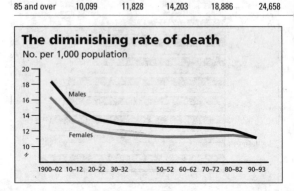

The diminishing rate of death

No. per 1,000 population

Males

Females

1900–02 10–12 20–22 30–32   50–52 60–62 70–72 80–82 90–93

a In some years the totals include a small number of persons whose age was not stated.

1950-52	1960-62	1970-72	1980-82	1990-92	1993
307,312	318,850	335,166	330,495	312,521	317,393
12.6	12.5	12.4	12.1	11.1	11.1
14,105	12,234	9,158	4,829	3,315	2,749
2,585	1,733	1,485	774	623	575
1,317	971	1,019	527	372	321
919	871	802	652	396	393
1,498	1,718	1,778	1,999	1,349	1,047
2,289	1,857	2,104	1,943	2,059	1,862
5,862	3,842	3,590	3,736	4,334	4,371
11,074	8,753	7,733	6,568	6,979	6,608
27,637	26,422	24,608	19,728	15,412	15,579
53,691	63,009	64,898	54,159	40,424	38,692
86,435	87,542	105,058	105,155	87,849	90,112
79,768	83,291	82,905	98,488	106,376	105,660
20,131	26,605	30,027	31,936	43,032	49,424

291,597	304,871	322,968	330,269	328,218	340,459
11.2	11.2	11.3	11.4	11.1	11.5
10,293	8,887	6,666	3,561	2,431	2,081
2,098	1,334	1,183	585	485	428
880	627	654	355	259	234
625	522	459	425	255	279
1,115	684	718	733	520	453
1,717	811	900	772	714	648
5,018	2,504	2,110	2,099	1,989	2,091
8,989	6,513	5,345	4,360	4,340	4,178
18,875	16,720	15,594	12,206	9,707	9,955
37,075	36,078	36,177	32,052	25,105	23,875
75,220	73,118	75,599	72,618	61,951	63,727
92,848	105,956	109,539	117,760	115,467	114,875
36,844	51,117	68,024	82,743	104,994	117,635

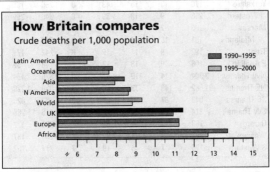

How Britain compares
Crude deaths per 1,000 population

Legend: 1990–1995 / 1995–2000

Categories: Latin America, Oceania, Asia, N America, World, UK, Europe, Africa

Axis: 6 7 8 9 10 11 12 13 14 15

Death: the causes

Mostly natural

	1935	1950	1960
Total deaths	**561,234**	**590,136**	**603,328**
from natural causes	536,275	568,119	576,747
of which:			
Tuberculosis (all forms)	33,485	20,405	4,058
Whooping cough	2,110	485	48
Meningococcal infection	...	327	118
Measles	1,825	271	33
Cancer – malignant disease	71,997	97,465	112,222
Diabetes mellitus	5,471	4,342	4,202
Mental disorders	...	...	...
Nervous system diseases	...	...	...
Cerebrovascular disease	50,922	75,154	88,262
Heart disease	119,453	169,202	173,579
Respiratory disease excl. asthma	75,208	55,796	57,397
Ulcer of stomach/duodenum	5,272	5,820	5,386
Liver disease & cirrhosis	...	...	...
from accidents & violence	**26,139**	**22,017**	**26,581**
of which:			
Motor vehicle accidents	6,859	4,842	7,496
Suicide	5,794	4,788	5,583

AIDS

Cases by exposure category, cumulative totals to December 31st 1994

	Sexual intercourse		Injecting drug		Other & undeter-	Cases cumul-	
	Males	Females	use	Blood[b]	mined	ative	Deaths
UK	8,344	543	591	565	256	10,304	7,019
England	7,902	504	366	504	234	9,510	6,434
Wales	98	8	4	24	7	141	118
Scotland[c]	305	32	220	33	14	604	429
N Ireland[c]	39	4	1	4	1	49	38
Northern	107	8	4	37	3	159	114
Yorkshire	170	13	16	43	8	250	185
N Western	266	9	18	39	8	340	259
Mersey	98	7	8	24	4	141	109
W. Midlands	181	16	7	39	6	249	184
Trent	192	9	14	19	8	242	171
E Anglian	106	9	18	13	2	148	97
NW Thames	3,304	114	110	43	55	3,626	2,454
NE Thames	1,682	149	73	68	64	2,036	1,229
SE Thames	943	87	56	67	29	1,182	825
SW Thames	314	49	14	14	25	416	286
Oxford	163	13	16	52	7	251	172
Wessex	197	14	7	27	8	253	187
S Western	179	7	5	19	7	217	162

a 1992.
b Blood/blood factor and tissue recipients.
c Data for Scotland and Northern Ireland are for 1991.

1970	1980	1985	1990	1993
655,382	**661,519**	**670,656**	**641,799**	**657,852**
629,067	**637,030**	**648,082**	**617,296**	**638,996**
1,950	1,059	896	651	586
22	6	4	8	...
163	81	111	189	190
51	34	12	2	4
131,158	146,308	158,017	161,718	159,702
5,581	5,477	8,077	8,486	6,823
1,608	3,928	12,989	14,439	9,097
7,134	7,367	12,390	12,711	10,188
91,691	82,800	83,665	76,409	71,287
213,451	225,839	221,162	198,350	203,566
87,367	80,746	49,614	41,286	68,246
4,280	5,019	5,427	4,815	4,687
1,671	2,696	3,074	3,623	3,542
26,315	**24,489**	**22,574**	**21,282**	**19,797**[a]
7,884	6,863	5,720	5,701	4,747[a]
4,386	4,917	5,105	4,643	4,628[a]

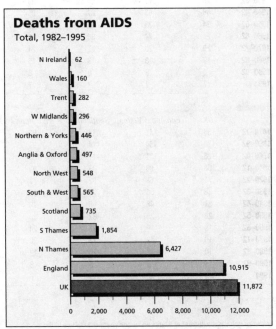

Deaths from AIDS
Total, 1982–1995

Region	Deaths
N Ireland	62
Wales	160
Trent	282
W Midlands	296
Northern & Yorks	446
Anglia & Oxford	497
North West	548
South & West	565
Scotland	735
S Thames	1,854
N Thames	6,427
England	10,915
UK	11,872

Infant mortality

Overall

	UK	England & Wales	Scotland	N. Ireland
1870–72	150	156	126	96
1890–92	145	149	125	107
1900–02	142	146	124	113
1910–22	110	110	109	101
1920–22	82	80	94	86
1930–32	67	65	84	75
1940–42	59	55	77	80
1950–52	30	29	37	40
1960–62	22	22	26	27
1970–72	18	18	19	22
1980–82	12	11	12	13
1990–92	7	7	7	7
1994	6	6	6	6

Male

	UK	England & Wales	Scotland	N. Ireland
1870–72	163	169	135	105
1890–92	159	164	136	115
1900–02	156	160	136	123
1910–12	121	121	120	110
1920–22	92	90	106	95
1930–32	75	72	94	83
1940–42	66	62	87	89
1950–52	34	33	42	45
1960–62	25	24	30	30
1970–72	20	20	22	24
1980–82	13	13	13	15
1990–92	8	8	8	8
1994	7	7	7	7

Female

	UK	England & Wales	Scotland	N. Ireland
1870–72	136	141	115	86
1890–92	130	134	114	99
1900–02	128	131	111	103
1910–12	98	98	97	92
1920–22	71	69	82	77
1930–32	58	55	73	66
1940–42	51	48	66	70
1950–52	26	25	32	36
1960–62	19	19	22	24
1970–72	16	15	17	20
1980–82	10	10	10	12
1990–92	6	6	6	6
1994	5	5	6	6

Infant mortality is the number of deaths under one year per 1,000 live births.

Regional differences		Class matters	
1993		*Infant deaths by father's occupation, 1986–90, England & Wales*	
Yorkshire & Humberside	7.3		
West Midlands	7.1		
North	6.7	Unskilled manual	13.1
East Midlands	6.6	Semi-skilled manual	10.5
North-West	6.5	Skilled manual	8.4
Greater London	6.4	Armed forces	7.8
South-East	5.9	Intermediate & junior	
South-West	5.8	non-managerial	7.5
East Anglia	4.8	Employers & managers	6.6
		Professional	6.6

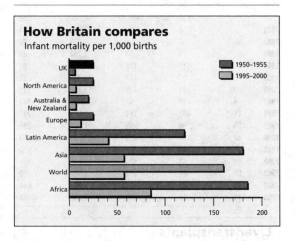

How Britain compares

Infant mortality per 1,000 births

- 1950–1955
- 1995–2000

(UK, North America, Australia & New Zealand, Europe, Latin America, Asia, World, Africa)

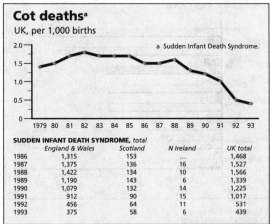

Cot deaths[a]

UK, per 1,000 births

a Sudden Infant Death Syndrome.

SUDDEN INFANT DEATH SYNDROME, *total*				
	England & Wales	*Scotland*	*N Ireland*	*UK total*
1986	1,315	153	...	1,468
1987	1,375	136	16	1,527
1988	1,422	134	10	1,566
1989	1,190	143	6	1,339
1990	1,079	132	14	1,225
1991	912	90	15	1,017
1992	456	64	11	531
1993	375	58	6	439

Diseases and transplants

Notifications of infectious diseases, UK

	1955	1960	1965	1970
Scarlet fever	38,850	36,326	28,982	14,402
Measles	...	...	502,066[a]	307,318[a]
Whooping cough	88,061	66,628	14,498	19,788
Dysentery	49,734	52,011	33,813	14,213
Food poisoning	...	...	5,001[a]	7,566[a]
Tuberculosis				
total	47,071	28,381	19,333	14,167
respiratory	41,293	24,837	16,231	11,377
other	5,778	3,544	3,102	2790

Organ transplants, UK

	Lung	Heart and lung	Heart	Kidney	Liver
1981	...	0	24	905	11
1982	...	0	36	1,033	21
1983	...	1	53	1,144	20
1984	...	10	116	1,443	51
1985	...	37	137	1,336	88
1986	3	51	176	1,493	127
1987	4	72	243	1,485	172
1988	16	101	274	1,575	241
1989	39	94	295	1,732	295
1990	52	95	329	1,730	359
1991	72	79	281	1,628	420
1992	90	53	325	1,640	506
1993	96	36	310	1,684	550
1994	116	52	328	1,748	644
1995	114	59	337	1,796	688

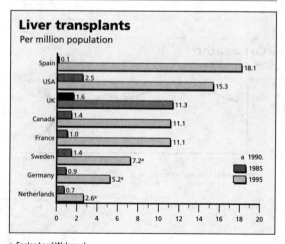

Liver transplants
Per million population

Country	1985	1995
Spain	0.1	18.1
USA	2.5	15.3
UK	1.6	11.3
Canada	1.4	11.1
France	1.0	11.1
Sweden	1.4	7.2[a]
Germany	0.9	5.2[a]
Netherlands	0.7	2.6[a]

a 1990.

a England and Wales only.
b Excludes Northern Ireland.

1975	1980	1985	1990	1994
10,235	12,936	7,451	9,505	8,031
148,643[b]	147,938	104,774	15,642	23,517
9,923	22,873	24,244	16,862	4,837
9,375	3,595	6,112	3,042	7,539
10,276[b]	12,021	21,364	55,988	86,894
12,612	10,486	6,647	5,897	6,229
9,649	7,789	5,292	4,476	4,587
2,963	2,697	1,404	1,469	1,642

Occupational hazards

Deaths due to occupationally related lung disease[b], Great Britain

	Asbestosis without mesothelioma	Mesothelioma	Pneumoconiosis	Total
1982	128	504	314	983
1983	121	573	317	1,059
1984	129	624	314	1,101
1985	140	615	324	1,111
1986	166	702	337	1,249
1987	144	808	279	1,272
1988	152	862	281	1,326
1989	157	899	317	1,406
1990	164	881	328	1,398
1991	163	1,010	287	1,484
1992	...	...	274	...
1993	...	...	301	...

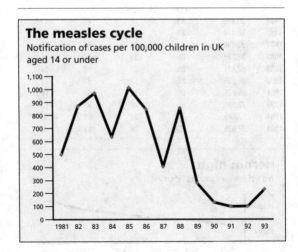

The measles cycle

Notification of cases per 100,000 children in UK aged 14 or under

Drugs

Addicts[a]
1994

	Heroin	Methadone	Dipipanone
1989	12,484	2,951	349
1990	14,497	4,992	387
1991	15,086	7,997	350
1992	16,964	10,011	320
1993	18,919	12,229	283
1994	22,313	15,632	296

New addicts
UK

	1973	1981	1986	1987	1988
Heroin	508	1,660	4,855	4,082	4,630
Methadone	328	431	659	627	576
Cocaine	132	174	520	431	462
Morphine	226	355	343	250	203
Dipipanone	28	473	116	113	124
Dextromoramide	28	59	97	101	80
Pethidine	27	45	33	37	44
Opium	0	0	23	17	18
Others	2	4	4	5	2
Total addicts notified	806	2,248	5,325	4,593	5,212

Seizures of controlled drugs

UK	Total	By authority, %			HM Customs & Excise[c]
		Police			
		Total	Metropolitan	Other	
1985	30,466	88	28	60	12
1986	30,478	83	27	56	17
1987	30,690	84	28	56	16
1988	38,235	86	33	53	14
1989	52,131	86	33	53	14
1990	60,859	88	30	57	12
1991	69,805	89	29	61	11
1992	72,065	89	26	63	11
1993	87,485	92	23	68	8
1994	107,629	93	24	69	7

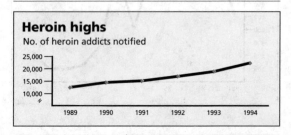

Heroin highs
No. of heroin addicts notified

Cocaine	Morphine	Other	Total[a]
888	760	378	14,785
1,085	839	410	17,755
1,525	406	382	20,820
1,951	321	324	24,703
2,463	255	282	27,976
3,110	267	235	33,952

1989	1990	1991	1992	1993	1994
4,883	5,819	6,328	7,658	9,063	10,607
682	1,469	2,180	2,493	3,362	3,990
527	633	882	1,131	1,375	1,636
259	296	185	161	120	130
109	154	155	158	128	120
75	78	89	76	60	32
36	39	37	49	44	44
15	14	12	5	25	12
1	4	1	0	2	–
5,639	6,923	8,007	9,663	11561	13,469

Deaths of drug addicts

UK	Total	Not primarily associated with drug misuse	Overdose	Other
1981	140	57	80	3
1982	183	65	113	5
1983	195	72	123	0
1984	145	38	103	4
1985	166	63	86	17
1986	233	97	125	11
1987	266	108	138	20
1988	289	108	163	18
1989	310	124	157	29
1990	375	147	187	41
1991	429	183	201	45
1992	525	201	304	20
1993	562	261	262	22

a Notified under the Misuse of Drugs Act to Home Office.
b Addicts may use more than one notifiable drug so total may be smaller than sum.
c In terms of weight, customs seize well over 80%.

Smoking

Cigarette smokers
% of persons over 16 years who smoke cigarettes

	1974	1978	1982	1986	1990	1994
Great Britain	45	40	35	33	30	27
England	45	40	35	32	30	26
Wales	46	40	35	31	31	27
Scotland	48	45	42	36	34	30
Northern Ireland	...	...	...	...	32	...
North	46	41	41	35	32	28
Yorkshire & Humberside	43	39	35	34	29	28
North West	48	43	36	35	34	27
West Midlands	45	39	35	34	30	24
East Midlands	44	39	33	31	29	26
East Anglia	39	38	30	31	26	24
South East	46	39	34	32	30	29
South West	41	39	34	29	27	24

Serious habits
% of persons over 16 years who smoke more than 20 cigarettes a day

	1980		1986		1992	
	Males	Females	Males	Females	Males	Females
Great Britain	21	13	15	10	12	9
England	20	13	14	9	12	8
Wales	25	16	14	10	12	8
Scotland	27	16	19	15	16	13
North	26	17	16	11	13	13
Yorks & Humberside	20	14	14	11	12	10
North West	25	16	15	9	12	9
West Midlands	19	12	17	10	12	7
East Midlands	22	13	15	8	11	7
East Anglia	20	9	13	9	11	6
Greater London	21	13	14	10	13	7
Rest of South East	18	11	13	8	11	7
South West	15	11	13	7	12	7

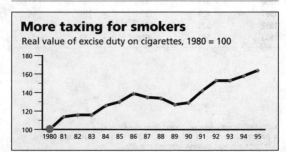

More taxing for smokers
Real value of excise duty on cigarettes, 1980 = 100

Who smokes most
% of persons over 16 years who smoke cigarettes

1974		1994	
Wales	46	Scotland	30
Scotland	45	Wales	27
England	45	England	26
North West	48	South East	29
North	46	North	28
South East	46	Yorkshire & Humberside	28
West Midlands	45	North West	27
East Midlands	44	East Midlands	26
Yorkshire & Humberside	43	West Midlands	24
South West	41	East Anglia	24
East Anglia	39	South West	24

Class seriousness
% of population over 16 years who smoke more than 20 cigarettes a day
1994

	Males	Females
Professional	6	3
Employers and managers	9	6
Intermediate and junior non-manual	9	5
Skilled manual	14	9
Semi-skilled manual	14	11
Unskilled manual	17	13
Total	12	8

How Britain compares
Tobacco consumption per year, kg per head of adult population

	1974–76	1990	2000
UK	2.6	1.9	1.6
Bulgaria	3.6	4.1	4.3
France	2.8	2.3	2.1
Germany	3.2	2.3	2.1
Greece	3.2	3.0	3.3
Ireland	3.2	2.4	2.1
Italy	2.2	1.9	2.0
Netherlands	3.8	3.0	2.7
Poland	3.4	3.5	3.7
Portugal	1.3	1.9	2.0
Spain	2.5	2.4	2.6
Sweden	1.9	1.5	1.3
Switzerland	3.7	2.9	2.3
USA	3.8	2.6	2.2
Canada	3.8	2.6	2.2
Japan	3.5	2.4	1.9

Health spending

Government spending on the NHS

Years ending 31 March, £m (figures in brackets are amount expressed in 1994/95 prices)

	Current expenditure	Capital expenditure	Total
1965–66	1,215 (11,780)	104 (1,008)	1,319
1966–67	1,333 (12,404)	114 (1,061)	1,447
1967–68	1,453 (13,192)	135 (1,226)	1,588
1968–69	1,565 (13,410)	144 (1,234)	1,709
1969–70	1,653 (13,537)	144 (1,179)	1,797
1970–71	1,941 (14,704)	170 (1,288)	2,111
1971–72	2,195 (15,275)	210 (1,462)	2,405
1972–73	2,491 (16,102)	255 (1,648)	2,746
1973–74	2,759 (16,116)	296 (1,729)	3,055
1974–75	3,793 (18,638)	302 (1,484)	4,095
1975–76	5,065 (19,910)	405 (1,592)	5,470
1976–77	5,826 (19,891)	423 (1,444)	6,249
1977–78	6,486 (19,735)	410 (1,248)	6,896
1978–79	7,369 (20,892)	466 (1,321)	7,835
1979–80	8,673 (20,781)	522 (1,251)	9,195
1980–81	11,256 (23,421)	688 (1,432)	11,944
1981–82	12,435 (23,098)	832 (1,546)	13,267
1982–83	13,528 (23,849)	857 (1,511)	14,385
1983–84	14,497 (24,264)	886 (1,483)	15,383
1984–85	15,322 (24,516)	990 (1,584)	16,312
1985–86	16,343 (24,760)	1,091 (1,653)	17,434
1986–87	17,822 (26,026)	1,160 (1,694)	18,982
1987–88	19,669 (27,695)	1,212 (1,707)	20,881
1988–89	21,771 (28,709)	1,309 (1,726)	23,080
1989–90	22,958 (28,108)	2,071 (2,536)	25,029
1990–91	26,063 (29,183)	1,848 (2,069)	27,911
1991–92	30,051 (32,156)	1,791 (1,920)	31,842
1992–93	33,801 (35,319)	1,612 (1,684)	35,413
1993–94	36,320 (37,313)	919 (935)	37,239
1994–95	39,208 (39,208)	619 (619)	39,827

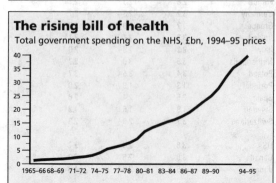

The rising bill of health

Total government spending on the NHS, £bn, 1994–95 prices

How Britain compares
Spending on health as % of domestic spending

	1960	1970	1980	1992
UK	3.9	4.6	5.9	6.6	7.1
OECD average	3.9	5.1	7.0	8.1	8.1
Australia	4.8	5.6	7.1	8.6	8.8
Austria	4.4	5.5	7.7	8.5	8.8
Belgium	3.4	4.2	6.5	8.1	8.2
Canada	5.3	7.2	7.5	9.9	10.1
Denmark	3.6	5.9	6.7	7.0	6.5
Finland	3.8	5.7	6.4	8.9	9.4
France	4.3	5.9	7.5	9.1	9.4
Germany	4.9	6.0	8.4	9.1	8.7
Greece	2.6	3.7	4.0	4.8	5.4
Iceland	3.4	5.4	6.5	8.3	8.5
Ireland	3.8	5.1	8.1	8.0	7.1
Italy	3.6	5.2	6.6	8.3	8.5
Japan	3.0	4.6	6.5	6.8	6.9
Luxembourg	…	4.7	6.8	6.6	7.4
Netherlands	4.0	5.9	8.0	8.7	8.6
New Zealand	4.2	5.1	7.2	7.7	7.7
Norway	3.2	4.9	7.1	8.4	8.3
Portugal	…	3.0	5.1	6.2	6.0
Spain	1.6	3.6	5.4	6.5	7.0
Sweden	4.7	7.1	9.2	8.8	7.9
Switzerland	3.3	5.1	7.0	8.0	9.3
Turkey	…	…	3.7	4.1	4.1
USA	5.3	7.4	9.2	13.3	14.0

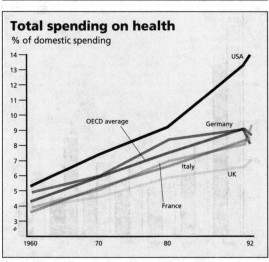

Total spending on health
% of domestic spending

Hospital services

Beds and treatment

	Hospital beds per 1,000 population			Cases treated per bed		Finished consultant episodes, 1994	
	1981	1986	1994	1981	1994	'000s	% in NHS trusts
England	7.5	6.7	4.5	16.4	36.4	7,983.5	69
Wales	8.2	7.7	6.0	16.4	30.0	508.0	54
Scotland	11.3	10.9	8.6	13.1	21.6	952.3	46
Northern Ireland	11.1	10.2	6.7	14.6	26.6	289.9	64
Northern	7.8	7.5	5.5	16.4	32.5	556.1	45
Yorkshire	8.0	7.1	4.7	16.1	37.2	653.4	92
North Western	7.6	7.1	5.3	18.1	35.6	757.9	36
Mersey	8.6	7.4	4.4	14.2	42.6	450.4	99
West Midlands	6.8	6.2	4.1	16.4	39.7	870.0	46
Trent	6.7	6.2	4.3	16.5	37.0	764.2	79
East Anglia	6.9	6.3	4.6	16.8	34.7	335.0	78
NW Thames	7.8	6.6	4.2	15.5	30.4	451.7	79
NE Thames	7.6	6.9	4.7	16.7	34.6	615.1	75
SE Thames	7.6	6.4	3.7	17.0	40.7	565.3	75
SW Thames	8.6	7.1	5.0	12.8	29.3	438.7	79
Oxford	5.7	4.9	3.4	20.4	42.0	374.2	50
Wessex	6.7	6.0	5.1	17.3	38.0	492.0	75
South Western	7.8	6.7	4.5	15.2	37.7	564.9	88

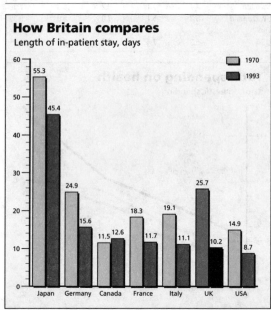

How Britain compares
Length of in-patient stay, days

NHS waiting lists

Regional differences
Waiting lists at end September 1994, '000s

	Ordinary admissions			Day case admissions			
	Total waiting '000s	Months waited, % under 6	6–12	over 12	Total waiting '000s	Months waited, % under 6	6–12	over 12
UK	745.9		92.5ᶜ	7.5	499.1	…	…	…
England	628.8	67.2	25.7	7.1	442.3	77.8	18.3	4.0
Wales	42.8		87.5ᶜ	2.5	16.6	…	…	…
Scotland	51.7	78.9	16.3	4.8	28.1	83.0	11.1	5.9
Northern Ireland	22.7	64.4	22.2	13.4	12.1	75.1	15.8	9.0
Northern & Yorks	88.6	63.9	26.6	9.4	60.8	76.9	18.3	4.8
North Western	93.4	71.3	25.8	2.9	70.5	82.1	16.6	1.3
West Midlands	63.5	66.6	26.6	6.8	49.2	77.1	19.0	3.8
Trent	58.3	69.1	24.5	6.4	36.8	80.3	16.1	3.6
Anglia/Oxford	65.0	70.2	24.6	5.2	37.3	80.9	16.2	2.8
N Thames	100.9	61.3	27.0	11.7	71.4	71.5	21.4	7.1
S Thames	86.1	62.8	27.3	10.0	66.0	73.4	20.8	5.8
South & West	72.0	75.1	22.1	2.7	49.7	83.6	15.3	1.1

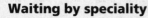

Waiting by speciality
Distribution of patients waiting by speciality, ordinary and day cases in England, September 1995

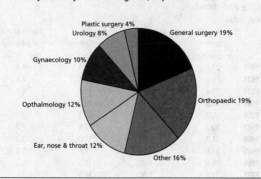

Plastic surgery 4%
Urology 8%
General surgery 19%
Gynaecology 10%
Orthopaedic 19%
Opthalmology 12%
Ear, nose & throat 12%
Other 16%

a Includes Northern Ireland figures for urology.
b Great Britain only.
c Under 12.

Doctors and dentists

General medical practitioners

	1982		1993			
	No.[a]	Average list size	No.[a]	Average list size	GP fund-holders	Opticians[b]
UK	28,065	2102	32,426	1,850	10,036	[c]
England	22,786	2,155	26,289	1,902	8,509	6,619
Wales	1,431	2,013	1,702	1,736	530	530
Scotland	3,040	1,778	3,475	1,542	855	981
Northern Ireland	808	1,981	960	1,763	142	254
Northern	1,458	2,194	1,671	1,878	533	414
Yorkshire	1,742	2,120	2,023	1,861	861	587
North Western	1,870	2,197	2,093	1,937	486	649
Mersey	1,167	2,182	1,274	1,940	609	444
West Midlands	2,459	2,176	2,755	1,958	956	819
Trent	2109	2,251	2,516	1,915	1,038	762
East Anglia	918	2,078	1,162	1,750	372	366
NW Thames	1,855	2,147	1,982	2,024	641	942
NE Thames	1,849	2,171	2,057	2,004	348	886
SE Thames	1,785	2,147	1,598	1,948	497	780
SW Thames	1,428	2,198	2,013	1,951	555	811
Oxford	1,117	2,190	1,409	1,887	600	518
Wessex	1,361	2,055	1,669	1,779	465	584
South Western	1,668	2,003	2,067	1,706	548	535

GPs and dentists
UK, '000s

	No. of doctors[a] in practice	Average no. of patients per doctor	No. of dentists in practice	Average no. of persons per dentist
1961	23.6	2.25	11.9	4.4
1971	24.0	2.39	12.5	4.5
1976	25.4	2.29	13.6	4.1
1981	27.5	2.15	15.2	3.7
1986	30.2	1.99	17.3	3.3
1987	30.7	1.97	17.6	3.2
1988	31.2	1.94	18.0	3.2
1989	31.5	1.91	18.4	3.1
1990	31.6	1.90	18.6	3.1
1991	31.7	1.90	18.6	3.1
1992	32.0	1.87	18.6	3.1
1993	30.3[d]	1.90[d]	19.1	3.0
1994	28.1[d]	1.83[d]	...	...
1995	28.4[d]	1.82[d]	...	...

a Unrestricted principals.
b Includes optometrists and Ophthalmic Medical practitioners.
c May practise in more than one region.
d England and Wales.

General dental practitioners

	1982	1993		
	No.	No.	Average list size	No. registered as % of pop.
UK	15,708	19,012	1,829	59
England	13,258	15,773	1,834	60
Wales	678	843	2,015	58
Scotland	1,369	1,851	1,408	51
Northern Ireland	403	545	1,806	60
Northern	645	909	2,047	60
Yorkshire	898	1,113	2,085	63
North Western	1,003	1,270	1,958	62
Mersey	630	773	2,004	64
West Midlands	1,226	1,454	2,143	59
Trent	966	1,302	2,231	61
East Anglia	483	611	2,146	63
NW Thames	1,458	1,457	1,364	56
NE Thames	1,114	1,228	1,711	55
SE Thames	1,176	1,370	1,494	55
SW Thames	1,127	1,258	1,368	57
Oxford	670	837	1,697	55
Wessex	778	953	1,937	62
South Western	1,084	1,238	1,820	64

Primary health care nursing staff
Whole time equivalents, rate per 1,000 population

	Community psychiatric nurses		Midwives		Health visitors		District nurses	
	1981	1993	1981	1993	1981	1993	1981	1993
England	2	9	7	8	20	21	31	20
Wales	3	...	7	...	19	...	43	...
Scotland	...	7	3	6	29	33	45	40
Northern Ireland	...	8	4	10	29	33	41	44
Northern	2	11	7	8	20	22	33	28
Yorkshire	2	10	7	10	20	23	31	17
North Western	2	11	9	11	23	28	38	22
Mersey	4	10	9	9	20	21	31	20
West Midlands	1	8	8	9	20	20	31	19
Trent	2	7	10	10	19	20	30	18
East Anglia	3	8	10	9	17	16	29	15
NW Thames	2	7	5	6	21	21	26	18
NE Thames	2	9	7	6	18	20	27	18
SE Thames	1	7	6	7	19	17	34	17
SW Thames	5	8	6	7	22	20	33	20
Oxford	3	7	7	6	20	25	32	23
Wessex	3	9	6	7	20	20	29	21
South Western	3	12	4	11	20	20	30	18

Prescriptions

Numbers and costs

UK

	Prescriptions dispensed [a]	Average total cost per prescription	Average no. of prescriptions per person	Average prescription cost per person [b]
	m	£		£
1961	233.2	0.41	4.7	1.9
1971	304.5	0.77	5.6	4.3
1981	370.0	3.46	6.6	23.0
1986	397.5	5.11	7.0	36.0
1990	442.2	6.73	7.8	52.1
1991	463.6	7.23	8.6	53.6
1992	483.8	7.79	8.6	65.5
1993	506.7	8.18	9.4	66.8

Regional variations [c]

	No. of prescription items per person			Average cost per person [d]	No. exempt from charges, %
	1981	1991	1993	£ 1993	1993
United Kingdom	6.6	8.6	9.4	66.82	...
England	6.5	8.4	9.2	65.08	82.1
Wales	8.6	10.8	11.5	77.70	83.9
Scotland	6.2	9.0	9.8	73.00	87.3
Northern Ireland	8.1	9.9	10.9	74.30	91.9
Northern	7.0	9.3	10.0	70.09	83.3
Yorkshire	6.9	9.1	9.8	65.51	82.7
North Western	7.5	10.0	10.8	70.96	83.6
Mersey	7.2	9.8	10.7	73.92	84.9
West Midlands	6.6	8.7	9.5	63.95	83.2
Trent	6.6	8.8	9.6	65.21	82.1
East Anglia	6.4	8.0	8.8	64.90	79.8
NW Thames	5.6	7.3	8.0	60.40	80.1
NE Thames	6.2	7.9	8.7	66.64	83.5
SE Thames	6.3	8.0	8.9	62.84	82.6
SW Thames	5.9	7.2	7.8	61.22	79.2
Oxford	5.6	6.9	7.6	58.00	76.8
Wessex	6.9	8.0	8.6	62.89	80.4
South Western	6.5	8.2	8.9	64.79	81.8

a Items dispensed by community pharmacists and appliance contractors only.
b Based on number of people on NHS prescribing list.
c Figures relate to NHS prescriptions dispensed by community pharmacists, appliance contractors, dispensing doctors and prescriptions submitted by prescribing doctors for items personally administered. Figures for Wales are for 1993–94.
d Cost is the cost of medicines before any discounts and does not include any dispensing costs or fees.

=== Part X ===
EDUCATION

School enrolment

Pupils in school
'000s

	1965–66	*1970–71*	*1975–76*	*1980–81*
UK	9,084	10,232	11,301	10,633
England	{ 7,856	8,361	9,258	8,720
Wales		512	576	545
Scotland	921	1,006	1,094	1,005
Northern Ireland	307	353	374	363

Age, % of all in age group

2 to 4	9.5	13.7	23.7	40.4
5 to 10	99.1	98.8	100.0	100.7
11	100.3	100.2	100.1	101.4
12 to 14	100.2	100.5	100.0	100.5
15	61.0	70.6	99.5	97.7
16	27.7	35.6	50.6	29.0
17	14.8	20.3	20.7	17.8
18 and over	5.1	7.0	6.8	2.3

Age, % of all males in age group

14	99.6	100.6	100.0	100.0
15	61.0	70.9	99.6	97.3
16	28.7	36.3	50.6	27.4
17	16.2	21.3	21.0	17.6

Age, % of all females in age group

14	99.9	101.1	100.0	100.2
15	60.9	70.3	99.5	98.1
16	26.7	34.9	50.8	30.6
17	13.2	19.3	20.4	17.8

School sizes
% of pupils on register in schools of size, 1993–4

	Primary				
	50 or under	*51–100*	*101–200*	*201 or over*	*Total no. of schools, '000s*
UK	8.2	12.8	30.2	48.7	23.4
England	5.5	11.8	31.5	51.2	18.7
Wales	15.6	16.0	32.9	35.5	1.7
Scotland	21.2	13.7	21.6	43.5	2.3
Northern Ireland	16.0	25.9	23.0	35.1	1.0
North	8.3	12.0	35.1	44.7	1.3
Yorkshire & Humberside	6.2	11.7	33.8	48.2	2.0
North West	2.7	5.3	31.3	60.8	2.5
West Midlands	5.1	10.5	27.2	57.1	2.1
East Midlands	8.6	16.8	33.1	41.6	1.8
East Anglia	11.3	20.9	30.2	37.6	0.9
Greater London	...	1.0	23.0	76.0	2.0
Rest of South East	4.4	12.4	35.6	47.6	4.0
South West	9.2	21.8	30.5	38.4	2.0

1985–86	*1989–90*	*1990–91*	*1991–92*	*1994–95*
9,565	9,199	9,260	9,368	9,707
7,830	7,557	7,617	7,712	8,012
495	480	482	487	498
894	821	821	826	846
346	340	341	343	351
42.6	43.3	44.1	45.0	48.1
99.9	98.9	98.9	98.0	99.1
102.5	99.6	99.0	98.8	98.5
101.7	100.1	99.8	99.2	98.6
97.3	100.3	99.5	98.3	96.1
32.1	37.5	40.6	43.8	38.4
18.8	23.6	25.5	28.2	28.1
3.0	3.3	3.8	4.4	3.5
100.6	100.6	99.8	99.6	97.9
97.4	100.1	99.4	98.2	95.7
30.9	35.7	38.4	41.9	37.2
18.5	22.7	24.3	26.7	26.7
100.5	100.4	100.0	99.7	98.6
97.8	100.5	99.6	98.4	96.6
33.4	39.5	42.8	45.8	40.0
19.0	24.6	26.8	29.9	29.7

Secondary

400 or under	*401–800*	*801–1,000*	*1,001 or over*	*Total no. of schools, '000s*
11.7	40.5	21.2	26.6	4.5
10.7	40.7	21.5	27.2	3.6
4.4	43.6	18.5	33.5	0.2
17.4	33.8	22.3	26.5	0.4
23.7	47.4	17.2	11.6	0.2
20.2	36.8	18.1	24.9	0.2
21.9	34.4	16.5	27.3	0.4
3.1	39.6	28.9	28.4	0.5
9.8	43.9	22.2	24.1	0.4
13.2	46.0	16.7	24.1	0.3
15.6	48.0	13.3	23.1	0.2
2.2	37.5	25.2	35.1	0.4
8.5	42.7	23.4	25.3	0.8
10.1	38.7	19.9	31.3	0.3

Pupil/teacher ratios

Pupils per teacher

England	1965–66	1970–71	1975–76	1980–81
Nursery	24.9	19.1	21.1	19.7
Primary	28.2	27.0	24.0	22.6
Secondary	18.3	17.9	17.0	16.6
Non-maintained	13.8	13.7	13.4	12.5
Special	11.2	10.2	8.6	7.6
All schools	21.9	21.4	19.4	18.2
Wales				
Nursery	20.7	19.9	19.4	19.0
Primary	25.0	25.0	22.8	21.7
Secondary	19.0	18.3	17.1	16.6
Non-maintained	13.3	13.8	12.3	12.1
Special	10.9	10.4	10.9	7.7
All schools	21.7	21.4	19.6	18.5
Scotland				
Nursery	...	36.6	24.5	25.3
Primary	...	27.9	22.4	20.3
Secondary	...	16.1	15.1	14.4
Non-maintained	...	17.3	16.3	15.1
Special	...	11.6	9.7	6.8
All schools	...	22.1	18.6	16.9
Northern Ireland				
Nursery	24.7	27.6	30.0	23.5
Primary	29.5	28.9	26.4	23.6
Secondary	19.8	18.6	17.2	15.2
Non-maintained	18.7	17.9	17.4	16.5
Special	11.4	10.7	9.8	8.4
All schools	24.7	23.5	21.3	18.9

Class sizes

Average numbers, maintained schools only

	One-teacher classes			
	Primary		Secondary	
	1981	*1994*	*1981*	*1994*
England	25.2	26.9	20.8	21.4
Wales	...	...	...	...
Scotland	...	...	...	...
North	24.1	26.6	20.5	21.5
Yorkshire & Humberside	24.7	27.0	21.3	21.6
North West	26.0	27.5	20.7	21.5
West Midlands	25.1	27.0	20.8	21.7
East Midlands	26.0	26.6	21.2	20.9
East Anglia	24.5	25.8	21.0	21.0
Greater London	23.1	26.7	19.6	21.7
Rest of South East	26.2	26.8	21.1	21.3
South West	26.1	26.9	21.7	21.5

1985–86	1989–90	1990–91	1991–92	1993–94
19.6	19.3	18.9	18.9	19.5
22.1	21.8	22.0	22.0	22.7
15.9	15.0	15.3	15.5	16.4
11.3	10.9	10.8	10.6	10.6
6.8	5.9	5.8	5.8	6.1
17.4	17.0	17.2	17.2	17.9
20.2	20.8	20.6	20.4	20.6
22.1	22.3	22.3	22.3	22.3
16.1	15.3	15.4	15.6	15.9
10.7	10.5	9.8	9.7	9.6
7.0	6.5	6.3	6.3	6.4
18.2	18.1	18.2	18.2	18.4
...	26.3	25.7	26.2	25.9
20.4	19.7	19.5	19.5	19.5
13.5	12.4	12.2	12.4	12.8
12.2	10.8	10.6	10.4	10.5
5.4	4.7	4.5	4.5	4.5
...	15.3	15.2	15.3	15.5
23.5	24.0	24.7	24.5	24.7
23.4	23.2	22.9	22.6	21.7
14.9	14.9	14.7	15.1	15.1
15.8	12.2	11.0	10.6	10.0
8.1	7.1	6.9	6.9	6.8
18.5	18.3	18.1	18.3	17.8

All classes			
Primary		Secondary	
1981	1994	1981	1994
25.5	27.2	21.5	21.8
...	25.6	...	20.1
23.8	24.7	19.9	19.4
24.7	26.9	21.2	22.0
25.1	27.4	21.9	21.9
26.2	27.9	21.4	21.8
25.4	27.4	21.3	22.0
26.3	27.0	22.0	21.3
24.9	26.2	22.2	21.6
23.5	27.0	20.2	22.1
26.6	27.0	21.8	21.6
26.4	27.1	22.2	21.8

Independent schools

Facts and figures

	1985	1990	1992	1994
No. of schools				
Boys'	640	477	447	404
Girls'	455	432	406	386
Mixed	1,367	1,558	1,594	1,641
Total	2,462	2,467	2,447	2,431
No. of full-time pupils by age and sex				
2 to 4	28,253	36,011	38,268	37,958
5 to 10	179,310	207,156	207,675	200,363
11 to 15	263,051	259,082	259,409	247,686
16 and over	73,720	81,372	78,247	79,109
Total boys[a]	301,449	319,699	318,423	308,635
Total girls[a]	257,608	283,304	285,177	278,330
Total[a]	559,057	603,003	603,600	586,965
Attending boys' schools				
Boys	180,850	146,239	135,622	119,656
Girls	5,071	2,337	2,170	1,700
Attending girls' schools				
Boys	2,143	2,540	2,544	2,279
Girls	151,192	151,958	146,252	137,171
Attending mixed schools				
Boys	118,456	170,920	180,257	186,590
Girls	101,345	129,009	136,755	139,337
Boarding schools				
Boys'	417	292	254	208
Girls'	225	200	177	159
Mixed	398	498	511	499
Total	1,040	990	942	866
No. of boarders				
Boys	81,498	73,810	67,768	60,165
Girls	44,422	44,101	41,450	36,744
Total	125,920	117,911	109,218	96,909
Teaching staff				
Full-time	40,067	46,232	47,926	47,864
Part-time	7,180	8,179	8,384	8,160
Total	47,247	54,411	56,310	56,024
Pupil/teacher ratio				
England	11.4	10.9	10.7	10.3
Wales	10.6	10.0	9.7	9.6
Scotland	11.2	10.7	10.7	10.6

a Includes part-time pupils aged 2–4.

The costs
ISIS registered independent schools and average fees per term, 1996

	No. of schools	Boarding fee, £	Weekly boarding fee, £	Average day fee, £	Average fee, £
Wales	25	3,108	2,946	1,471	1,783
Scotland	50	3,593	2,965	1,365	1,686
Ireland	14	1,854	1,921	466	560
North	194	3,288	2,949	1,347	1,507
West Midlands	139	3,618	2,906	1,537	1,940
East Midlands	165	3,645	2,930	1,580	1,992
East Anglia	93	3,229	2,837	1,542	1,771
Greater London	165	4,154	3,954	1,725	1,790
South East	278	3,636	3,173	1,752	2,259
South & West	188	3,651	3,009	1,554	2,128
All	1,311	3,571	3,042	1,533	1,870

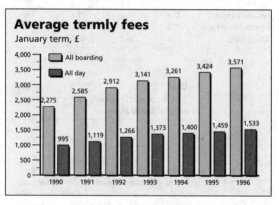

Average termly fees
January term, £

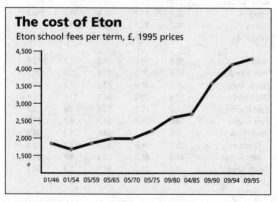

The cost of Eton
Eton school fees per term, £, 1995 prices

Sixteen plus

School leavers
16 year-olds participating in school or further education, '000s
1985–86

	Staying on at school	Going to FE Full-time	Going to FE Part-time	Participation in education, %
UK	253.8	180.1	165.1	67
England	184.4	162.3	130.1	65
Wales	13.5	8.2	7.3	65
Scotland	47.9	5.7	22.4	87
Northern Ireland	8.0	3.9	5.3	60
North	9.3	10.5	8.9	61
Yorkshire & Humb	18.9	15.3	15.8	63
North West	20.0	26.3	25.3	72
West Midlands	18.4	21.0	17.5	68
East Midlands	14.0	13.7	13.5	68
East Anglia	7.2	5.8	5.0	60
Greater London	32.6	15.1	11.2	59
Rest of South East	45.6	38.4	22.0	64
South West	18.4	16.2	10.9	65

Making the grade
%

Males
% of 16-year-olds achieving GCSEs or SCE standard grade

	5 or more grades A–C	5 or more grades A–G	1 or more grade A–G	None	'000s All 16-yr-olds in schools
Great Britain	36.6	81.2	89.2	10.8	314.7
England	36.2	81.3	88.9	11.1	268.0
Wales	31.8	72.2	86.5	13.5	16.6
Scotland	42.8	84.6	93.6	6.4	30.1
North	32.4	78.9	87.3	12.7	17.3
Yorkshire & Humb	31.6	78.3	87.6	12.4	28.1
North West	35.0	78.8	87.2	12.8	36.1
West Midlands	32.8	79.9	88.4	11.6	30.6
East Midlands	34.9	83.1	90.4	9.6	23.3
East Anglia	38.0	85.2	91.3	8.7	11.7
South East	38.6	82.1	88.8	11.2	94.6
Greater London	33.4	76.6	85.9	14.1	32.8
Rest of South East	41.3	85.0	90.4	9.6	61.8
South West	40.3	85.4	91.7	8.3	26.3

	1993–94		
Staying on at school	Going to FE		Participation in education, %
	Full-time	Part-time	
251.7	217.0	54.9	80
192.1	194.5	39.5	79
9.0	10.6	3.2	68
39.5	4.7	7.4	87
11.1	7.2	4.8	99
9.6	11.7	3.4	71
17.9	18.4	6.5	77
17.9	30.1	6.5	75
19.6	22.3	4.8	78
17.2	14.6	3.3	76
9.6	7.7	1.6	80
28.4	25.1	3.4	82
50.8	46.2	6.5	84
21.1	18.4	3.5	83

Females
% of 16-year-olds achieving GCSEs or SCE
or SCE standard grade

% 17–19 yr-olds achieving 5 or more grades A–C	5 or more grades A–C	5 or more grades A–G	1 or more grade A–G	None	'000s All 16-yr-olds in schools	% 17–19 yr-olds achieving 5 or more grades A–C
20.8	45.8	86.3	92.1	7.9	298.6	23.0
20.0	45.2	86.3	91.8	8.2	254.3	21.6
26.0	41.5	80.1	91.5	8.5	15.5	33.5
24.1	54.1	89.7	95.4	4.6	28.8	28.6
12.6	40.8	83.9	90.7	9.3	16.6	14.8
14.3	40.1	83.6	90.6	9.4	26.4	15.5
13.1	44.1	83.9	90.5	9.5	34.4	13.5
15.4	41.9	85.8	91.9	8.1	28.6	16.5
18.3	43.4	87.4	93.1	6.9	21.7	20.0
18.8	49.7	90.1	93.5	6.5	11.2	22.4
32.1	47.3	86.9	91.6	8.4	90.4	33.3
17.6	41.8	82.3	88.7	11.3	32.2	18.7
50.5	50.4	89.5	93.3	6.7	58.2	52.8
20.6	50.5	90.5	94.0	6.0	25.0	23.6

Qualifications

Subject passes
Pupils achieving GCSE grades A–C equivalent in final year of schooling, %

	Males			Females		
	1988–89	*1991–92*	*1993–94*	*1988–89*	*1991–92*	*1993–94*
English	38	41	45	53	57	62
Any science	35	39	43	33	39	43
Biology	13	7	7	19	9	8
Chemistry	17	10	9	13	8	7
Physics	21	11	10	10	6	5
Double award science	7	23	32	7	24	34
Mathematics	36	38	42	32	37	42
Any modern language	19	20	25	30	33	40
French	17	18	20	27	29	33
History	16	15	18	18	20	24
Geography	21	22	23	18	19	21
Craft, design & technology[a]	19	18	19	5	8	10

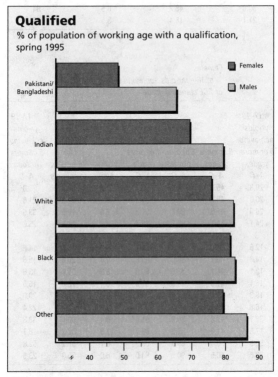

Qualified
% of population of working age with a qualification, spring 1995

Females
Males

Pakistani/Bangladeshi
Indian
White
Black
Other

40 50 60 70 80 90

a England only.

The three Rs and science
Pupils reaching expected standards, 1994, %

England	Teacher assessment		Tests	
	Males	Females	Males	Females
7-yr-olds				
English				
Handwriting	76	87	76	85
Reading	76	85	76	85
Spelling	67	80	65	77
Writing	64	76	61	74
All elements	75	85	...	...
Mathematics	79	83	...	...
of which: arithmetic	80	84	80	84
Science	85	87	...	...
14-yr-olds				
English	55	72	49	66
Mathematics	62	67	60	63
Science	63	65	64	63

How literate and numerate?
Adult literacy and numeracy standards[a], by age on leaving full-time education, 1994, %

England & Wales	Low literacy	High literacy	Low numeracy	High numeracy
Under 16	14	9	31	11
16	8	19	16	23
17–18	4	30	8	30
19–20	3	31	7	40
21 and over	...	46	3	54
All adults[a]	8	21	18	25

Who thinks what's important
Public opinion on subjects regarded as essential or very important in secondary schools, 1993–94, %

	Arts	Sciences	Technology/ technical studies	Foreign languages	Education for citizenship
Austria	43	67	60	91	64
Belgium	29	57	53	88	66
Denmark	36	46	...	79	46
Finland	31	53	39	87	35
France	31	63	47	87	67
Netherlands	31	64	42	85	41
Portugal	55	76	66	85	73
Spain	44	65	63	72	66
Sweden	31	65	38	87	70
Switzerland	58	63	52	77	65
UK	26	66	57	56	36
USA	47	85	36	53	77

a Percentage of adults aged 22 to 74.

Student numbers

New students

Full-time and part-time students in higher education in England, '000s

HE Institution	1990–91		1991–92	
	Full-time	Part-time	Full-time	Part-time
Postgraduate				
HE	66.9	70.2	76.8	81.4
of which mature	37.7	64.0	42.1	74.9
1st degree				
HE	436.0	112.1	491.0	125.2
of which mature	170.8	109.6	195.1	122.7
Other undergraduate				
HE	68.1	94.7	75.7	91.7
of which mature	34.8	81.8	38.4	80.1
Total	571.0	277.0	643.5	298.3
Higher education in further education				
Postgraduate	0.3	2.0	0.4	2.2
1st degree	4.0	1.9	5.3	2.1
Other	17.5	85.3	21.5	87.0
Total	21.8	89.2	27.2	91.3
of which mature	10.9	67.9	13.8	71.2
Grand total	592.8	366.2	670.7	389.6
of which mature	254.2	323.3	289.4	348.9
% mature	42.9	88.3	43.1	89.6
% of total students				
HE Institution				
Postgraduate	11	19	11	21
1st degree	74	31	73	32
Other	11	26	11	24
Higher education in further education				
Postgraduate	0	1	0	1
1st degree	1	1	1	1
Other	3	23	3	22

What they study

Enrolments in further education, '000s, 1993–94

	Full-time		Part-time		All
	Male	Female	Male	Female	
Combined & general	131	141	200	359	831
Languages & humanities	35	57	111	251	454
Business & finance	60	84	79	206	429
Engineering & technical	76	5	213	18	312
Science	33	59	62	94	248
Education	8	6	25	42	81
Social sciences	3	14	10	46	73
Other	14	13	20	17	64
Total	360	379	720	1,033	2,492

a Provisional.

| 1992–93 | | 1993–94 | | 1994–95ᵇ | |
Full-time	Part-time	Full-time	Part-time	Full-time	Part-time
87.6	95.5	92.4	107.4	103.4	137.4
45.1	88.3	49.3	99.7	55.4	127.9
557.4	138.6	619.8	152.6	667.2	152.8
233.3	136.0	272.6	150.0	300.8	149.8
86.6	94.5	92.0	87.4	88.8	78.9
45.8	80.3	50.4	80.6	46.9	72.5
731.6	328.6	804.2	347.4	859.4	369.1
0.5	2.5	0.6	2.2	0.6	2.3
7.2	2.5	11.5	2.9	11.3	3.3
27.0	84.6	32.1	84.1	31.8	96.6
34.7	89.6	44.2	89.2	43.7	102.2
17.6	72.8	22.0	75.2	21.8	85.3
766.3	418.2	848.4	436.6	903.1	471.3
341.8	377.4	394.3	405.5	424.9	435.5
44.6	90.2	46.5	92.9	47.0	92.4
11	23	11	25	11	29
73	33	73	35	74	32
11	23	11	20	10	17
0	1	0	1	0	0
1	1	1	1	1	1
4	20	4	19	4	20

What they study

Enrolments in higher education, '000s, 1993–94

| | Full-time | | Part-time | | All |
	Male	Female	Male	Female	
Combined & general	61	74	8	11	154
Languages & humanities	66	96	10	14	186
Business & finance	77	76	67	64	284
Engineering & technical	124	23	70	8	225
Science	145	121	40	111	417
Education	21	58	15	35	129
Social sciences	57	66	15	21	159
Other	…	…	57	55	112
Total	551	514	282	319	1,666

Universities ranked

Total graduates		First class honours	%
London	10,703	Cambridge	26
Leeds	3,320	Oxford	17
Manchester	3,224	Bath	14
Cambridge	3,058	Manchester IST	12
Oxford	2,975	York	11
Birmingham	2,878	Nottingham	11
Sheffield	2,688	Surrey	10
Liverpool	2,653	London	9
Newcastle	2,458	Bristol	9
Bristol	2,355	City	9
Nottingham	2,290	Manchester	9
Warwick	2,010	Southampton	9
Southampton	1,927	Brunel	9
Reading	1,832	Loughborough	8
Loughborough	1,798	Reading	8
Durham	1,781	Durham	8
Hull	1,728	Salford	8
Exeter	1,649	Birmingham	8
Lancaster	1,644	Leicester	8
Leicester	1,580	Leeds	8
Salford	1,423	Newcastle	8
Sussex	1,408	Aston	8
Kent	1,372	Sheffield	8
Bradford	1,326	East Anglia	8
East Anglia	1,280	Sussex	7
Manchester IST	1,222	Kent	7
York	1,107	Exeter	7
Essex	1,001	Warwick	7
Aston	962	Bradford	7
Bath	942	Lancaster	6
Keele	920	Liverpool	6
Surrey	868	Essex	5
City	840	Hull	5
Brunel	709	Keele	5

Further study	%		
Oxford	17	Manchester	12
Essex	16	East Anglia	12
York	15	Surrey	12
Cambridge	15	Manchester IST	12
Bath	15	Kent	12
Liverpool	14	Leicester	11
Southampton	14	Warwick	11
Durham	13	Nottingham	11
London	13	Hull	11
Leeds	13	Salford	10
Brunel	13	Keele	10
Sheffield	13	Newcastle	10
Bristol	12	Sussex	10
Birmingham	12	Loughborough	10

Permanent employment	%	Full-time staff	%
Aston	62	London	101
Brunel	52	Cambridge	86
Bradford	51	Oxford	81
Bath	50	Surrey	69
Loughborough	49	Bath	67
Exeter	48	Bristol	65
Manchester	46	Manchester	63
Leeds	46	Leicester	63
Surrey	46	Nottingham	62
Warwick	46	York	62
Newcastle	45	Newcastle	61
Nottingham	45	Manchester IST	60
Oxford	44	Birmingham	59
Reading	44	Liverpool	55
Sheffield	44	Brunel	54
York	43	Sheffield	53
Manchester IST	43	Reading	52
Durham	42	Warwick	49
Hull	42	Leeds	49
Birmingham	41	Southampton	48
City	41	Sussex	48
Salford	40	City	47
Liverpool	40	Loughborough	46
Lancaster	40	East Anglia	46
Cambridge	40	Keele	45
East Anglia	39	Durham	44
Kent	39	Lancaster	42
Southampton	39	Exeter	42
Bristol	36	Kent	40
London	35	Bradford	38
Leicester	33	Essex	37
Sussex	33	Hull	36
Keele	32	Aston	30

Seeking employment	%	Birmingham	7
Leeds	11	Essex	7
Keele	10	Bradford	7
York	10	Sheffield	7
Salford	9	Manchester IST	7
Reading	9	Exeter	7
Leicester	9	Loughborough	7
Newcastle	9	Nottingham	6
East Anglia	9	London	6
Southampton	9	Warwick	6
Manchester	9	Durham	6
Hull	8	Aston	6
Sussex	8	Kent	6
Liverpool	7	Bath	5

How Britain compares

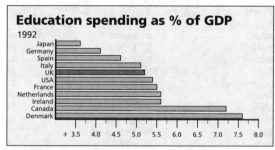

Education spending as % of GDP
1992

Japan
Germany
Spain
Italy
UK
USA
France
Netherlands
Ireland
Canada
Denmark

3.5 4.0 4.5 5.0 5.5 6.0 6.5 7.0 7.5 8.0

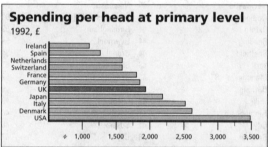

Spending per head at primary level
1992, £

Ireland
Spain
Netherlands
Switzerland
France
Germany
UK
Japan
Italy
Denmark
USA

1,000 1,500 2,000 2,500 3,000 3,500

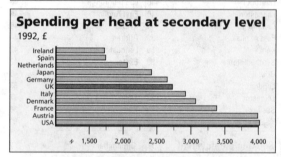

Spending per head at secondary level
1992, £

Ireland
Spain
Netherlands
Japan
Germany
UK
Italy
Denmark
France
Austria
USA

1,500 2,000 2,500 3,000 3,500 4,000

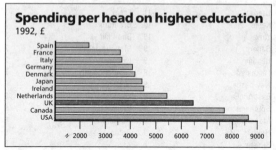

Spending per head on higher education
1992, £

Spain
France
Italy
Germany
Denmark
Japan
Ireland
Netherlands
UK
Canada
USA

2000 3000 4000 5000 6000 7000 8000 9000

Note: Germany data are for western Germany.

Part XI

CRIME AND PUNISHMENT

Regional variations in crime

Total crime
Registered offences per 100,000 population

	1975	1980	1985[b]	1990[b]	1993[a]
England	4,296	5,501	7,317	9,047	10,846
Wales	3,976	4,762	6,276	7,979	9,626
Scotland[b]	...	7,075	8,994	10,502	10,605
Northern Ireland	2,423	3,620	4,151	3,599	4,058
North	4,731	6,299	9,162	11,892	13,009
Yorkshire & Humberside	4,491	5,608	7,449	10,000	13,154
North West	4,819	6,209	8,924	10,056	11,281
West Midlands	3,543	5,176	7,122	8,304	10,552
East Midlands	4,057	5,179	6,542	8,844	11,393
East Anglia	3,312	4,013	5,021	6,697	8,296
South East	4,612	5,796	7,345	8,896	10,278
Greater London	...	...	...	...	12,321
Rest of South East	...	...	...	...	8,815
South West	3,220	3,922	5,375	7,374	9,516

Violence against the person
Registered offences per 100,000 population

	1975	1980	1985	1990	1993
England	144	198	245	364	397
Wales	147	183	237	381	458
Scotland[b]	...	143	208	266	270
Northern Ireland	162	155	222	212	282
North	168	230	281	399	417
Yorkshire & Humberside	192	241	302	433	419
North West	138	202	240	311	367
West Midlands	130	217	280	387	407
East Midlands	202	258	311	465	503
East Anglia	115	161	180	301	334
South East	132	178	221	352	393
Greater London	...	...	...	...	536
Rest of South East	...	...	...	...	290
South West	106	146	189	304	337

Sexual offences
Registered offences per 100,000 population

	1975	1980	1985	1990	1993
England	48	43	44	58	61
Wales	47	37	33	52	63
Scotland[b]	...	44	50	64	72
Northern Ireland	16	24	42	50	73
North	50	43	44	54	54
Yorkshire & Humberside	66	53	52	67	63
North West	45	41	37	47	48
West Midlands	48	46	45	51	53
East Midlands	66	60	50	67	67

Clear-up rate, %

	1987	1988	1989	1990	1991	1992	1993
England	32	35	33	31	29	25	25
Wales	43	42	43	40	35	35	34
Scotland[b]	34	34	33	32	31	32	34
Northern Ireland	43	45	43	38	36	34	36
North	41	43	40	36	35	24	25
Yorkshire & Humberside	38	42	39	37	31	26	19
North West	34	38	37	38	39	36	34
West Midlands	37	43	40	37	32	28	27
East Midlands	39	40	38	36	30	28	28
East Anglia	38	39	40	38	36	32	29
South East	23	25	24	21	21	20	21
Greater London[c]	...	...	...	...	17	16	17
Rest of South East	...	...	...	...	25	24	24
South West	35	38	37	32	30	22	23

Clear-up rate, %

	1987	1988	1989	1990	1991	1992	1993
England	74	75	76	76	77	75	76
Wales	87	85	89	88	88	88	88
Scotland[b]	79	78	81	82	81	78	77
Northern Ireland	71	68	58	62	62	64	62
North	79	80	80	78	79	76	79
Yorkshire & Humberside	81	79	80	84	82	84	77
North West	71	75	77	76	76	74	73
West Midlands	76	80	80	82	81	80	77
East Midlands	80	79	80	80	81	79	80
East Anglia	83	85	85	86	85	86	82
South East	65	66	68	67	69	69	71
Greater London[c]	...	...	...	...	63	61	65
Rest of South East	...	...	...	...	78	78	78
South West	85	83	88	85	85	76	83

Clear-up rate, %

	1987	1988	1989	1990	1991	1992	1993
England	74	74	74	75	74	73	73
Wales	96	90	93	95	93	93	93
Scotland[b]	78	78	77	79	77	76	77
Northern Ireland	91	84	86	92	87	80	74
North	81	80	80	84	83	80	84
Yorkshire & Humberside	81	82	76	84	77	82	73
North West	77	78	79	81	80	80	79
West Midlands	72	78	78	75	76	75	74
East Midlands	78	79	77	81	80	74	76

For footnotes see over page.

Sexual offences (cont.)
Registered offences per 100,000 population

	1975	1980	1985	1990	1993
East Anglia	40	39	37	55	55
South East	42	39	44	61	68
Greater London	...	...	...	...	87
Rest of South East	...	...	...	...	55
South West	46	36	40	54	61

Robbery
Registered offences per 100,000 population

	1975	1980	1985	1990	1993
England	23	32	58	75	118
Wales	15	11	10	16	26
Scotland[b]	...	72	86	91	109
Northern Ireland	128	84	116	103	106
North	14	13	22	30	59
Yorkshire & Humberside	18	17	25	41	95
North West	27	28	59	71	133
West Midlands	17	29	50	68	129
East Midlands	23	19	26	40	75
East Anglia	9	7	12	21	31
South East	33	53	99	121	162
Greater London	...	...	...	...	331
Rest of South East	...	...	...	...	40
South West	8	10	15	33	60

Burglary
Registered offences per 100,000 population

	1975	1980	1985	1990	1993
England	1,059	1,270	1,765	2,017	2,703
Wales	1,081	1,170	1,512	1,570	2,136
Scotland[b]	...	1,522	1,960	1,994	1,911
Northern Ireland	924	1,283	1,303	932	964
North	1,359	1,687	2,644	2,939	3,426
Yorkshire & Humberside	1,273	1,417	1,955	2,474	4,218
North West	1,408	1,609	2,615	2,459	2,861
West Midlands	906	1,341	1,987	2,006	3,044
East Midlands	1,012	1,168	1,317	1,754	2,950
East Anglia	660	715	1,022	1,372	2,028
South East	1,007	1,217	1,526	1,829	2,120
Greater London	...	...	...	...	2,366
Rest of South East	...	...	...	...	1,944
South West	653	757	1,099	1,538	2,302

Clear-up rate, %

	1987	1988	1989	1990	1991	1992	1993
East Anglia	83	79	84	86	83	79	79
South East	66	65	66	64	64	66	66
Greater London[c]	...	...	...	...	54	58	59
Rest of South East	...	...	...	...	76	76	75
South West	79	81	82	85	88	74	79

Clear-up rate, %

	1987	1988	1989	1990	1991	1992	1993
England	21	23	26	26	23	22	21
Wales	58	45	57	58	48	47	50
Scotland[b]	29	29	29	28	27	24	27
Northern Ireland	19	23	23	18	17	19	15
North	38	42	43	37	35	34	29
Yorkshire & Humberside	40	41	41	39	34	28	27
North West	23	28	32	31	29	27	25
West Midlands	33	40	40	43	33	26	24
East Midlands	38	47	45	39	33	34	33
East Anglia	44	43	50	48	45	41	38
South East	15	16	18	18	16	16	16
Greater London[c]	...	...	...	...	13	13	14
Rest of South East	...	...	...	...	31	31	31
South West	29	31	36	39	34	25	25

Clear-up rate, %

	1987	1988	1989	1990	1991	1992	1993
England	27	29	27	25	23	19	19
Wales	32	32	34	33	26	28	27
Scotland[b]	19	18	17	16	15	14	16
Northern Ireland	30	29	27	22	22	19	20
North	37	39	35	34	30	19	17
Yorkshire & Humberside	31	36	34	30	24	17	11
North West	29	31	33	34	35	32	30
West Midlands	41	44	38	33	29	23	25
East Midlands	32	35	32	31	25	23	23
East Anglia	29	28	31	30	27	25	21
South East	15	15	14	13	14	14	16
Greater London[c]	...	...	...	...	11	11	14
Rest of South East	...	...	...	...	17	16	17
South West	23	24	25	21	20	13	15

a In England and Wales, offences of trafficking in controlled drugs were included only from January 1983.
b Figures for Scotland are not strictly comparable with others because of differences in the legal system, recording practices and classification.
c The Metropolitan Police use a different method for assessing the clear-up rate, hence the lower figure.

Rising crime[a]

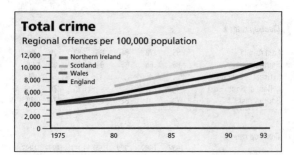

Total crime
Regional offences per 100,000 population

- Northern Ireland
- Scotland
- Wales
- England

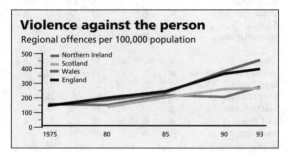

Violence against the person
Regional offences per 100,000 population

- Northern Ireland
- Scotland
- Wales
- England

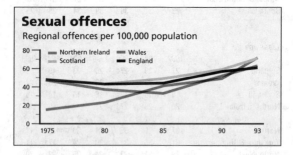

Sexual offences
Regional offences per 100,000 population

- Northern Ireland
- Scotland
- Wales
- England

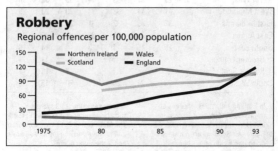

Robbery
Regional offences per 100,000 population

- Northern Ireland
- Scotland
- Wales
- England

Offences, convictions and guns

Total crime
Offences per 100,000 population, 1992

1	North	13,009	8	West Midlands	10,552
2	Yorkshire & Humberside	13,154	9	South East	10,278
3	Greater London	12,321	10	Wales	9,626
4	East Midlands	11,393	11	South West	9,516
5	North West	11,281	12	Rest of South East	8,815
6	England	10,846	13	East Anglia	8,296
7	Scotland	10,605	14	Northern Ireland	4,058

The guilty young
Offenders found guilty or cautioned per 100,000 population, 1993

	Age 10–13	Age 14–17	Age 18–20	Age 21 and over
England	1,159	4,183	4,594	776
Wales	1,319	4,723	5,507	861
North	2,005	5,563	5,261	808
Yorkshire & Humberside	1,423	4,862	4,629	762
North West	1,279	4,719	5,635	997
West Midlands	1,393	4,505	4,771	782
East Midlands	1,280	4,284	4,394	729
East Anglia	919	3,836	4,318	716
South East	905	3,706	4,248	753
Greater London	743	3,853	4,717	955
Rest of South East	1,012	3,613	3,932	606
South West	773	3,215	3,988	631

Gunning for trouble
Offences recorded by the police in which firearms were reported to have been used

	1986	1990	1991	1992	1993
England	9,037	9,986	11,676	12,939	13,565
Wales	326	387	453	366	386
Scotland	1,525	1,484	1,888	1,950	1,767
North	561	704	755	808	740
Yorkshire & Humberside	1,161	1,369	1,494	1,948	2,146
North West	1,179	1,187	1,411	1,605	2,065
West Midlands	1,020	949	1,063	1,328	1,372
East Midlands	973	796	904	1,078	1,044
East Anglia	221	361	378	413	328
South East	3,641	4,320	5,386	5,496	5,454
Greater London	2,404	2,764	3,706	3,584	3,513
Rest of South East	1,237	1,556	1,680	1,912	1,941
South West	281	300	285	263	416

a Figures for Scotland are not comparable with others because of the differences in the legal system, recording practices and classification.

Recent trends in crime

Rises and falls
Notifiable offences by police force area, 1994

	Total no. of offences[a]	Violent crime[b]	Burglary	Vehicle crime	Criminal damage[a]
		% of total			
Avon & Somerset	165,765	6	23	34	12
Bedfordshire	52,062	6	25	34	13
Cambridgeshire	61,294	6	23	26	12
Cheshire	72,516	6	27	26	14
Cleveland	75,248	4	24	30	12
Cumbria	40,039	6	25	25	14
Derbyshire	83,485	6	29	27	16
Devon & Cornwall	108,780	5	28	26	12
Dorset	53,780	5	17	25	12
Durham	59,768	6	21	28	12
Essex	103,683	5	23	25	15
Gloucestershire	60,547	5	26	30	11
Gtr. Manchester	311,718	5	29	32	12
Hampshire	138,004	5	21	26	15
Hertfordshire	54,173	5	22	33	17
Humberside	134,847	5	33	25	14
Kent	151,996	6	18	27	16
Lancashire	109,669	4	25	30	9
Leicestershire	97,483	7	27	29	13
Lincolnshire	46,467	6	24	20	16
London, City of	5,261	3	13	12	5
Merseyside	135,501	8	24	23	16
Metrolpolitan Police	784,041	10	21	24	12
Norfolk	55,880	5	25	25	14
Northamptonshire	57,298	6	25	27	18
Northumbria	180,039	5	32	27	16
North Yorkshire	58,703	4	28	27	11
Nottinghamshire	145,584	7	24	24	17
South Yorkshire	152,451	4	34	30	13
Staffordshire	93,178	8	29	28	16
Suffolk	38,440	7	20	19	16
Surrey	46,556	7	22	26	14
Sussex	103,548	5	23	24	14
Thames Valley	184,852	4	21	31	15
Warwickshire	42,272	4	26	32	15
West Mercia	81,669	5	20	27	16
West Midlands	308,207	6	29	29	15
West Yorkshire	288,449	5	30	28	15
Wiltshire	37,167	8	22	23	14
Dyfed-Powys	19,758	13	18	18	15
Gwent	37,312	8	18	25	16
North Wales	42,537	7	24	23	16
South Wales	155,927	5	24	33	19
England & Wales	5,035,954	6	25	27	14

a Excluding offences of value £20 and under.

% change on previous year

Total	Violence against the person	Sexual offences	Robbery	Burglary	Vehicle crime	Criminal damage
-5	18	22	-8	-8	-9	3
-11	2	0	7	-18	-13	-2
-6	7	7	-21	-6	-12	12
-6	9	17	-19	-13	-15	9
3	6	9	39	-2	2	8
-4	11	2	-19	-6	-10	5
-5	-3	3	18	-6	-13	11
-10	12	-9	-5	-7	-14	-13
4	8	39	8	-3	8	18
-5	11	3	-9	-8	-9	-2
-8	8	-23	-2	-13	-16	4
0	22	48	5	-8	-6	30
-9	-8	-10	-1	-7	-9	-1
-4	7	-25	4	-10	-5	8
-3	4	11	-3	-10	-2	6
-3	2	-13	4	-8	2	4
-4	15	17	1	-13	-9	4
-6	3	7	1	-8	-12	21
-1	29	31	11	4	-5	0
-10	2	26	-25	-14	-10	2
-6	-47	0	-43	-13	-22	6
-2	4	5	-8	-2	-6	13
-8	18	9	5	-6	-19	-16
-13	7	1	-14	-23	-20	3
-3	-5	26	2	-9	-10	16
-7	-3	5	-1	-9	-9	-2
6	4	-1	52	3	13	48
-5	0	-2	-1	-13	-8	21
0	4	4	13	-2	-5	7
-5	6	6	0	-11	-6	6
-9	1	3	1	-15	-13	13
-11	25	23	-23	-21	-19	2
-3	5	8	8	-9	-12	11
-7	18	11	24	-5	-13	-9
-6	-3	-13	4	-12	-5	0
1	4	13	9	-7	-5	26
-5	-5	-10	18	-9	-5	6
-4	2	3	-6	-7	-8	7
-8	-5	-5	-7	-11	-11	3
-14	8	-31	32	-25	-17	-5
-4	6	-14	-32	-6	-9	3
-9	-9	-37	-15	-15	-15	6
-3	2	-8	-13	-2	2	-9
-5	7	2	4	-8	-10	2

b Offences of violence against the person, sexual offences and robbery.

Driving offences

Overall offences
'000s

	England & Wales	Scotland	Northern Ireland
1935	432.8	35.4	19.6
1940	208.1	23.1	13.9
1945	148.4	16.6	18.8
1950	357.9	31.8	23.8
1955	407.9	38.7	27.7
1960	622.5	60.8	33.8
1965	856.7[a]	82.5	27.1
1970	991.1	84.5	21.8
1975	1,194.7[b]	173.4[b]	24.6
1980	1,294.1	236.9	28.7
1985	1,052.0	220.3	27.3
1990	704.6	296.2	27.2
1991	713.1	305.6	20.1
1994	638.7	330.7	21.5

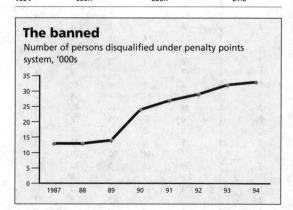

The banned
Number of persons disqualified under penalty points system, '000s

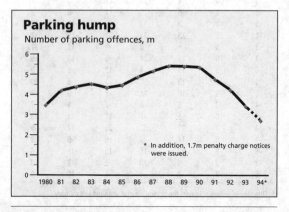

Parking hump
Number of parking offences, m

* In addition, 1.7m penalty charge notices were issued.

Offences of driving after consuming alcohol or taking drugs

	Total proceedings	Total found guilty	% attracting custodial sentence		Average sentence, months	
	1993	1993	1987	1993	1987	1993
UK	119,863	104,122	2.9	4.1	3.0	3.1
England	98,864	85,665	3.0	5.1	2.9	3.0
Wales	6,294	5,533	2.3	4.0	3.4	3.5
Scotland	9,943	9,117	3.1	3.2	3.2	3.3
North	6,360	5,651	3.3	4.3	3.2	3.3
Yorkshire & Humberside	9,513	8,439	3.7	5.7	2.8	3.0
North West	15,047	13,330	3.7	5.8	2.9	3.0
West Midlands	12,034	10,421	3.2	5.7	3.0	3.3
East Midlands	6,837	5,791	3.6	7.0	2.9	2.8
East Anglia	3,134	2,829	2.3	3.6	2.5	3.1
South East	37,932	32,076	2.5	4.6	2.9	2.9
Greater London	18,610	15,094	2.2	5.5	3.0	2.9
Rest of South East	19,322	16,982	2.7	3.7	2.9	3.0
South West	8,007	7,128	2.9	4.0	2.7	3.2

Breath tests
England and Wales

	Total no. of tests '000	No. positive or refused, '000	% positive or refused
1982	206.6	88.6	43
1983	241.2	98.4	41
1984	207.6	87.6	42
1985	250.3	95.7	38
1986	303.0	97.8	32
1987	399.8	111.4	28
1988	443.3	111.7	25
1989	540.9	108.0	20
1990	596.6	102.4	17
1991	562.5	90.3	16
1992	531.3	87.8	17
1993	599.6	89.4	15
1994	678.5	93.3	14
1995	702.7	94.4	13

a 1964.
b 1974.

Prisons

Locked up
Daily average prison population, '000s

	England & Wales	Scotland	N Ireland	Total
1935	11.3	1.7	0.3	13.3
1940	9.4	1.3	0.2	10.9
1945	14.7	1.9	0.4	17.0
1950	20.5	1.7	0.4	22.6
1951	21.8	1.8	0.4	24.0
1952	23.7	2.1	0.4	26.2
1953	23.6	2.1	0.4	26.1
1954	22.4	2.1	0.4	24.9
1955	21.1	2.1	0.4	23.6
1956	20.8	2.2	0.4	23.4
1957	22.6	2.4	0.4	25.4
1958	25.4	2.6	0.4	28.4
1959	26.6	2.9	0.4	29.9
1960	27.1	2.8	0.4	30.3
1961	29.0	3	0.4	32.4
1962	31.1	3.2	0.4	34.7
1963	30.9	3.5	0.4	34.8
1964	29.6	3.2	0.4	33.2
1965	30.4	3.4	0.5	34.3
1966	33.1	3.8	0.6	37.5
1967	35.0	4.2	0.7	39.9
1968	32.5	4.5	0.7	37.7
1969	34.7	4.8	0.7	40.2
1970	39.0	5	0.9	44.9
1971	39.8	5.3	1.1	46.2
1972	38.3	5.2	1.6	45.1
1973	36.8	4.8	2.1	43.7
1974	36.9	4.7	2.6	44.2
1975	39.8	4.9	2.7	47.4
1976	41.4	4.9	2.6	48.9
1977	41.6	4.9	2.6	49.1
1978	41.8	5.1	2.8	49.7
1979	42.2	4.6	2.7	49.5
1980	42.2	4.9	2.5	49.6
1981	43.3	4.5	2.5	50.3
1982	43.7	4.9	2.5	51.1
1983	43.8	5.1	2.4	51.3
1984	43.3	4.8	2.2	50.3
1985	46.3	5.3	2.1	53.7
1986	46.9	5.6	1.9	54.4
1987	49.0	5.4	1.9	56.3
1988	50.0	5.2	1.9	57.1
1989	48.6	5.0	1.8	55.4
1990	45.6	4.7	1.8	52.1
1991	45.9	4.8	1.8	52.5
1992	45.8	5.3	1.8	52.9
1993	44.6	5.6	1.9	52.1
1994	48.8	5.6	1.9	56.3

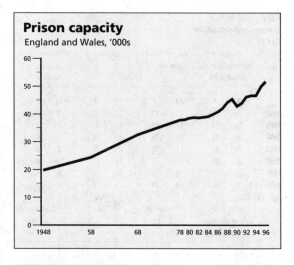

Prison capacity

England and Wales, '000s

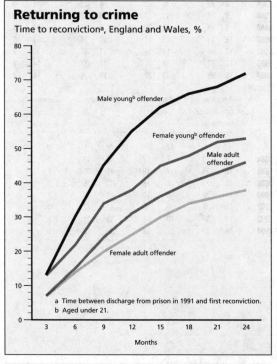

Returning to crime

Time to reconviction[a], England and Wales, %

Male young[b] offender

Female young[b] offender

Male adult offender

Female adult offender

a Time between discharge from prison in 1991 and first reconviction.
b Aged under 21.

Months

Sentencing facts

Who gets what
% of persons sentenced
Age 14–17

	Absolute or conditional discharge		Supervision order		Fine		Community service order	
	M	F	M	F	M	F	M	F
1984	18	33	11	13	32	35	7	2
1986	19	37	11	10	31	32	7	3
1988	20	42	11	10	29	28	8	4
1990	25	48	11	10	26	22	8	3
1992	31	53	11	12	18	15	10	4
1993	31	51	16	19	11	12	8	4
1994	30	52	18	20	12	9	7	3

Age 18–20

	Absolute or conditional discharge		Probation order		Fine		Community service order	
	M	F	M	F	M	F	M	F
1984	8	23	10	22	8	23	14	5
1986	9	24	11	23	9	24	14	6
1988	9	27	12	23	9	27	14	6
1990	13	34	13	21	13	34	14	6
1992	17	40	13	19	17	40	15	7
1993	17	37	12	17	17	37	14	7
1994	16	36	13	20	16	36	14	7

Age 21+

	Absolute or conditional discharge		Probation order		Fine		Community service order	
	M	F	M	F	M	F	M	F
1984	9	22	7	17	45	43	7	3
1986	10	24	7	19	41	38	7	3
1988	10	27	8	18	42	35	7	3
1990	13	32	8	18	43	32	7	4
1992	17	36	9	16	37	27	9	5
1993	18	34	10	17	38	31	11	6
1994	16	32	11	19	36	28	11	7

Attendance centre order		Care order		Young offenders institution		Otherwise dealt with		Total immediate custody		Total community sentence	
M	F	M	F	M	F	M	F	M	F	M	F
12	4	1	2	14	2	1	1	14	2	33	27
11	4	1	1	14	2	1	1	14	2	34	26
10	3	1	1	14	3	1	1	14	3	35	25
10	2	0	0	9	2	2	2	9	2	36	26
11	3	...	...	10	2	2	3	10	2	39	27
13	5	...	...	11	3	3	2	11	3	44	33
13	6	...	...	11	3	3	2	11	3	44	34

Attendance centre order		Young offenders institution		Otherwise dealt with		Total immediate custody		Total community sentence	
M	F	M	F	M	F	M	F	M	F
2	0	21	6	1	1	21	6	26	27
2	...	22	6	1	1	22	6	27	29
1	0	21	5	1	1	21	5	27	29
2	...	15	3	2	2	15	3	29	27
2	0	15	3	2	2	15	3	30	26
1	0	17	5	2	2	17	5	30	26
1	0	19	5	2	2	19	5	32	29

Imprisonment fully suspended		Imprisonment partly suspended		Imprisonment unsuspended		Otherwise dealt with		Total immediate custody		Total community sentence	
M	F	M	F	M	F	M	F	M	F	M	F
11	8	2	1	18	5	2	1	20	6	14	20
12	8	1	1	20	6	1	1	21	7	14	22
12	8	1	1	19	6	2	1	20	7	15	21
10	8	1	0	17	5	2	2	17	6	15	21
8	7	0	0	17	6	3	2	18	6	18	22
1	2	...	...	18	7	3	2	18	7	23	24
1	2	...	...	20	8	2	2	20	8	25	28

Custody numbers

Male prisoners
Annual average population in custody in England and Wales, '000s

	Convicted unsentenced	Young offenders	Adults	All males
1987	1.5	8.6	27.7	47.2
1990	1.8	6.1	28.2	44.0
1991	1.9	5.7	28.6	44.3
1992	1.9	5.3	28.9	44.2
1993	2.6	5.0	27.2	43.0
1994	3.0	5.2	29.3	47.0

Female prisoners
Annual average population in custody in England and Wales, '000s

	Convicted unsentenced	Young offenders	Adults	All females
1987	0.07	0.21	1.09	1.77
1990	0.08	0.14	1.07	1.60
1991	0.10	0.14	1.03	1.56
1992	0.11	0.13	1.06	1.58
1993	0.11	0.14	1.00	1.56
1994	0.14	0.16	1.14	1.81

Lifers
Annual population serving life sentences in England and Wales, mid-year

	Male	of which young offenders	Female	of which young offenders	Total
1984	1,856	113	61	4	1,917
1985	1,991	118	60	8	2,051
1986	2,126	116	68	9	2,194
1987	2,265	106	74	8	2,339
1988	2,427	106	76	10	2,503
1989	2,592	103	85	5	2,677
1990	2,704	121	91	4	2,795
1991	2,800	100	96	5	2,896
1992	2,904	87	96	4	3,000
1993	2,990	77	105	4	3,095
1994	3,081	83	111	5	3,192

How Britain compares
Rate of imprisonment per 100,000 population, 1993

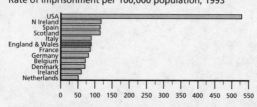

Part XII
PEOPLE AND CULTURE

Marriage and divorce

Men getting married
'000s

	1938	1950	1960	1970
Bachelors	375.9	354.4	352.6	412.4
Divorced men	4.8	26.9	19.7	38.1
Widowers	28.4	26.7	21.3	20.5
Under 21	14.1	23.2	46.6	81.4
21–24	117.7	141.2	161.0	209.7
25–29	156.2	121.3	94.6	91.1
30–34	60.1	47.3	32.8	30.3
35–44	33.9	41.6	27.0	26.0
45–54	13.0	17.3	14.9	14.5
55 and over	12.4	14.9	15.9	17.9

Women getting married
'000s

	1938	1950	1960	1970
Spinsters	387.0	361.2	356.8	415.9
Divorced women	4.1	23.9	19.0	36.2
Widows	18.0	22.9	17.8	18.9
Under 21	67.6	99.9	141.9	186.0
21–24	151.3	148.2	139.9	171.6
25–29	110.2	77.6	48.0	51.2
30–34	38.1	29.6	19.4	18.3
35–44	25.0	30.3	20.8	18.6
45–54	9.6	13.5	13.1	13.2
55 and over	5.5	7.6	9.8	12.1

Divorce
Divorces per thousand women

	1961	1971	1976	1981	1986	1991	1994
Under 25	2.4	7.5	14.5	22.3	30.7	27.7	22.2
25 to 29	4.3	13.0	20.4	26.7	28.6	31.3	29.6
30 to 34	3.8	10.5	18.3	20.2	22.0	25.1	26.1
35 to 44	2.7	6.7	12.6	14.9	15.8	17.2	18.0
45+	0.9	2.8	4.0	3.9	4.1	4.5	4.9

Divorces per thousand men

	1961	1971	1976	1981	1986	1991	1994
Under 25	1.4	5.0	13.6	17.7	30.9	25.9	20.0
25 to 29	3.9	12.5	21.4	27.6	31.2	32.9	28.5
30 to 34	4.1	11.8	18.9	22.8	25.1	28.5	28.3
35 to 44	3.1	7.9	14.1	17.0	18.0	20.1	20.7
45+	1.1	3.1	4.5	4.8	5.2	5.6	6.1

Divorces by duration of marriage, %

	1961	1971	1976	1981	1986	1991	1994
Up to 4	11.3	13.4	18.0	20.5	24.5	23.3	22.6[a]
5 to 9	30.6	30.5	30.2	29.1	27.5	27.0	28.2[a]
10 to 14	22.9	19.4	18.7	19.6	17.5	18.3	18.3[a]
15 to 19	13.9	12.6	12.8	12.8	12.9	12.8	12.3[a]
20+	21.2	24.2	20.3	18.0	17.6	18.6	18.7[a]

a 1993.

1980	1990	1993
314.8	276.5	245.6
87.7	88.2	85.8
15.9	10.7	9.8
52.6	15.9	8.7
141.8	92.3	64.9
98.8	122.8	114.0
48.1	57.0	63.8
39.4	50.0	50.6
19.4	22.0	23.8
18.3	15.5	15.4

1980	1990	1993
319.1	279.4	247.8
83.4	85.6	84.2
16.0	10.4	9.2
127.5	45.6	26.6
133.3	119.0	92.9
65.8	103.2	104.5
34.1	42.8	49.7
30.7	39.0	40.1
15.0	16.8	18.8
12.0	8.9	8.7

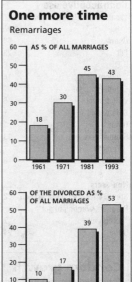

One more time
Remarriages

AS % OF ALL MARRIAGES

18 — 1961
30 — 1971
45 — 1981
43 — 1993

OF THE DIVORCED AS % OF ALL MARRIAGES

10 — 1961
17 — 1971
39 — 1981
53 — 1993

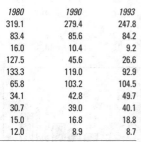

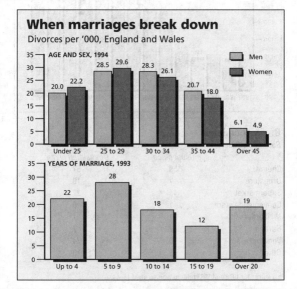

When marriages break down
Divorces per '000, England and Wales

AGE AND SEX, 1994
Men / Women

	Men	Women
Under 25	20.0	22.2
25 to 29	28.5	29.6
30 to 34	28.3	26.1
35 to 44	20.7	18.0
Over 45	6.1	4.9

YEARS OF MARRIAGE, 1993

Up to 4	5 to 9	10 to 14	15 to 19	Over 20
22	28	18	12	19

Family planning

Contraceptive use
Women aged 16–49, Great Britain, %

	1976ᵇ	1983ᵃ	1986	1989	1993
Users	68	75	71	69	72
Pill	29	28	23	22	25
IUD	6	6	7	5	5
Condom	14	13	13	15	17
Cap/diaphragm	2	1	2	1	1
Withdrawal	5	4	4	4	3
Safe period	1	1	1	1	1
Other	1	1	1	1	1
Sterilisation	13	22	23	23	24
Female	7	11	12	11	12
Male	6	10	11	12	12
Non-users	32	25	29	31	29
Sterile after another operation	2	2	3	5	2
Pregnant/wanting to get pregnant	7	7	7	7	8
Other	24	16	19	19	21

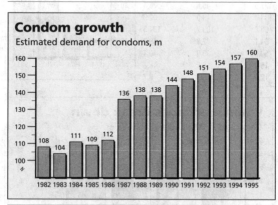

Condom growth
Estimated demand for condoms, m

1982	1983	1984	1985	1986	1987	1988	1989	1990	1991	1992	1993	1994	1995
108	104	111	109	112	136	138	138	144	148	151	154	157	160

Buying condoms
Sources, all users, %, 1996

	Usual place	Occasional place
Chemist	59	57
Drugstore	7	19
Supermarket	15	27
Convenience store	1	5
Mail order	1	1
Garage	2	7
Vending	10	24
Other	5	10

a Figures for 1976 and 1983 refer to women aged 18–44.

Abortion

% of total, Great Britain

	1971	1981	1986	1991	1994
Single women					
Under 16	4.3	4.3	3.9	2.8	3
16 to 19	36.1	38.7	34.0	27.3	24
20 to 34	55.9	54.6	59.9	67.1	69
35 to 44	1.9	2.0	2.2	2.7	4
Total no., '000s	63.4	96.4	115.2	127.6	118.2
Married women					
16 to 19	1.4	2.0	1.5	1.2	1
20 to 34	63.9	66.8	66.8	69.7	68
35 to 44	31.9	29.8	30.8	28.2	30
45+	0.9	1.0	0.9	0.9	1
Total no., '000s	58.6	55.5	47.2	42.0	38.5
All women[b]					
Under 16	2.1	2.4	2.5	1.9	2
16 to 19	18.0	22.8	22.2	18.9	16
20 to 34	60.9	60.6	62.9	68.3	69
35 to 44	16.8	13.3	12.1	10.7	12
45+	0.8	0.4	0.3	0.3	…
Total no., '000s	133.1	136.9	171.5	181.9	176.3

Births outside marriage

Per 1,000 births

Country	1960	1992
Sweden	11	50
Denmark	8	46
France	6	33
UK	5	31
USA	5	30
Canada	4	29
Australia	5	24
Germany	6	15
Netherlands	1	12
Spain	2	10

BIRTHS OUTSIDE MARRIAGE
% of all live births in UK

b Includes women who are divorced, separated or whose marital status is not known.

Income and wealth

From Dover to Derry
Average weekly gross household income, 1993 prices[a], £

	1985–86	1986–87	1988–89	1989–90	1990–91	1993
UK	324.5	338.7	359.1	356.4	368.9	353.0
England	329.9	348.0	368.7	367.2	378.9	358.5
Wales	291.7	286.3	302.3	293.6	299.6	306.1
Scotland	302.5	293.6	316.6	309.6	322.9	334.1
Northern Ireland	277.5	287.1	269.5	259.7	288.7	325.9
North	270.1	273.0	312.5	296.3	290.5	291.1
Yorkshire & Humberside	278.3	289.4	307.8	294.0	311.3	317.7
North West	293.2	320.4	319.7	323.3	338.2	335.2
West Midlands	300.4	311.3	325.9	330.2	336.8	301.0
East Midlands	312.6	313.5	330.6	347.7	358.4	341.7
East Anglia	323.2	304.7	364.5	362.8	358.5	346.9
Greater London	...	...	...	...	466.2	431.7
Rest of South East[b]	387.4	418.1	442.6	441.2	452.4	419.2
South West	334.8	346.6	363.1	354.1	375.0	330.5

Low and high incomes
% of households by weekly income, 1993

	Under £80	£80–£175	£175–375	£375–£649	£650+
UK	11.7	21.6	30.3	23.8	12.7
England	11.4	21.5	30.1	23.9	13.2
Wales	13.8	24.7	31.1	21.8	8.6
Scotland	13.4	19.8	32.1	24.5	10.3
Northern Ireland	14.8	26.5	28.8	19.3	10.5
North	16.4	22.8	31.2	23.6	6.0
Yorkshire & Humberside	12.8	19.6	32.6	27.0	7.9
North West	13.5	22.9	28.7	23.6	11.5
West Midlands	12.6	27.6	32.1	19.9	7.9
East Midlands	9.7	20.6	33.8	25.4	10.5
East Anglia	9.5	23.7	34.4	18.9	13.4
Greater London	12.2	19.4	25.1	22.3	20.9
Rest of South East	8.5	18.9	27.8	25.4	19.5
South West	9.8	22.4	33.0	25.0	9.8

Rich London

Average gross weekly earnings, Men, April 1995, £

1	Greater London	498.2
2	Rest of South East	387.6
3	North West	354.2
4	Scotland	350.7
5	South West	349.6
6	West Midlands	346.3
7	East Anglia	341.2
8	East Midlands	338.2
9	Yorkshire & Humberside	337.1
10	North	331.7
11	Wales	331.4
12	Northern Ireland	330.9

Personal disposable income per head 1994, £

1	Greater London	9,677
2	Rest of South East	8,539
3	Scotland	8,210
4	East Anglia	8,190
5	South West	7,942
6	West Midlands	7,733
7	East Midlands	7,686
8	North West	7,572
9	Northern Ireland	7,536
10	Yorkshire & Humberside	7,473
11	North	7,423
12	Wales	7,245

Most to dispose of
Distribution of disposable household income, quintile groups of individuals

Net income before housing costs, %

	Bottom fifth	Next fifth	Middle fifth	Next fifth	Top fifth
1979	10	14	18	23	35
1987	9	13	17	23	39
1994–95	7	11	17	24	40

Net income after housing costs

	Bottom fifth	Next fifth	Middle fifth	Next fifth	Top fifth
1979	10	14	18	23	35
1987	8	12	17	23	40
1990–91	6	12	17	23	43

How the wealth is held
Net wealth of the personal sector by type, %

	1971	1981	1994
Dwellings (net of mortgage debt)	26	36	28
Other fixed assets	10	10	5
Non-marketable tenancy rights	12	12	7
Building society shares and deposits	7	8	8
National savings, notes and coins and bank deposits	13	10	9
Stocks, shares and unit trusts	23	8	10
Life assurance and pension funds	15	16	33
Other financial assets net of liabilities	-6	0	…
Total, £bn at 1994 prices	1,172	1,416	2,551

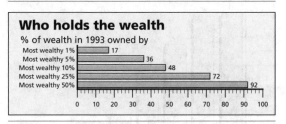

Who holds the wealth
% of wealth in 1993 owned by

Most wealthy 1% — 17
Most wealthy 5% — 36
Most wealthy 10% — 48
Most wealthy 25% — 72
Most wealthy 50% — 92

Marketable wealth
% of wealth owned by

	1976	1981	1986	1991	1993
Most wealthy 1%	21	18	18	17	17
Most wealthy 5%	38	36	36	35	36
Most wealthy 10%	50	50	50	47	48
Most wealthy 25%	71	73	73	71	72
Most wealthy 50%	92	92	90	92	92
Total wealth, £bnᶜ	280	565	955	1,711	1,809

a Adjusted for national consumer price inflation.
b Includes Greater London 1985–86 to 1989–90.
c Includes value of dwellings.

Consumerism

Consumer goods
% households owning, 1994–95 (1980–81 in brackets)

	Microwave oven	Washing machine	Tumble dryer	Dish-washer	Fridge-freezer[a]
UK	67	89 (77)	50 (22)	18 (4)	86 (47)
England	67	89 (76)	51 (22)	19 (4)	86 (48)
Wales	68	88 (81)	43 (23)	12 (2)	84 (50)
Scotland	67	93 (83)	56 (24)	19 (3)	83 (39)
Northern Ireland	66	93 (70)	39	13	76
North	67	91 (88)	46 (19)	12 (1)	85 (42)
Yorkshire & Humberside	72	92 (84)	52 (24)	12 (2)	86 (40)
North West	69	90 (77)	50 (21)	18 (2)	84 (40)
West Midlands	67	89 (77)	51 (21)	16 (2)	85 (42)
East Midlands	69	91 (84)	52 (22)	18 (3)	85 (45)
East Anglia	61	85 (80)	48 (27)	21 (5)	81 (59)
South East	64	87 (69)	49 (23)	23 (6)	88 (55)
Greater London	56	82 (61)	42 (20)	18 (4)	85 (50)
Rest of South East	69	89 (75)	53 (25)	25 (7)	89 (59)
South West	71	87 (72)	56 (22)	21 (5)	89 (54)

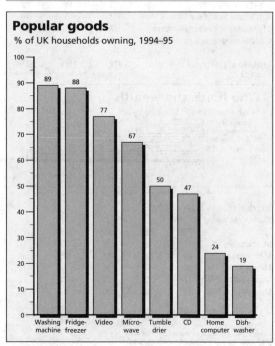

Popular goods

% of UK households owning, 1994–95

Washing machine 89, Fridge-freezer 88, Video 77, Microwave 67, Tumble drier 50, CD 47, Home computer 24, Dish-washer 19

a 1980–81 deep freezers only.

Telephone	Television	CD player	Video	Home computer[b]	Central heating	Second home
91 (73)	98 (97)	46	76	23	84 (59)	3
92 (74)	98 (97)	46	77	24	84 (52)	3
86 (67)	98 (98)	36	71	24	82 (51)	3
89 (74)	98 (97)	46	77	20	86 (39)	3
90 (57)	97 (91)	46	77	17	87 (64)	1
88 (64)	98 (98)	41	76	24	89 (64)	2
92 (68)	98 (97)	43	77	22	78 (52)	4
89 (71)	99 (98)	40	77	24	77 (54)	4
91 (71)	98 (97)	44	78	23	81 (54)	3
92 (73)	99 (98)	49	79	22	87 (65)	3
90 (73)	98 (98)	39	66	23	90 (68)	5
93 (80)	98 (96)	52	78	25	88 (62)	3
92 (79)	98 (95)	45	73	23	86 (54)	4
94 (80)	99 (97)	55	80	27	89 (67)	3
94 (72)	98 (96)	46	74	23	83 (57)	3

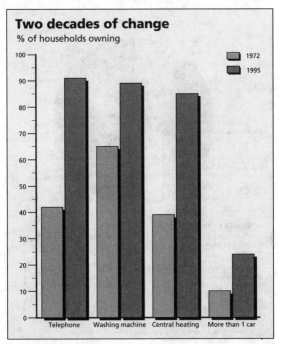

Two decades of change
% of households owning

1972
1995

b 1992–93.

Consumer spending and saving

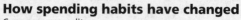

How spending habits have changed
Consumer expenditure

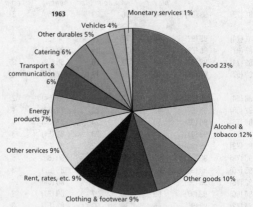

1963

- Monetary services 1%
- Vehicles 4%
- Other durables 5%
- Catering 6%
- Transport & communication 6%
- Energy products 7%
- Other services 9%
- Rent, rates, etc. 9%
- Clothing & footwear 9%
- Other goods 10%
- Alcohol & tobacco 12%
- Food 23%

1994

- Monetary services 4%
- Vehicles 5%
- Other durables 4%
- Catering 9%
- Transport & communication 10%
- Energy products 6%
- Other services 13%
- Rent, rates, etc. 13%
- Clothing & footwear 6%
- Other goods 11%
- Alcohol & tobacco 9%
- Food 11%

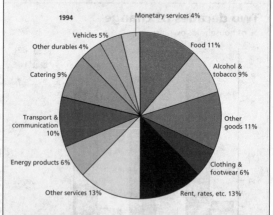

CONSUMER EXPENDITURE, % of total

	1940	1950	1960	1970	1980	1992	1994
Transport & communication	5	7	7	10	16	17	18
Housing	11	9	10	13	14	15	16
Food	30	29	28	20	17	12	11
Recreation, entertainment & education	3	4	5	5	9	10	10
Alcoholic beverages	8	8	6	7	7	6	6
Clothing	11	11	10	9	7	6	6
Household goods & services	6	9	12	11	7	7	7
Fuel & power	5	4	4	5	5	4	3
Tobacco	6	8	7	5	4	3	3
Other[a]	17	11	12	14	14	20	20

a Includes insurance, catering, other services and adjustments for tourists'
  expenditure and expenditure abroad.

How bills are paid
%

	1976	1981	1984	1990	1992	1994
Cash	93	88	86	78	76	75
Non-cash	7	12	14	22	24	25
Non-cash payments:						
Cheque	68	68	64	52	46	38
Standing order/ direct debit	21	20	22	23	25	27
Plastic cards	7	9	13	20	25	32
of which:						
Credit/charge card	6	8	12	15	14	15
Retailer card	...	1	...	1	1	1
Debit card	0	0	0	4	11	16
Other	2	2	1	4	4	2

Savings by working status
% of adults

	Employed						
	Full-time	Part-time	Retired	Not working	Male	Female	All
Building society account	69	71	68	55	64	66	65
Bank account	89	83	81	70	83	79	81
Premium bonds	29	28	39	20	28	28	28
Company shares	16	11	13	5	14	9	12
Government privatisation shares	12	8	14	6	13	8	10
National Savings Bank investment/ ordinary account	10	12	10	9	10	10	10
Unit & investment trusts	10	8	12	5	11	7	9
National Savings certificates/bonds	5	7	14	6	8	7	7
Personal equity plan	8	5	7	3	8	4	6

Savings by age and sex
% of adults, 1993

	16–34	34–64	65+	Males	Females
Building society account	62	68	62	64	66
Bank account	77	85	77	83	79
Premium bonds	16	35	34	28	28
Unit trusts	4	13	7	11	7
Shares	8	16	9	14	9
Government privatisation shares	5	14	12	13	8
National Savings Bank investment/ ordinary account	10	10	10	10	10
National Savings certificates/ bonds	5	7	13	8	7
Personal equity plans	...	...	...	8	4

A history of prices

Prices since 1900
*Actual prices and (**in bold**) revalued to 1996 prices, £*

	1900	1990	1930	1996	1960
Railway fare: London to	1.66	5.00	8.40	59.00	82.00
Glasgow 2nd class return	**82.90**	**189.60**	**102.90**	**71.30**	**82.00**
Atlantic crossing by ship	12.33[a]	16.00[b]	67	970	945
(to New York): cheapest	**784**	**613**	**821**	**1172**	**945**
Cunard ticket available					
Atlantic crossing by air:	...	...	154.35	323.00	216.00
London to New York (return)	...	...	**1,890**	**390**	**216**
cheapest ticket available					
London to Nairobi (return)	...	178	199	517	307
cheapest ticket available	...	**6,758**	**2,441**	**625**	**307**
Bottle of whisky including tax	0.18[c]	0.71[d]	1.95[e]	8.80	10.70
	8.80	**24.80**	**23.10**	**10.60**	**10.70**
Car:	225[f]	170	494	6,180	7,145
Ford, cheapest model	**13,230**	**6,450**	**6,050**	**7,470**	**7,145**
Monet painting of	793[g]	1,744[h]	20,000	4,000,000	3,393,111
Waterloo Bridge, Effet de	**43,440**	**79,980**	**245,000**	**4,832,000**	**3,393,111**
soleil (oil on canvas, 1903)					
English dinner at The Savoy:	0.38[i]	0.78	2.38	28.75	35.85
soup, main course,	**19.00**	**29.60**	**29.20**	**34.70**	**35.85**
pudding, coffee					
Top of the range camera:	20	19	145	1,200	2,200
Sanderson, Leica, Nikon	**998**	**705**	**1,776**	**1,450**	**2,200**
Telephone call: 3 minutes	0.25[j]	0.33	0.13	0.41	0.10
London to Glasgow	**12.50**	**12.50**	**1.60**	**0.50**	**0.10**
Telephone call: 3 minutes	...	15.00	3.00	2.33	1.11
London to New York	...	**570.00**	**36.70**	**2.80**	**1.11**
Opera ticket at Covent Garden:	0.13	0.33	0.18	3.00	4.00
least expensive	**6.50**	**12.50**	**2.20**	**3.60**	**4.00**
Opera ticket at Covent Garden:	1.50	1.40	2.10	101.00	140.00
most expensive	**74.90**	**53.10**	**25.70**	**122.00**	**140.00**
Household coal per short ton	1.18	1.24	4.22	120.66	160.00
	58.90	**47.00**	**51.70**	**145.80**	**160.00**
The Economist	0.03	0.05	0.08	1.60	2.00
	1.50	**1.90**	**1.00**	**1.90**	**2.00**
Theatre ticket: Theatre Royal,	0.08[k]	0.08[l]	0.30	7.50	8.50
least expensive	**2.20**	**3.10**	**3.70**	**9.10**	**8.50**
Theatre ticket: Theatre Royal,	0.60[k]	0.75[l]	1.50	25.00	32.50
most expensive	**16.80**	**28.70**	**18.40**	**30.20**	**32.50**
Gold per oz	4.24	4.25	12.56	273.72	261.61
	211.70	**161.20**	**153.80**	**330.70**	**261.61**
Hotel room:	...	1.50	6.00	189.00	240.00
Hyde Park Hotel, single	...	**56.90**	**73.50**	**228.30**	**240.00**
Most expensive Jaguar,	...	310[h]	2,197	43,200	58,800
two-seater	...	**14,220**	**26,910**	**52,180**	**58,800**
Pair of men's handmade	0.84[m]	1.99	4.98[n]	125.00	220.00
shoes	**36.40**	**75.50**	**86.50**	**151.00**	**220.00**
Standard Dunhill pipe	0.38[o]	1.25	8.38	108.00	147.00

Man's suit:	...	4.20[p]	30.00	269.00	269.00
Daks 2-piece	...	**146.60**	**367.50**	**324.90**	**269.00**
London taxi ride,	0.30	0.11	0.11	1.60	2.20
one mile	**15.00**	**4.20**	**1.30**	**1.90**	**2.20**
Lighter, gold-plated	1.75	2.25	7.25	185.00	225.00
	50.80	**85.30**	**88.80**	**223.50**	**225.00**
Potatoes per 7lbs	0.02	0.02	0.08	0.91	1.56
	1.00	**0.80**	**1.00**	**1.10**	**1.56**

Actual and (in bold) revalued to 1996 prices, pence

Bread:	0.5	0.7	2.4	42	52
unsliced loaf per 400g	**25**	**27**	**29**	**51**	**52**
Milk per pint	0.7	1.2	3.3	30	35
	35	**46**	**40**	**36**	**35**
Postage stamp:	0.42	0.42	1.25	22	25
London to Scotland	**21**	**16**	**15**	**27**	**25**
Postage stamp:	0.01	0.63	1.25	37	41
London to America	**0.5**	**24**	**15**	**45**	**41**
The Times	0.83[m]	0.83	3.30	35	30
	36	**31**	**40**	**42**	**30**
Underground ticket:	0.83	0.63	2.08	70	110
Victoria to South Kensington	**41**	**24**	**25**	**25**	**110**
Mars bar	...	0.8	2.5	21	30
	...	**30**	**31**	**25**	**30**

Note: all food prices are July 1914 average instead of 1900, and 1933 instead of 1930.

a 1895.
b 1934.
c 1906.
d 1939.
e 1961.
f 1904.
g 1905.
h 1932.
i 1900 price includes fourth course of fish.
j 1912.
k 1922.
l 1935.
m 1913.
n 1949.
o 1910.
p 1938.
q 1926.
r 1933.

Food and drink

The weekly diet
Estimated household consumption, grammes per person per week, GB

	1965	1975	1985	1994
Cheese	91	107	111	106
Butter	173	160	80	39
Margarine	86	74	107	43
Beef and veal	229	264	185	131
Mutton and lamb	167	120	93	54
Pork	79	77	98	77
Poultry	100	162	196	229
Fish	164	127	139	145
Fresh green vegetables	406	328	277	245
Fresh potatoes	1,509	1,244	1,161	812
Fresh fruit	533	496	525	645
Other fresh vegetables & frozen vegetables	432	483	614	674
Bread	1,151	925	878	758
Tea	74	62	49	38
Instant coffee	7	14	15	13
Sugar	498	320	238	144
Eggs[a]	4.78	4.14	3.15	1.86

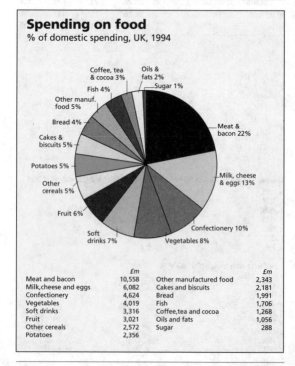

Spending on food
% of domestic spending, UK, 1994

Coffee, tea & cocoa 3%
Oils & fats 2%
Sugar 1%
Fish 4%
Other manuf. food 5%
Bread 4%
Cakes & biscuits 5%
Potatoes 5%
Other cereals 5%
Fruit 6%
Soft drinks 7%
Vegetables 8%
Meat & bacon 22%
Milk, cheese & eggs 13%
Confectionery 10%

	£m		£m
Meat and bacon	10,558	Other manufactured food	2,343
Milk, cheese and eggs	6,082	Cakes and biscuits	2,181
Confectionery	4,624	Bread	1,991
Vegetables	4,019	Fish	1,706
Soft drinks	3,316	Coffee, tea and cocoa	1,268
Fruit	3,021	Oils and fats	1,056
Other cereals	2,572	Sugar	288
Potatoes	2,356		

Drinking trends

UK consumption of alcohol, litres per head

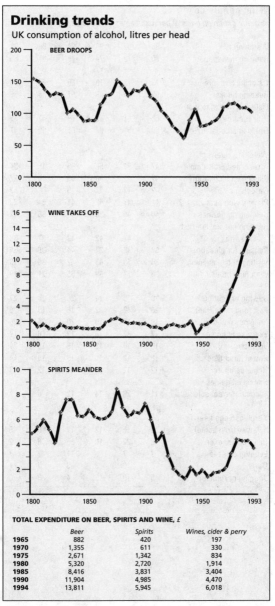

BEER DROOPS

WINE TAKES OFF

SPIRITS MEANDER

TOTAL EXPENDITURE ON BEER, SPIRITS AND WINE, £

	Beer	Spirits	Wines, cider & perry
1965	882	420	197
1970	1,355	611	330
1975	2,671	1,342	834
1980	5,320	2,720	1,914
1985	8,416	3,831	3,404
1990	11,904	4,985	4,470
1994	13,811	5,945	6,018

a Number per person per week.

Leisure

What people do
% participation on basis of participating at least once a week, 1994

	All	16–24	25–34	35–44	45–59	60+
Watching TV	96	97	95	94	96	98
Reading newspapers	80	72	74	75	87	86
Listening to the radio	73	73	70	80	76	69
Reading books	60	55	59	57	58	69
Listening to CDs, tapes or records	58	81	66	69	51	35
Drinking alcohol at home	56	51	64	61	59	47
Watching videos of recorded programmes	47	50	57	55	45	34
Playing with children	47	43	66	68	40	27
Gardening	42	12	32	49	60	52
Playing with pets	41	41	42	45	54	28
Reading magazines	40	45	38	41	36	42
Reading special interest magazines	39	42	42	42	37	33
Cooking for pleasure	37	38	37	44	36	34
Visiting pub in evening	36	59	43	42	35	13
Watching other videos	30	57	39	35	21	10
Sewing or knitting	20	9	14	26	23	27
Fast food restaurant	20	42	32	16	13	5
Religious meeting	19	10	10	20	24	26
Exercise at home	17	17	16	19	16	17
Voluntary work	16	10	13	15	19	21
Pub at lunchtime	15	18	15	15	15	14
Home computer	12	12	14	21	12	3
Specialist games computer/console	11	26	14	12	6	1
Aerobics/yoga/keep fit (away from home)	9	15	12	11	6	5
Billiards/snooker	8	22	10	5	6	2
Evening classes	7	7	5	11	7	7
Darts	5	10	3	3	7	1
Jogging or running	5	10	12	4	3	0

% participation on basis of participating at least once a quarter, 1994

	All	16–24	25–34	35–44	45–59	60+
Going to the pub	61	69	72	68	63	40
Eating out as an occasion	61	57	62	57	65	61
Had people round at home	60	58	68	60	58	58
Eating take-away at home	51	67	72	66	44	20
Long walk for pleasure	48	49	49	47	54	42
Motoring for pleasure	45	42	41	44	48	49
Home entertaining	45	44	51	48	41	41
DIY or house repair	44	31	62	57	50	27
Holiday in UK	43	38	42	45	43	47
Visiting the library	41	38	44	42	35	44
Eating out – fast food	40	64	66	41	31	10
Going to the cinema	35	66	51	35	24	10
Holiday abroad	32	32	32	34	39	26
Short break holiday	31	29	34	29	30	32
Board games playing	30	35	42	38	25	17
Sports or leisure centre	28	45	37	40	19	9
Historic building	26	25	28	27	22	29
Swimming	25	33	40	30	20	7
Going to a disco or nightclub	24	63	32	20	16	2
Theatre	23	15	21	24	28	26
Museum/art gallery	21	23	24	22	19	18
Spectator sports	18	20	20	25	20	10
Visited a fun fair	16	29	22	23	11	3
Eating take-away at another place	15	30	22	12	10	4
Playing individual sport	13	17	17	16	10	8
Team sport playing	13	26	15	16	11	4
Exhibition	12	8	14	10	15	13
Bingo	10	9	6	8	10	14
Theme park visiting	9	9	14	13	9	5
Betting shop	8	10	9	7	8	6
Camping/caravanning	8	11	9	6	11	4
Pop or rock concert	7	15	8	9	6	0
Classical concert or opera	7	1	6	10	11	8
Fishing	4	5	6	3	5	2
Horse racing	3	0	5	3	3	2
Dog racing	3	0	7	3	2	1
Circus visiting	2	6	3	2	1	0

Newspapers and magazines

Daily papers
January–June average circulation, '000s

	Daily Telegraph	Financial Times	Guardian	Independent	Times
1950	...	58	140	...	254
1955	...	79	156	...	222
1960	1,177	122	199	...	263
1965	1,351	152	276	...	258
1970	1,402	175	303	...	402
1975	1,353	186	336	...	327
1980	1,446	198	375	...	316
1985	1,221	229	487	...	480
1990	1,086	292	433	414	432
1991	1,075	289	431	394	406
1992	1,044	292	418	377	390
1993	1,025	290	416	347	366
1994	1,008	297	403	280	485
1995	1,006	294	390	294	547

Sunday papers
January–June average circulation, '000s

	Independent on Sunday	Observer	Sunday Telegraph	Sunday Times	Mail on Sunday
1950	...	422	...	...	...
1955	...	564	...	606	...
1960	...	704	...	943	...
1965	...	829	662	1,275	...
1970	...	848	756	1,464	...
1975	...	761	757	1,396	...
1980	...	1,018	1,032	1,419	...
1985	...	746	690	1,258	1,605
1990	352[a]	567	587	1,187	1,889
1991	385	579	576	1,177	1,940
1992	385	541	562	1,203	1,960
1993	385	509	578	1,224	2,030
1994	335	501	625	1,221	1,984
1995	327	464	692	1,253	1,959

Magazines
UK average circulation figures from start of ABC membership, first half of year, '000s

	The Economist	Time	Newsweek
1975	58.7	...	...
1980	70.4	65.5	32.5
1985	79.9	59.4	30.3
1990	96.5	71.2	31.9
1994	99.7	92.9	29.9
1995	106.5	101.3	31.5

a July–December.

Daily Express	Daily Mail	Daily Mirror	Star	Sun	Today
4,116	2,245	4,567	...	2,071	...
4,036	2,068	4,725	...	1,759	...
4,143	2,066	4,565	...	1,407	...
3,981	2,325	4,957	...	1,361	...
3,607	1,917	4,697	...	1,509	...
2,894	1,730	4,018	...	3,435	...
2,325	1,985	3,651	1,033	3,837	...
1,875	1,828	3,272	1,435	4,066	...
1,562	1,670	3,130	919	3,937	581
1,565	1,720	2,957	879	3,693	490
1,538	1,689	2,868	808	3,588	495
1,497	1,775	2,680	773	3,517	538
1,367	1,794	2,493	747	4,071	587
1,279	1,788	2,518	738	4,080	566

News of the World	People	Sunday Express	Sunday Mirror	Sunday Sport
8,444	5,089	2,967	5,094	...
7,971	5,075	3,235	5,539	...
6,456	5,323	3,556	5,275	...
6,175	5,509	4,187	5,022	...
6,215	5,242	4,281	4,885	...
5,646	4,219	3,786	4,284	...
4,472	3,900	3,100	3,856	...
4,787	3,090	2,405	3,211	...
5,036	2,588	1,727	2,911	452
4,808	2,338	1,623	2,806	371
4,725	2,130	1,692	2,768	316
4,620	2,032	1,727	2,674	258
4,774	2,012	1,563	2,567	270
4,744	2,066	1,403	2,560	313

Business Week	New Statesman	Private Eye	The Spectator
...	37.3	...	...
4.4	34.0	...	15.7
5.9	24.3	226.5	19.3
8.0	...	197.6	25.6
11.0	19.1	186.1	51.5
11.3	16.2	191.8	54.6

Television

Viewing trends
Daily hours of viewing per household

	Total hours	ITV	BBC1	BBC2	C4	Satellite
1969	4.5	2.4	2.1	...	...	...
1972	4.8	2.7	1.9	0.3	...	...
1976	5.1	2.7	2.1	0.4	...	...
1980	5.1	2.5	2.0	0.6	...	...
1982	4.9	2.4	1.9	0.6	...	...
1986	5.3	2.4	1.9	0.6	0.5	...
1990	5.1	2.3	1.9	0.5	0.5	...
1994	6.0	2.3	1.9	0.7	0.7	0.4

Box-watching hours
Monthly average daily hours of viewing per person, 1994

	BBC1	BBC2	ITV	C4	Satellite	Total
January	1.19	0.23	1.38	0.26	0.14	4.01
February	1.19	0.29	1.31	0.27	0.16	4.01
March	1.14	0.20	1.29	0.25	0.16	3.45
April	1.08	0.24	1.25	0.22	0.15	3.34
May	1.04	0.20	1.22	0.22	0.14	3.23
June	1.01	0.24	1.17	0.20	0.13	3.15
July	0.59	0.20	1.13	0.20	0.12	3.05
August	1.02	0.23	1.12	0.22	0.14	3.14
September	1.09	0.20	1.23	0.22	0.14	3.29
October	1.09	0.20	1.29	0.23	0.14	3.37
November	1.15	0.23	1.31	0.23	0.16	3.49
December	1.20	0.26	1.32	0.24	0.17	3.59
Average	1.10	0.26	1.25	0.23	0.15	3.36

Channel ratings
% average monthly share of audience, 1995

	BBC1	BBC2	ITV	C4	Satellite
January	32	11	39	11	8
February	32	11	37	12	8
March	33	11	37	12	8
April	31	13	36	12	8
May	33	11	36	12	9
June	30	12	38	12	8
July	31	14	35	12	9
August	31	12	35	13	10
September	31	11	38	11	10
October	31	11	38	11	9
November	31	12	38	11	9
December	34	12	35	10	9

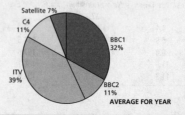

Satellite 7%
C4 11%
BBC1 32%
ITV 39%
BBC2 11%
AVERAGE FOR YEAR

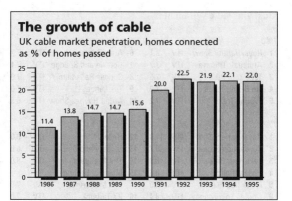

The growth of cable
UK cable market penetration, homes connected
as % of homes passed

Year	Value
1986	11.4
1987	13.8
1988	14.7
1989	14.7
1990	15.6
1991	20.0
1992	22.5
1993	21.9
1994	22.1
1995	22.0

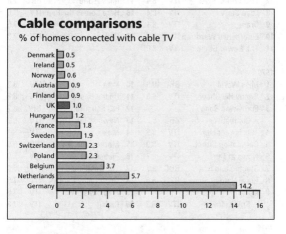

Cable comparisons
% of homes connected with cable TV

Denmark	0.5
Ireland	0.5
Norway	0.6
Austria	0.9
Finland	0.9
UK	1.0
Hungary	1.2
France	1.8
Sweden	1.9
Switzerland	2.3
Poland	2.3
Belgium	3.7
Netherlands	5.7
Germany	14.2

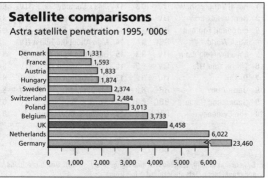

Satellite comparisons
Astra satellite penetration 1995, '000s

Denmark	1,331
France	1,593
Austria	1,833
Hungary	1,874
Sweden	2,374
Switzerland	2,484
Poland	3,013
Belgium	3,733
UK	4,458
Netherlands	6,022
Germany	23,460

Television: top programmes

Most viewed programmes[a]

m

1960

1	Royal Variety Show	ITV	8.1
2	Armchair Theatre	ITV	7.7
3	Take Your Pick	ITV	7.5
4	No Hiding Place	ITV	7.2
5	Wagon Train	ITV	7.2
6	Army Game	ITV	7.2
7	Bootsie and Snudge	ITV	7.1
8	Sunday Palladium	ITV	7.0
9	The Larkins	ITV	7.0
10	Arthur Haynes Show	ITV	6.9

1965

1	Royal Variety Show	ITV	11.0
2	Coronation Street	ITV	9.7
3	Take Your Pick	ITV	8.8
4	Riviera Police	ITV	8.6
5	No Hiding Place	ITV	8.5
6	Double Your Money	ITV	8.4
7	This Week	ITV	8.4
8	Love Story	ITV	8.4
9	Crane	ITV	8.1
10	Emergency Ward Ten	ITV	8.0
11	The Power Game	ITV	8.0
12	Hello Dolly	ITV	8.0
13	Steptoe and Son	BBC	8.0
14	The Avengers	ITV	8.0
15	Music of Lennon & McCartney	ITV	7.9
16	It's Tarbuck	ITV	7.8
17	Miss World	BBC	7.8
18	Here Comes the Pops	ITV	7.6
19	Blackmail	ITV	7.6
20	Professional Boxing	ITV	7.3

1970

1	Miss World	BBC	10.6
2	Benny Hill Show	ITV	9.3
3	Eurovision Song Contest	BBC	9.2
4	This is Your Life	ITV	8.9
5	Coronation Street	ITV	8.9
6	News at Ten	ITV	8.7
7	Steptoe and Son	BBC	8.7
8	Royal Variety Show	BBC	8.5
9	Apollo 13 Splashdown	ITV	8.3
10	Kate	ITV	8.2
11	On the Buses	ITV	8.2
12	633 Squadron	BBC	8.2
13	News at Ten	ITV	8.2
14	Max	ITV	8.1
15	Morecambe & Wise	BBC	8.0
16	Please Sir!	ITV	8.0
17	The Dustbinmen	ITV	8.0
18	Opportunity Knocks	ITV	7.9
19	A Family at War	ITV	7.9
20	Callan	ITV	7.8

1975

1	Royal Variety Show	ITV	10.3
2	Benny Hill Show	ITV	9.5
3	European Football	BBC	9.4
4	Miss World	BBC	9.4
5	Love thy Neighbour	ITV	9.3
6	This is Your Life	ITV	9.3
7	Dr No	ITV	9.2
8	Dad's Army	BBC	8.9
9	Generation Game	BBC	8.9
10	The Sweeney	ITV	8.8
11	Cilla's Comedy Six	ITV	8.8
12	Coronation Street	ITV	8.8
13	Edward the Seventh	ITV	8.8
14	Man About the House	ITV	8.8
15	Bless this House	ITV	8.7
16	Tommy Cooper Hour	ITV	8.4
17	The Two Ronnies	BBC	8.4
18	My Old Man	ITV	8.3
19	News at Ten	ITV	8.3
20	Upstairs, Downstairs	ITV	8.3

a Soap operas are only featured with their highest entry in the 20. Omnibus editions and repeat broadcasts are included in this fiigure

1980

1	Live and Let Die	ITV	23.5	11	Morecambe & Wise	ITV	18.7
2	To the Manor Born	BBC	21.6	12	The Two Ronnies	BBC	18.6
3	Dallas	BBC	20.3	13	Paint Your Wagon	ITV	18.5
4	This is Your Life	ITV	19.8	14	Robin's Nest	ITV	18.4
5	My Wife Next Door	ITV	19.3	15	Generation Game	BBC	18.3
6	Jim'll Fix It	BBC	19.2	16	Benny Hill Show	ITV	18.1
7	Blankety Blank	BBC	19.1	17	Dick Emery Show	ITV	18.1
8	Coronation Street	ITV	19.0	18	Keep it in the Family	ITV	18.1
9	Dick Emery Show	BBC	18.9	19	Little and Large	ITV	18.1
10	All Creatures Great and Small	BBC	18.7	20	George and Mildred	ITV	17.8

1985

1	EastEnders	BBC	23.6	11	Hollywood Wives	ITV	18.0
2	Coronation Street	ITV	21.4	12	Boxing	ITV	18.0
3	Wish You Were Here	ITV	19.0	13	Night of 100 Stars	ITV	17.7
4	Open All Hours	BBC	19.0	14	Game for a Laugh	ITV	17.6
5	Last of the Summer Wine	ITV	18.8	15	Superman II	ITV	17.6
6	Prince and Princess of Wales	ITV	18.6	16	Fresh Fields	ITV	17.5
				17	Dr No	ITV	17.5
7	It'll Be Alright on the Night	ITV	18.6	18	From Russia with Love	ITV	17.3
8	The Two Ronnies	BBC	18.5	19	Goldfinger	ITV	17.0
9	That's Life	BBC	18.4	20	Only Fools and Horses	ITV	16.9
10	Crossroads	ITV	18.1				

1990

1	Coronation Street	ITV	22.8	10	News and Weather	BBC	16.6
2	EastEnders	BBC	20.8	11	Inspector Morse	ITV	16.2
3	Neighbours	BBC	20.6	12	Octopussy	ITV	15.9
4	Only Fools and Horses	BBC	18.0	13	Blind Date	ITV	15.8
				14	Wish You Were Here	ITV	15.8
5	It'll Be Alright on the Night	ITV	17.9	15	This is Your Life	ITV	15.7
6	E.T.	BBC	17.5	16	The Bill	ITV	15.3
7	A View to a Kill	ITV	16.9	17	For Your Eyes Only	ITV	15.2
8	Generation Game	BBC	16.7	18	Watching	ITV	14.8
9	World Cup (W. Germany v England)	BBC	16.7	19	Strike it Lucky	ITV	14.6
				20	Bergerac	BBC	14.2

1995

1	Panorama Special	BBC	22.8	7	EastEnders	BBC	17.0
2	Coronation Street	ITV	19.4	8	Casualty	BBC	16.8
3	Heartbeat	ITV	18.7	9	Keeping Up Appearances	BBC	16.7
4	National Lottery Live	BBC	18.2				
5	Auntie's Bloomers	BBC	17.8	10	News and Weather (Christmas)	BBC	16.7
6	One Foot in the Grave (Christmas)	BBC	17.8				

Video

The rise and peaks of video

	Video tapes			Video hardware	
	Consumer sales		Rental market		
				VCR sales	Penetration
	Units sold, m	Value, £m	Value, £m	m	% of households
1986	6	55	367	…	…
1987	12	110	420	…	…
1988	20	184	478	2.4	64.1
1989	38	345	569	2.3	68.0
1990	40	374	564	2.2	71.1
1991	45	440	544	2.2	73.6
1992	48	506	511	2.2	75.8
1993	60	643	457	2.4	77.7
1994	66	698	438	2.5	79.4
1995	73	789	457	2.6	81.5

Top 20

1995, all genres

1. The Lion King
2. Riverdance – The Show
3. The Aristocats
4. The Fox and the Hound
5. Four Weddings and a Funeral
6. Pinocchio
7. Coronation Street Special
8. Batman Forever
9. The Mask
10. Star Wars
11. The Return of Jafar
12. Pulp Fiction
13. Robson and Jerome – So Far So Good
14. Return of the Jedi
15. Power Rangers – The Movie
16. The Empire Strikes Back
17. Bottom Live – The Big No. 2 Tour
18. Miracle on 34th Street
19. Roy Chubby Brown – Clitoris Allsorts
20. Forrest Gump

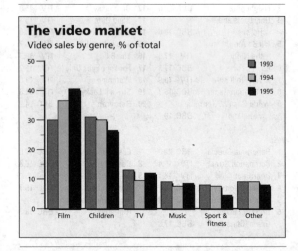

The video market

Video sales by genre, % of total

Music sales

The domestic market

UK sales, '000s

	Singles	LPs	Tapes	CDs	Retail value $m
1972	46.2	59.3	8.1	...	258
1973	54.6	81.0	15.5	...	379
1974	62.7	89.5	20.2	...	486
1975	56.9	91.6	20.2	...	531
1976	56.9	83.8	18.2	...	459
1977	62.1	81.7	19.6	...	475
1978	88.8	86.1	21.2	...	680
1979	89.1	74.5	23.6	...	845
1980	77.9	67.4	25.2	...	1022
1981	77.4	64.0	28.7	...	867
1982	78.6	57.8	31.5	...	809
1983	74.0	54.3	35.8	0.3	745
1984	77.0	54.1	45.3	0.8	734
1985	73.8	52.9	55.4	3.1	862
1986	67.4	52.3	69.6	8.4	1,089
1987	63.4	52.2	74.4	18.2	1,499
1988	60.1	50.2	80.9	29.2	1,973
1989	61.1	37.9	83.0	41.7	1,981
1990	58.9	24.7	75.1	50.9	2,118
1991	56.3	12.9	66.8	62.8	2,155
1992	52.9	6.7	56.4	70.5	1,998
1993	56.3	5.0	55.7	92.9	1,976
1994	63.0	4.5	56.0	116.4	2,366
1995	70.7	3.6	53.4	139.2	2,572

World music sales

	Sales, $m			1995 % share
	1973	1983	1995	
UK	379	745	2,572	6.5
USA	2,001	3,814	12,102	30.5
Japan	700	1,322	7,552	19.0
Germany[b]	430	897	3,270	8.2
France	314	669	2,392	6.0

b Western.

Cinema and theatre

New British films

	Titles produced	Production cost, £m 1994 prices	Average budget, £m 1994 prices
1981	24	119.2	5.0
1982	40	253.4	6.3
1983	51	431.4	8.5
1984	53	438.5	8.3
1985	54	415.5	7.7
1986	41	247.4	6.0
1987	55	279.0	5.1
1988	48	241.0	5.0
1989	30	132.5	4.4
1990	60	248.0	4.1
1991	59	260.3	4.4
1992	47	190.4	4.1
1993	69	230.8	3.3
1994	84	458.7	5.5

Cinema visits: a British revival
Millions

	1983	1988	1994
UK	66	84	124
France	191[a]	125	126
Germany	125	109	133
Italy	162	93	98
Japan	170	145	123
USA	1,197	1,085	1,290
EU	659	559	663

Average no. of admissions per head of population

	1983	1988	1994
UK	1.2	1.5	2.1
France	…	2.2	2.2
Germany	2.0	2.2	2.2
Italy	2.9	1.6	1.7
Japan	1.4	1.2	1.0
USA	5.1	4.4	5.0
EU	2.3	1.7	1.9

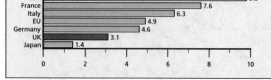

Screen comparisons
No. of screens per 100,000 pop., 1994 or latest available year

USA	9.8
France	7.6
Italy	6.3
EU	4.9
Germany	4.6
UK	3.1
Japan	1.4

a 1984.

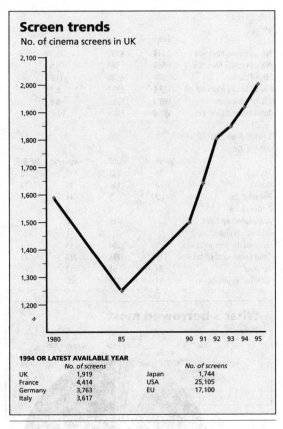

Screen trends
No. of cinema screens in UK

1994 OR LATEST AVAILABLE YEAR

	No. of screens		No. of screens
UK	1,919	Japan	1,744
France	4,414	USA	25,105
Germany	3,763	EU	17,100
Italy	3,617		

London theatres

	Paid attendances in West End theatres, m	Gross box office revenue, £m 1994 prices	No. of productions opening
1983	8.9	112.8	201
1984	10.0	135.9	203
1985	10.8	156.7	256
1986	10.2	165.1	213
1987	10.9	183.2	212
1988	10.9	187.7	228
1989	10.9	191.7	237
1990	11.3	203.2	187
1991	10.9	201.6	192
1992	10.9	202.7	193
1993	11.5	220.8	198
1994	11.2	217.8	208

Books

Libraries
UK

	1975[a]	1993–94	% change
No. of public libraries	3,714	4,499	21.1
No. of mobile libraries	655	692	5.6
No. of staff	30,988	27,320	-11.8
No. of books stocked, *m*	123.4	131.7	6.7
No. of issues, *m*	589.3	550.6	-6.6
Total expenditure, £m	161.4	740.6	10.8[b]

Library expenditure
1992–3, £m

	National	Public	University	HE & FE[c]
Staff	51	383	112	43
Books	10	110	31	13
Periodicals	3	6	41	6
Audio-visual	...	9	3	...
Automated systems	...	16	10	...
On-line services	...	...	1	...
Overheads, premises etc.	...	254	15	...
Total gross expenditure	115	778	213	71
Income	23	51	11	...
Total net expenditure	92	727	202	...

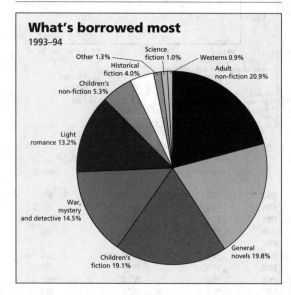

What's borrowed most
1993–94

- Other 1.3%
- Science fiction 1.0%
- Westerns 0.9%
- Historical fiction 4.0%
- Adult non-fiction 20.9%
- Children's non-fiction 5.3%
- Light romance 13.2%
- War, mystery and detective 14.5%
- Children's fiction 19.1%
- General novels 19.8%

a Data for 1975 may be greater than listed due to low response rates from Scotland and Northern Ireland.
b In real terms.
c Higher education and further education.

What is published
Titles published in the UK

	All titles		Average price, £	No. of paperbacks
	1989	1994	1994	1994
Children's books	6,255	7,072	5.44	3,589
School text-books	1,794	2,752	14.39	2,165
Adult fiction	7,321	8,704	8.73	5,392
Adult non-fiction	16,094	23,973	19.27	15,468
Scientific, technical, medical	11,720	17,498	40.32	8,706
Academic/professional books	19,146	29,739	28.56	16,278

Market sectors
Spending, 1993, £m

	Paperback	Hardback	Total
Fiction			
General novels	90	110	190
Crime/thriller/western	75	20	95
Romance	75	20	95
Other	45	25	80
Children's books	105	155	260
Non-fiction			
School text-books	110	105	215
Scientific, technical & medical	175	150	325
Academic & professional	105	200	305
Reference	50	235	285
Arts	115	220	335
Leisure interests	125	270	395
Other	45	75	120
Total	1,115	1,585	2,700

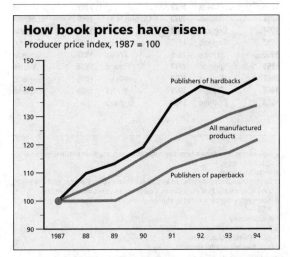

How book prices have risen
Producer price index, 1987 = 100

Publishers of hardbacks

All manufactured products

Publishers of paperbacks

Sport

Attendances

	Soccer[a]			Cricket[c]		Tennis	Golf[d]
	England	Scotland[b]		Test	County	Wimbledon	Open
	m	m		'000s	'000s	'000s	'000s
1960/61	28.6	...	**1965**	...	...	277[e]	33
1965/66	27.2	4.1	**1970**	...	...	284	73
1970/71	28.2	4.2	**1975**	...	...	339	76
1975/76	24.9	3.7	**1980**	...	...	334	132
1980/81	21.9	2.9	**1985**	372.2	296.8	395	142
1985/86	16.5	3.2	**1986**	285.2	328.1	400	134
1986/87	17.4	4.0	**1987**	234.6	313.8	396	139
1987/88	18.0	4.6	**1988**	245.8	304.7	411	207
1988/89	18.5	4.1	**1989**	343.0	369.6	400	161
1989/90	19.5	3.9	**1990**	269.2	332.4	348	209
1990/91	19.5	3.8	**1991**	316.8	363.3	378	192
1991/92	20.5	3.8	**1992**	306.7	298.7	373	150
1992/93	20.7	4.1	**1993**	370.7	306.3	393	124
1993/94	21.7	4.4	**1994**	391.3	366.2	384	135[f]
1994/95	21.9	3.7	**1995**	426.0	370.3	385	180

Rugby

International Championship winners

1947	Wales/England	**1964**	Scotland/Wales	**1981**	France
1948	Ireland	**1965**	Wales	**1982**	Ireland
1949	Ireland	**1966**	Wales	**1983**	France/Ireland
1950	Wales	**1967**	France	**1984**	Scotland
1951	Ireland	**1968**	France	**1985**	Ireland
1952	Wales	**1969**	Wales	**1986**	France/Scotland
1953	England	**1970**	France	**1987**	France
1954	Eng/France/Wales	**1971**	Wales	**1988**	Wales/France
1955	France/Wales	**1972**	[g]	**1989**	France
1956	Wales	**1973**	Quintuple tie	**1990**	Scotland
1957	England	**1974**	Ireland	**1991**	England
1958	England	**1975**	Wales	**1992**	England
1959	France	**1976**	Wales	**1993**	France
1960	France/England	**1977**	France	**1994**	Wales
1961	France	**1978**	Wales	**1995**	England
1962	France	**1979**	Wales	**1996**	England
1963	England	**1980**	England		

---

a Figures may have been affected by changes to league system and introduction of Premier League.

b Includes cup ties.

c Cricket attendances are affected by play at different venues and are totals for all days in all tests or fiirst class games. County fiiures do not include members.

d Golf fiigures may be affected by change of venue for each Open Championship.

e 1966.

f Approximately.

g Fixtures uncompleted.

h Year in which season ended.

i Cups now named after sponsors.

Cricket

County Championship winners

1951	Warwickshire	1966	Yorkshire	1981	Nottinghamshire
1952	Surrey	1967	Yorkshire	1982	Middlesex
1953	Surrey	1968	Yorkshire	1983	Essex
1954	Surrey	1969	Glamorgan	1984	Essex
1955	Surrey	1970	Kent	1985	Middlesex
1956	Surrey	1971	Surrey	1986	Essex
1957	Surrey	1972	Warwickshire	1987	Nottinghamshire
1958	Surrey	1973	Hampshire	1988	Worcestershire
1959	Yorkshire	1974	Worcestershire	1989	Worcestershire
1960	Yorkshire	1975	Leicestershire	1990	Middlesex
1961	Hampshire	1976	Middlesex	1991	Essex
1962	Yorkshire	1977	Middx/Kent	1992	Essex
1963	Yorkshire	1978	Kent	1993	Middlesex
1964	Worcestershire	1979	Essex	1994	Warwickshire
1965	Worcestershire	1980	Middlesex	1995	Warwickshire

Football

	League champions [h]	F.A. Cup winners [i]	League Cup winners [j]
1966	Liverpool	Everton	W. Bromwich Albion
1967	Manchester United	Tottenham Hotspur	Queens Park Rangers
1968	Manchester City	W. Bromwich Albion	Leeds United
1969	Leeds United	Manchester City	Swindon Town
1970	Everton	Chelsea	Manchester City
1971	Arsenal	Arsenal	Tottenham Hotspur
1972	Derby County	Leeds United	Stoke City
1973	Liverpool	Sunderland	Tottenham Hotspur
1974	Leeds United	Liverpool	Wolves
1975	Derby County	West Ham United	Aston Villa
1976	Liverpool	Southampton	Manchester City
1977	Liverpool	Manchester United	Aston Villa
1978	Nottingham Forest	Ipswich Town	Nottingham Forest
1979	Liverpool	Arsenal	Nottingham Forest
1980	Liverpool	West Ham United	Wolves
1981	Aston Villa	Tottenham Hotspur	Liverpool
1982	Liverpool	Tottenham Hotspur	Liverpool
1983	Liverpool	Manchester United	Liverpool
1984	Liverpool	Everton	Liverpool
1985	Everton	Manchester United	Norwich City
1986	Liverpool	Liverpool	Oxford United
1987	Everton	Coventry City	Arsenal
1988	Liverpool	Wimbledon	Luton Town
1989	Arsenal	Liverpool	Nottingham Forest
1990	Liverpool	Manchester United	Nottingham Forest
1991	Arsenal	Tottenham Hotspur	Sheffield Wednesday
1992	Leeds United	Liverpool	Manchester United
1993	Manchester United	Arsenal	Arsenal
1994	Manchester United	Manchester United	Aston Villa
1995	Blackburn Rovers	Everton	Liverpool
1996	Manchester United	Manchester United	Aston Villa

Holidays and outings

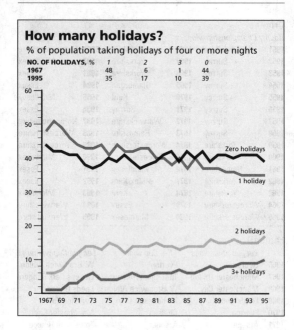

How many holidays?

% of population taking holidays of four or more nights

NO. OF HOLIDAYS, %	1	2	3	0
1967	48	6	1	44
1995	35	17	10	39

Zero holidays
1 holiday
2 holidays
3+ holidays

1967 69 71 73 75 77 79 81 83 85 87 89 91 93 95

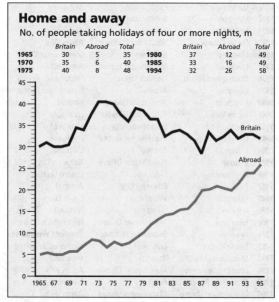

Home and away

No. of people taking holidays of four or more nights, m

	Britain	Abroad	Total		Britain	Abroad	Total
1965	30	5	35	**1980**	37	12	49
1970	35	6	40	**1985**	33	16	49
1975	40	8	48	**1994**	32	26	58

Britain
Abroad

1965 67 69 71 73 75 77 79 81 83 85 87 89 91 93 95

Heritage appeal

Historic properties and monuments, no. of paid admissions in England

1990			1994		
1	Tower of London	2,296,683	1	St Paul's Cathedral, London	2,600,000
2	Roman Baths and Pump Room, Bath	950,472	2	Tower of London	2,407,115
3	State Apartments, Windsor Castle	855,239	3	Windsor Castle[a]	1,090,668
4	Stonehenge, Wiltshire	703,221	4	Roman Baths and Pump Room, Bath	871,308
5	Warwick Castle	685,000	5	Warwick Castle	755,670
6	Shakespeare's birthplace, Stratford	603,899	6	Stonehenge, Wiltshire	696,605
7	Leeds Castle, Kent	540,483	7	Shakespeare's birthplace, Stratford	591,205
8	Tower Bridge, London	527,766	8	Hampton Court Palace	543,061
9	Hampton Court Palace	520,995	9	Leeds Castle, Kent	537,965
10	Blenheim Palace, Woodstock	511,630	10	Blenheim Palace, Woodstock	449,755
11	Beaulieu, Hampshire	493,216	11	Beaulieu, Hampshire	421,093
12	Chatsworth House, Derbyshire	421,663	12	Buckingham Palace, London	420,000
13	The Cutty Sark, Greenwich	411,000	13	Chatsworth House, Derbyshire	402,573
14	St George's Chapel, Windsor	372,068	14	Tower Bridge, London	400,506
15	Anne Hathaway's Cottage, Shottery	365,286	15	HMS Victory, Portsmouth	370,077
16	HMS Victory, Portsmouth	340,000	16	Royal Pavilion, Brighton	357,942
17	The Mary Rose, Portsmouth	333,126	17	Anne Hathaway's Cottage, Shottery	326,792
18	Royal Pavilion, Brighton	314,443	18	Dover Castle, Kent	296,289
19	Hever Castle, Kent	303,094	19	Fountains Abbey, North Yorkshire	290,606
20	Fountains Abbey, North Yorkshire	300,067	20	Harewood House, West Yorkshire	259,014
21	Dover Castle, Kent	271,978	21	Hever Castle, Kent	258,356
22	Castle Howard, North Yorkshire	222,876	22	Cabinet War Rooms, London	251,931
23	Christ Church College, Oxford	220,000	23	Christ Church College, Oxford	250,000
24	St Michael's Mount, Marazion	194,793	24	The Cutty Sark, Greenwich	248,000
25	Polesden Lacey, Surrey	192,738	25	Polesden Lacey, Surrey	195,935
26	Quarry Bank Mill, Styal	187,841	26	St Mary's Mount	187,680
			27	Quarry Bank Mill, Styal	184,542
			28	Buckler's Hard, Beaulieu	180,000
			27	Queen Mary's Dolls House	158,096

a Windsor Castle not split.

National Lottery

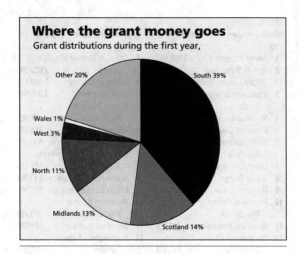

Where the grant money goes
Grant distributions during the first year,

- South 39%
- Scotland 14%
- Midlands 13%
- North 11%
- West 3%
- Wales 1%
- Other 20%

Regional breakdown of grants

	Charities		Non-charities		Grand total	
	£000	%	£000	%	£000	%
All England	59,371	9.36	50,462	7.96	109,833	17.32
Wales	107	0.02	5,099	0.80	5,206	0.82
Scotland	35,819	5.65	50,286	7.93	86,105	13.58
Northern Ireland	5,505	0.87	120	0.02	5,625	0.89
North East	2,365	0.37	13,818	2.18	16,183	2.55
Yorkshire & Humb	5,130	0.81	5,999	0.95	11,129	1.76
North West	25,857	4.08	15,988	2.52	41,845	6.60
West Midlands	38,726	6.11	14,691	2.32	53,417	8.42
East Midlands	5,244	0.83	7,576	1.19	12,820	2.02
East Anglia	8,599	1.36	5,291	0.83	13,890	2.19
N Home Counties	4,482	0.71	8,539	1.35	13,021	2.05
South East	3,721	0.59	5,708	0.90	9,429	1.49
London	120,393	18.99	52,572	8.29	172,965	27.28
South West	5,821	0.92	7,539	1.19	13,360	2.11
South of England	6,846	1.08	48,972	7.72	55,818	8.80
Unallocated	87	0.01	13,363	2.11	13,450	2.12
Total	328,073	51.74	306,023	48.26	634,096	100.00

General elections

Votes and seats since 1955

	1955	1959	1964
Conservative			
Votes recorded, '000	13,311	13,763	12,002
Share of vote, %	49.7	49.4	43.4
Seats	345	366	304
Labour			
Votes recorded, '000	12,418	12,216	12,206
Share of vote, %	46.4	43.8	44.1
Seats	277	258	317
Liberal Democrat			
Votes recorded, '000	722	1,643	3,099
Share of vote, %	2.7	5.9	11.2
Seats	6	6	9
Others			
Votes recorded, '000	309	241	349
Share of vote, %	1.2	0.9	1.3
Seats	2	0	0
Total electorate	**34,852**	**35,397**	**35,894**

	1979	1983	1987
Conservative			
Votes recorded, '000	13,698	13,013	13,736
Share of vote	43.9	42.4	42.2
Seats	339	397	375
Labour			
Votes recorded, '000	11,510	8,461	10,030
Share of vote	37.0	27.6	30.8
Seats	268	209	229
Liberal Democrat			
Votes recorded, '000	4,314	7,776	7,341
Share of vote	13.8	25.4	22.6
Seats	11	23	22
Others			
Votes recorded, '000	1,700	1,420	1,422
Share of vote	5.3	4.6	4.4
Seats	17	21	24
Total electorate	**41,573**	**42,704**	**43,666**

	1966	1970	Feb 1974	Oct 1974
	11,418	13,174	11,929	10,429
	41.9	46.4	38.1	35.8
	253	330	296	276
	13,066	12,186	11,661	11,407
	47.9	43.0	37.2	39.2
	363	287	301	319
	2,328	2,124	6,057	5,347
	8.5	7.5	19.3	18.3
	12	6	14	13
	453	875	1,695	2,008
	1.7	3.1	5.4	6.7
	2	7	24	27
	35,957	**39,615**	**40,256**	**40,256**

1992

14,093
41.9
336

11,560
34.4
271

5,999
17.8
20

1,961
5.8
24

43,719

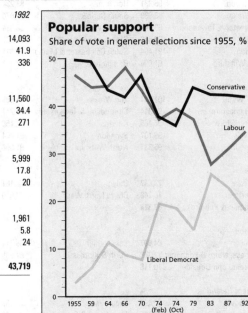

Popular support
Share of vote in general elections since 1955, %

Conservative

Labour

Liberal Democrat

1955 59 64 66 70 74 (Feb) 74 (Oct) 79 83 87 92

Parliamentary constituencies

How many electors?

Parliamentary electors, m

	UK	England	Wales	Scotland	N. Ireland
1984	42.99	35.80	2.15	3.96	1.08
1985	43.13	35.94	2.14	3.97	1.08
1986	43.39	36.16	2.16	3.99	1.09
1987	43.66	36.39	2.18	3.99	1.10
1988	43.71	36.45	2.18	3.97	1.11
1989	43.61	36.36	2.19	3.93	1.12
1990	43.67	36.39	2.21	3.94	1.13
1991	43.55	36.30	2.21	3.91	1.13
1992	43.73	36.44	2.22	3.93	1.14
1993	43.72	36.41	2.22	3.93	1.15
1994	43.79	36.46	2.22	3.95	1.16
1995	43.90	36.54	2.22	3.96	1.17

Biggest constituencies

No. of parliamentary electors, 1995

UK

Isle of Wight	101,391	Ryedale	90,861
East Hampshire	96,314	Westbury	89,111
East Berkshire	96,185	North Colchester	88,725
Eastleigh	96,107	Wokingham	88,248
Huntingdon	95,331	Horsham	88,234
The Wrekin	93,989	South Suffolk	88,070
Cirencester & Tewkesbury	93,241	Dudley West	88,034
Devizes	92,456	Grantham	87,927
Swindon	91,404	South Colchester & Maldon	87,811
North Wiltshire	91,096	Bridlington	87,421

England

Isle of Wight	101,391	The Wrekin	93,989
East Hampshire	96,314	Cirencester & Tewkesbury	93,241
East Berkshire	96,185	Devizes	92,456
Eastleigh	96,107	Swindon	91,404
Huntingdon	95,331	North Wiltshire	91,096

Wales

Pembroke	73,847	Delyn	68,161
Carmarthen	70,248	Clwyd North West	67,919
Ceredigion & Pembroke N	68,318		

Scotland

Gordon	84,897	East Lothian	68,714
Inverness, Nairn & Lochaber	72,378	Perth & Kinross	67,985
Kincardine and Deeside	70,116		

Northern Ireland

South Down	80,496	Lagan Valley	77,138
East Londonderry	80,025	Fermanagh & South Tyrone	73,468
Foyle	79,846		

How average are they?

Parliamentary constituencies as % of average electorate, 1995

	England	Wales	Scotland	N. Ireland
Less than 50%	0	0	1	0
50 but less than 60%	0	1	2	0
60 but less than 70%	8	0	1	0
70 but less than 80%	45	1	2	4
80 but less than 90%	84	6	12	0
90 but less than 100%	114	9	15	1
100 but less than 110%	137	11	17	8
110 but less than 120%	90	8	14	4
120 but less than 130%	35	2	6	0
130 but less than 140%	10	0	1	0
140 but less than 150%	1	0	0	0
150 but less than 160%	0	0	1	0
Total	524	38	72	17
Average electorate	69,742	58,429	55,022	68,790

Smallest constituencies

No. of parliamentary electors, 1995

UK

Western Isles	23,304	Newham North West	42,422
Caithness & Sutherland	31,298	Montgomery	42,718
Meirionnydd Nant Conwy	32,391	Roxburgh & Berwickshire	44,163
Orkney & Shetland	32,411	Glasgow, Cathcart	44,277
Glasgow, Provan	34,525	Glasgow, Govan	45,059
Tweeddale, Ettrick &L'dale	40,881	Surbiton	45,104
Glasgow, Garscadden	41,310	Glasgow, Pollok	45,223

England

Newham North West	42,422	Knowsley North	47,961
Surbiton	45,104	Chelsea	48,142
Greenwich	45,637	Walthamstow	48,804
Kensington	46,655	Liverpool, Riverside	49,158
Coventry South East	47,431	Hammersmith	49,548

Wales

Meirionnydd Nant Conwy	32,391	Cynon Valley	49,330
Montgomery	42,718	Aberavon	51,224
Caernarfon	47,012		

Scotland

Western Isles	23,304	Glasgow, Provan	34,525
Caithness and Sutherland	31,298	Tweeddale, Ettrick & L'dale	40,881
Orkney and Shetland	32,411		

Northern Ireland

Belfast South	51,547	Belfast West	54,260
Belfast East	42,278	East Antrim	65,407
Belfast North	53,930		

Ministers

Prime ministers

Sir Robert Walpole	Apr 1721	Earl of Derby	Jun 1866
Earl of Wilmington	Feb 1741	Benjamin Disraeli	Feb 1868
Henry Pelham	Aug 1743	William Ewart Gladstone	Dec 1868
Duke of Newcastle	Mar 1754	Benjamin Disraeli	Feb 1874
Duke of Devonshire	Nov 1756	William Ewart Gladstone	Apr 1880
Duke of Newcastle	Jul 1757	Marquess of Salisbury	Jun 1885
Earl of Bute	May 1762	William Ewart Gladstone	Feb 1886
George Grenville	Apr 1763	Marquess of Salisbury	Jul 1886
Marquess of Rockingham	Jul 1765	William Ewart Gladstone	Aug 1892
Earl of Chatham	Jul 1766	Earl of Rosebery	Mar 1894
Duke of Grafton	Oct 1768	Marquess of Salisbury	Jun 1895
Lord North	Jan 1770	Arthur James Balfour	Jul 1902
Marquess of Rockingham	Mar 1782	Sir Henry Campbell-Bannerman	
Earl of Shelburne	Jul 1782		Dec 1905
Duke of Portland	Apr 1783	Herbert Henry Asquith	Apr 1908
William Pitt	Dec 1783	David Lloyd George	Dec 1916
Henry Addington	Mar 1801	Andrew Bonar Law	Oct 1922
William Pitt	May 1804	Stanley Baldwin	May 1923
Lord Grenville	Feb 1806	James Ramsay MacDonald	
Duke of Portland	Mar 1807		Jan 1924
Spencer Perceval	Oct 1809	Stanley Baldwin	Nov 1924
Earl of Liverpool	Jun 1812	James Ramsay MacDonald	
George Canning	Apr 1827		Jun 1929
Viscount Goderich	Aug 1827	Stanley Baldwin	Jun 1935
Duke of Wellington	Jan 1828	Neville Chamberlain	May 1937
Earl Grey	Nov 1830	Winston Churchill	May 1940
Viscount Melbourne	Jul 1834	Clement Attlee	Jul 1945
Duke of Wellington	Nov 1834	Winston Churchill	Oct 1951
Sir Robert Peel	Dec 1834	Sir Anthony Eden	Apr 1955
Viscount Melbourne	Apr 1835	Harold Macmillan	Jan 1957
Sir Robert Peel	Aug 1841	Sir Alec Douglas-Home	Oct 1963
Lord John Russell	Jun 1846	Harold Wilson	Oct 1964
Earl of Derby	Feb 1852	Edward Heath	Jun 1970
Earl of Aberdeen	Dec 1852	Harold Wilson	Feb 1974
Viscount Palmerston	Feb 1855	James Callaghan	Apr 1976
Earl of Derby	Feb 1858	Margaret Thatcher	May 1979
Viscount Palmerston	Jun 1859	John Major	Nov 1990
Earl Russell	Oct 1865		

Chancellors of the Exchequer

Sir M. Hicks-Beach	1900	S. Baldwin	Oct 1922
Marquess of Lansdowne	Nov 1900	N. Chamberlain	Aug 1923
C. Ritchie	Aug 1902	P. Snowden	Jan 1924
A. Chamberlain	Oct 1903	W. Churchill	Nov 1924
H. Asquith	Dec 1905	P. Snowden	Jun 1929
D. Lloyd-George	Apr 1908	N. Chamberlain	Nov 1931
R. McKenna	May 1915	Sir J. Simon	May 1937
A. Bonar Law	Dec 1916	Sir K. Wood	May 1940
A. Chamberlain	Jan 1919	Sir J. Anderson	Sep 1943
Sir R. Horne	Apr 1921	H. Dalton	Jul 1945

Sir S. Cripps	Nov 1947	R. Jenkins	Nov 1967
H. Gaitskell	Oct 1950	I. Macleod	Jun 1970
R. Butler	Oct 1951	A. Barber	Jul 1970
H. Macmillan	Dec 1955	D. Healey	Mar 1974
P. Thorneycroft	Jan 1957	Sir G. Howe	May 1979
D. Heathcoat Amory	Jan 1958	N. Lawson	Jun 1983
S. Lloyd	Jul 1960	J. Major	Oct 1989
R. Maudling	Jul 1962	N. Lamont	Nov 1990
J. Callaghan	Oct 1964	K. Clarke	May 1993

Foreign ministers

Marquess of Salisbury (3rd)	1900	S. Lloyd	Dec 1955
Sir E. Grey (Vt)	Dec 1905	Earl of Home	Jul 1960
A. Balfour	Dec 1916	R. Butler	Oct 1963
Earl Curzon (M)	Oct 1919	P. Gordon Walker	Oct 1964
R. MacDonald	Jan 1924	M. Stewart	Jan 1965
(Sir) A. Chamberlain	Nov 1924	G. Brown	Aug 1966
A. Henderson	Jun 1929	M. Stewart	Mar 1968
Marquess of Reading	Aug 1931	Sir A. Douglas-Home	Jun 1970
Sir J. Simon	Nov 1931	J. Callaghan	Mar 1974
Sir S. Hoare	Jun 1935	A. Crosland	Apr 1976
A. Eden	Dec 1935	D. Owen	Feb 1977
Vt Halifax	Feb 1938	Lord Carrington	May 1979
A. Eden	Dec 1940	F. Pym	Apr 1982
E. Bevin	Jul 1945	Sir G. Howe	Jun 1983
H. Morrison	Mar 1951	J. Major	Jul 1989
(Sir) A. Eden	Oct 1951	D. Hurd	Oct 1989
H. Macmillan	Apr 1955	M. Rifkind	Jul 1995

Home ministers

Sir M. White-Ridley	1900	Sir D. Somervell	May 1945
C. Ritchie	Nov 1900	C. Ede	Aug 1945
A. Akers-Douglas	Aug 1902	Sir D. Maxwell-Fyfe	Oct 1951
H. Gladstone	Dec 1905	G. Lloyd-George	Oct 1954
W. Churchill	Feb 1910	R. Butler	Jan 1957
R. McKenna	Oct 1911	H. Brooke	Jul 1962
Sir J. Simon	May 1915	Sir F. Soskice	Oct 1964
Sir H. Samuel	Jan 1916	R. Jenkins	Dec 1965
Sir G. Cave (Vt)	Dec 1916	J. Callaghan	Nov 1967
E. Shortt	Jan 1919	R. Maudling	Jun 1970
W. Bridgeman	Oct 1922	R. Carr	Jul 1972
A. Henderson	Jan 1924	R. Jenkins	Mar 1974
Sir W. Joynson-Hicks	Nov 1924	M. Rees	Sep 1976
J. Clynes	Jun 1929	W. Whitelaw	May 1979
H. Samuel	Aug 1931	L. Brittan	Jun 1983
Sir J. Gilmour	Sep 1932	D. Hurd	Sep 1985
Sir J. Simon	Jun 1935	D. Waddington	Oct 1989
Sir S. Hoare	May 1937	K. Baker	Nov 1990
Sir J. Anderson	Sep 1939	K. Clarke	Apr 1992
H. Morrison	Oct 1940	M. Howard	May 1993

Monarchs

Kings and queens

Saxons and Danes	
Egbert	802
Ethelwulf	839
Ethelbald	855
Ethelbert	860
Ethelred	866
Alfred (the Great)	871
Edward I (the Elder)	899
Athelstan	925
Edmund I (the Magnificent)	939
Edred	946
Edwy	955
Edgar (the Peaceable)	959
Edward II (the Martyr)	975
Ethelred II (the Unready)[a]	978
Sweyn	1013
Edmund II (Ironside)[b]	1016
Canute	1016
Harold I[c]	1037
Hardicanute[c]	1040
Edward III (the Confessor)	1042
Harold II	1066
Edgar Atheling[d]	1066

House of Normandy	
William I	1066
William II	1087
Henry I	1100
Stephen	1135

House of Plantagenet	
Henry II	1154
Richard I	1189
John	1199
Henry III	1216
Edward I	1272
Edward II	1307
Edward III	1327
Richard II	1377

House of Lancaster	
Henry IV	1399
Henry V	1413
Henry VI	1422

House of York	
Edward IV	1461
Henry VI	1470
Edward IV	1471
Edward V	1483
Richard III	1483

House of Tudor	
Henry VII	1485
Henry VIII	1509
Edward VI	1547
Jane[e]	1553
Mary I	1553
Elizabeth I	1558

House of Stuart	
James I (VI of Scotland)	1603
Charles I	1625
Charles II	1649

Commonwealth[f]	1649

Charles II	1660
James II (VII of Scotland)	1685
William III and Mary II	1689
William III	1694
Anne	1702

House of Hanover	
George I	1714
George II	1727
George III	1760
George IV	1820
William IV	1830
Victoria	1837

House of Saxe-Coburg and Gotha	
Edward VII	1901

House of Windsor	
George V	1910
Edward VIII[g]	1936
George VI	1936
Elizabeth II	1952

a Restored (in Canute's absence) on Sweyn's death in 1014.
b Divided the kingdom with Canute for seven months.
c Ruled jointly 1035–37.
d October–December.
e 10–19 July.
f Oliver Cromwell, Lord Protector 1653–58; Richard Cromwell, Lord Protector 1658–59.
g January–December.

Sources

The land and the environment
Countryside Commission
Department of the Environment, *Digest of Environmental Protection and Water Statistics*
OECD, *Environmental Data*
ONS, *Regional Trends*
Whitaker's Almanac

Population
B.R. Mitchell, *British Historical Statistics*
ONS, *Annual Abstract of Statistics*
ONS, *Regional Trends*
OPCS
UNDP, *Human Development Report*

The economy
The Bank of England
Datastream
Dresdner Bank Statistical Survey
The Economist , *One Hundred Years of Economic Statistics*
GATT
IMF, *International Financial Statistics*
B.R. Mitchell, *British Historical Statistics*
OECD, *Economic Outlook; Main Economic Indicators; National Accounts*
ONS, *Economic Trends; Annual Abstract of Statistics; Regional Trends; The Pink Book; The Blue Book*
Times Newspapers Ltd, *The British Economy, Key Statistics 1900–1970*
UN Development Program, *Human Development Report*

Government finance
Bank of England
HM Treasury
Inland Revenue
B.R. Mitchell, *British Historical Statistics*
OECD, *Economic Outlook*

Labour
Department for Education and Employment
Crawford's Directory of City Connections
B.R. Mitchell, *British Historical Statistics*
TUC

Business and finance
The Banker
CBI
Datastream
Gallup
London Stock Exchange, *Stock Exchange Quarterly*

Morgan Stanley Capital International
National stockmarkets
ONS, *The Blue Book; Financial Statistics*
The Patent Office
The Times 1000

Tourism and transport
British Tourist Authority
Civil Aviation Authority
Department of Transport, *Road Accidents Great Britain; Transport Statistics Great Britain; Transport Statistics Report*
International Civil Aviation Organisation
International Road Federation, *World Road Statistics*
World Tourism Organisation

Housing
Building Societies Association
Census Reports
Council of Mortgage Lenders
Department for Education and Employment
Department of the Environment
Department of the Environment, Northern Ireland
Eurostat
Finance and Personnel Department of Northern Ireland
General Household Survey
General Register Office Scotland
General Register Office Northern Ireland
Northern Ireland Housing Executive
Mitchell B.R., *British Historical Statistics*
ONS, *Economic Trends; Family Expenditure Survey; Financial Statistics; Regional Trends; Social Trends*
Royal Institute of Chartered Surveyors Building Cost Information Service
Scottish Development Department
Scottish Office Environment Department
Welsh Office

Health
Council of Europe, *Organ Donation and Transplants*
General Household Survey and Northern Ireland Continuous Household Survey
General Register Office Scotland
General Register Office Northern Ireland
Government Actuary's Department
Department of Health and Social Services, Department of Northern Ireland
Health and Safety Executive
Home Office

MAFF National Food Survey
National Health Service in Scotland, Directorate of Information Services
OECD Health Data
ONS, *Annual Abstract; Family Expenditure Survey; Mortality Statistics; Population Trends; Regional Trends; Social Trends*
Public Health Laboratory Service, Communicable Disease Surveillance Centre
Scottish Centre for Infection and Environmental Health
Scottish Health Service Common Services Agency
Scottish Office
UN, *World Population Prospects*
UK Transplant Support Service Authority
Welsh Office
World Bank Development Report

Education
Department for Education and Employment *Statistical Bulletin, Education Statistics, Universities Statistics Record*
Eton College
Higher Education Statistics Unit
Independent Schools Information Service, *Annual Census*
OECD, *Education at a Glance*
ONS, *Annual Abstract; Regional Trends; Social Trends*
The Times Higher Education Supplement

Crime and punishment
Council of Europe, Directorate of Legal Affairs
Home Office, *Criminal Statistics England and Wales; Prison Statistics; Statistical Bulletin*
ONS, *Regional Trends*

People and culture
All England Lawn Tennis
APACS
Audit Bureau of Circulation
Bank of England
The Bookseller
British Airways
British Coal
British Film Institute, *Film and Television Yearbook*
British Screen
British Telecom
British Tourist Authority
British Video Association Yearbook

Cable and Satellite Europe
Cable and Satellite Express
The Cable Television Association
Centre National de la Cinématographie
Charities Aid Foundation
Chartered Institute for Public Finance and Accountancy
Cunard
Datamonitor Food Databases
Department of Employment, *New Earnings Survey*
Dunhill
Euromonitor
The Football League
Ford Motor Company
General Household Survey
J. Harbord and J. Wright, *40 Years of British Television*
Hyde Park Hotel
International Federation of Phonographic Industries
Jaguar Cars
Leisure Futures
Liverpool University
London Regional Transport
Mars (UK)
Metropolitan Police
ONS, *Annual Abstract; Family Spending; General Household Survey; Population Trends; Regional Trends; Social Trends*
The Premier League
Royal and Ancient Golf Club
Royal Opera House
Rothman's Football Yearbook
Rothman's Rugby Union Yearbook
Savoy Hotel
Scotch Whisky Association
Scottish Football League
Screen Digest
Screen Finance
Simpson (Piccadilly)
Society of Film Distributors
Society of West End Theatres
Sotheby's
Taylor Nelson AGB/BARB/AGB Television
Test and County Cricket Board
Theatre Royal, Drury Lane
The Times
Wisden Cricketers' Almanack

Government
Anthony King et al., *Britain at the Polls*
R. Allison, S Riddell, *The Royal Encyclopaedia*
ONS, *Electoral Statistics*
Vacher's Parliamentary Companion